# CHANGING THE SCHOOL CULTURE

## Per Dalin

with

## Hans-Günter Rolff

in co-operation with

## Bab Kleekamp

CASSELL

the
imtec
foundation

Cassell
Villiers House
41/47 Strand
London WC2N 5JE

387 Park Avenue South
New York
NY 10016-8810

First published in English 1993. German and Norwegian versions were published in 1991.
Reprinted 1995

**British Library Cataloguing in Publication Data**
A catalogue record for this book is available from the British Library.

ISBN 0-304-32745-X (hardback)
    0-304-32737-9 (paperback)

Typeset by Colset Private Limited, Singapore

Printed and bound in Great Britain by
Redwood Books, Trowbridge, Wiltshire

...OPMENT SERIES

David Reynolds

## CHANGING THE SCHOOL CULTURE

0304 327379

# Contents

# Series Editors' Foreword

We are pleased once more to make available in this series the work of leading international experts in our field. Per Dalin and his colleagues associated with IMTEC of Norway will be already known to many of those in the fields of school improvement, school evaluation and school effectiveness. Their Institutional Development Program (IDP) has been used in over a thousand schools in many parts of the world. Here, in this text, they present for the first time a coherent, integrated and stimulating summary of what their vast experience in these schools and countries has taught them. This clearly makes the volume a very important book indeed.

Their IDP has a number of central and core assumptions: that the school is the unit of change; that the 'subjective reality' of school members is important; that conflicts are in fact opportunities; and that schools need to become learning organizations in order to deal with the changed situational requirements of a rapidly changing social context.

The book outlines in fascinating detail the procedures that are part of their IDP: the initiation phase and the negotiation of the contractual relationship between the school and the outside 'change agent'; the diagnostic phase using the Guide to Institutional Learning (GIL); the prioritizing of goals and activities; and the management and sustaining of change at the level of the school culture.

There are of course a number of alternative schemes of school improvement that are available internationally, but what distinguishes the scheme outlined in this book is its comprehensiveness - it is concerned with change in school culture *and* organization, with internal *and* external change forces, with subjective *and* objective reality, with practitioner *and* expert knowledge, and with diagnosis *and* institutionally based action.

The comprehensiveness of the approach advocated in this book does not necessarily make it a simple one, but we have no doubt that in a world full of the simple peddling of the snake oil of school effectiveness 'recipes' and of school improvement 'quick fixes', the intellectual depth, rigour, experience and humanity of the ideas outlined in this book will have a lasting impact upon practitioners, policymakers and researchers alike.

David Hopkins
David Reynolds

July 1993

# Preface

IMTEC's school improvement programme has from its inception in 1976 been known as the 'Institutional Development Program' (IDP). We knew when we started this work that to change the pedagogical practice of the school would often mean changes in the attitudes and behaviour of teachers and educational leaders, and possibly changes in the school culture.

Our starting point was the school. We felt that the school had to be clear about its own needs before it involved itself in 'innovations'. The 1970s saw one 'innovation wave' after another. We felt that schools were often involved in work that may have involved change but where improvement was rare. One of the first major development tasks of IMTEC was therefore to develop a diagnostic instrument (GIL) to help the organization to diagnose its own strengths and weaknesses.

We learned quickly that to renew the practice of the school was a more complicated process than we had thought. It was not easy to get schools involved in diagnosis. Secondly, it was even more difficult to move from diagnosis to action. Thirdly, the process often stopped because of limited capacity for change in the individual schools. This resulted in a decision to start a two-year-long consultant development programme, a training programme that is still offered in several countries. A practical training programme under supervision working directly in schools gave a chance for meaningful exchange of experiences. This programme has been the basis for our reflections on the IDP.

The IDP has always been an ambitious development. We have encountered many difficult dilemmas. We have tried to connect theory and practice. We wanted to work both short and long term. We have developed comprehensive training programmes for consultants and for managers, and we also wanted to try the IDP in different cultures.

Our main orientation has been change theory and organizational theory. This area has seen tremendous change over the last 10 years. To us it has been both challenging and fun to try out new ideas and to learn from practice. We had to leave behind a lot of theoretical old baggage. In this area there are many short-lived 'theories', knowledge that is often based on single case studies in a given cultural context. To us it has been important to build a practice that could continuously be assessed and modified. Even if research has been of help to us, practice coupled with reflection has been even more useful.

Since the inception of the IDP we have been totally dependent on expertise and support from many of our partners in several countries. Prior to the IDP, I was involved in a major international research programme for the Organisation for Economic Co-operation and Development, a programme that started in

1970. Through this programme an international network of researchers and practitioners on educational change was developed. Later, colleagues from Norway (in particular from the municipalities of Trondheim and Bærum) took part in the first IDP programme.

The first report on the IDP was published in 1983 (Dalin and Rust, 1983). Since then a number of case descriptions, evaluations and analyses have followed. In the last few years the work in the Netherlands and Germany has been important for the further development of the programme. The NOVO foundation at the University of Amsterdam has been the leading force in the Netherlands. Around 100 Dutch IDP consultants have been through a two-year training programme, and many schools have used and still are using the IDP as a basis for development. Bab Kleekamp has been the driving force in this period. He has rich experience in the area of consultancy and his theoretical insight has been of great importance to the work of this book. In Germany the state-funded research and development centre in North Rhine-Westphalia (Landesinstitut für Schule and Weiterbildung) has been our partner. About 50 consultants have been trained through the German programme. The German version of this book was published in 1991 (*Institutionelles Schulentwicklungsprogramm*; Dalin and Rolff), and the Norwegian version in the same year. Chapters 3 and 5 were written by Hans-Günter Rolff for the German book, and are being used in a modified version for this publication. Hans-Günter Rolff and Herbert Buchen are the leaders of the development programme in Germany and both have been instrumental in the development of the German publication.

Several persons have in the last years been of particular importance for the development of the IDP. First and foremost I want to thank my colleagues in the Netherlands and Germany, Bab Kleekamp, Hans-Günter Rolff and Herbert Buchen, who more than others had to tolerate cultural differences and learn how to live with the unfinished and the unknown! Together with a team of trainers, among others Leo Horster, Klaus Isselburg, Mette Eldevik, Hermien Biekmann and Bea Pruijt, we have experienced a unique international co-operation. In addition, Klaus Isselburg has designed the figures in this book.

Per Dalin, *Oslo, June 1993*

# Chapter 1

# The Future of Schooling

As I walked down the beautiful sandy beach on the outskirts of Colombo in Sri Lanka I saw a small group of teenagers in intense discussion with two elderly fishermen. I stopped for a moment and discovered that this was more than a morning talk. The youngsters were organized: one was interviewing the two old men, another was making a drawing of the fishing boat, a third was describing the equipment and two were taking notes.

These youngsters were simply members of a learning group from the nearby lower secondary school. I got in touch with the teacher and she explained that she had organized all her 68 (!) children in learning groups all through the year. She saw her job as to design learning opportunities, to help those most in need, to organize learning resources so that the children could help each other and to secure quality of the process and the product.

This 'primitive' little school in the jungle of Sri Lanka had already made a quantum leap — away from the traditional classroom instruction, from instruction to learning, from the individual alone to the group and the individual as the focus of learning, from the teacher as instructor to the teacher as the designer and facilitator, and from the students as receivers of information to the students as creative learners.

I was impressed. One of the many major classroom changes that we have tried to accomplish in our rich industrialized societies for more than 50 years was accomplished under severe poverty and with very little in the way of learning resources and support. How was it possible?

We may have focused more on the *difficulties* of improving schools than on the *successes*. Research literature about educational change is full of warnings and studies of failures. This book is about how to change the culture of your school successfully, towards a learning organization, drawing on research and practice.

We see change as *learning*, the most natural of all human activities. It is part of our life before we are born. It is challenging and rewarding. It is vital. Without learning we will not grow up.

Changing schools is also a learning process. It involves individuals as well as teams, indeed every member of the entire organization. It is also challenging, and rewarding. And it is vital. Without successful change schools will not survive the future. This is the real message of this book.

## OUR VALUES

The more we have worked with schools undergoing change, we have discovered that *ad hoc* and piecemeal efforts at change are inadequate. What is needed is *systemic change* that involves a fundamental cultural change (Dalin, 1978). Our arguments can be summarized in six statements:

1   *The paradigm shift*: The world is changing dramatically; we are in the middle of a major paradigm shift, and add-on changes to the existing schools are inadequate. Meaningful educational changes demand new perspectives and basic changes in the culture of schools.

2   *The school as the unit of change*: The school is the unit of change, because it is the only place where the demands of society and the expectations and learning needs of students and teachers meet. Each school is unique. It must learn how to learn.

3   *Central authorities as partners*: The school is part of nation building. It is not alone; it needs the challenges and the support of central authorities. Many future problems are overwhelming and can only be dealt with as a result of close co-operation between the school and central authorities.

4   *The real needs*: School improvements, to be effective, must meet the real needs of students. To reach this goal is a complex process of developing ownership and a shared vision of short-term and long-term goals within each school.

5   *Change as learning*: Changes that have an impact on students' lives involve an in-depth learning process that can only be mastered by teachers and heads who themselves are learning, in teams that can draw on the talents of all members, and in the school as an organization involving all participants. Meaningful changes are dependent on *personal mastery*, an outcome of a continuous process of learning (Senge, 1990).

6   *The learning organization*: The goal is a learning organization that is able to respond creatively to changes in the environment; an organization that has embedded capacities for school-based curriculum changes, for staff development and supervision, for team development as well as management and organizational development; and, not least, that has institutionalized the process of ongoing school assessment.

We shall deal with each one of these statements below. This book is about how schools can become *learning organizations*. It is based on a project, IMTEC's Institutional Development Program (IDP), initiated in 1976 and developed in several countries, which successfully demonstrates how different schools are able to change their culture.

An overview of IDP will be given in Chapter 2, and the remainder of the book is a fairly detailed analysis of the road towards changing schools into learning organizations. The term itself may soon become a slogan, with little meaning. For us it is not a theoretical concept, it is *practice*. We want to show how schools, starting from where they are, can change their cultures and learn to become learning organizations. That is what this book is about. We now look closer at the above six statements.

# SOCIETY IS CHANGING: THE PARADIGM SHIFT

We live amid dramatic political, social, economic and organizational changes. Our perspectives are changing, as are our lives. Over the past hundred years the member countries of the Organisation for Economic Co-operation and Development (OECD) have gone through rapid changes in all facets of life and, in fact, the very basis for schooling, or the 'contract' between home and school, which the old school model was built upon, is changing rapidly.

*Homes* are smaller, siblings are of the same age group, both parents of children at school work outside the home (over 70 per cent in Scandinavia, 40 per cent in the FRG, and 90 per cent in the former GDR), and divorce affects 50 per cent of the families in our cities. Increasingly, society is involved in the upbringing of children, and in the resolution of conflicts in the home. The youth peer culture is taking over the leadership role from parents, teachers and other adults.

*Mass media* have to a large extent filled the vacuum that many young people experience in their lives. The megastars are the new high priests and prophets who set the trends and define the acceptable values. Young people in the Western hemisphere today spend more time in front of the television than in school. We know that socially and educationally disadvantaged youth often spend most of their time watching television and videos, unfortunately often showing less than positive programmes. In fact, many experience our time as a cultural ideological fight between the 'imagery' culture of the mass media and the written culture of the textbook (Postman, 1987).

The *workplace* is undergoing dramatic changes as well. Not only is the work different, it also demands new types of, often higher, qualifications. Work has also taken on another meaning for many of us. The workplace has filled many social needs that were earlier satisfied within the family and the local environment. We are looking not only for a job, but for a career. Our self-concept is to a large extent connected with *what* I am, and less and less with *who* I am. For many firms ownership of a company culture is so important that it attempts to satisfy a variety of economic, social and educational needs. In fact, the cost of training in industry is today higher than the total cost of the college and university systems in OECD countries. Much of this training deals with the development of the company culture and the quality of life in the workplace. The enterprises that survive the tough international competition will be those which have a capacity for learning, creative adaptation and change; organizations that can create their own future.

At the same time an unacceptably high proportion of our youth are unemployed, and many students go directly from school to unemployment. For these individuals, the knowledge that a career and an attachment to a work culture is so important for personal growth in today's society makes the unemployment situation even harder to cope with. Also, it will have a negative impact on the motivation for schooling, and will in turn become a vicious circle.

The *church* once played a significant role in forming attitudes and behaviour. Today, only a small proportion of people belong to the church. Holidays have increasingly become free time, immigrants bring in new perspectives on religion and morality, and youth find themselves more a part of a pluralistic society where they start without mental baggage; they have to define their own values and norms, often without the support of adults and the church.

We are seeing the skeleton of a new society that distinguishes more clearly than before between the *producers*, on the one hand, and the *consumers*, on the other. Prestige and values will be more and more attached to those who determine the production process in society (in all fields of the public and private economy), rather than to those at the receiving end. Many will play both roles, but those who only play the part of consumers may well be the disadvantaged in the future.

We have mentioned just a few factors that are changing the role of schooling in our societies. What characterizes these changes today is not only that they are so rapid, but that they occur in so many fields simultaneously. We talk about a *critical mass* factor. The pupils we work with today are different from those of 10 years ago; their 'social capital' is different (Coleman, 1987), their life opportunities are different, and their future is far more uncertain than was the case 10 years ago.

## OUR PERSPECTIVES ARE CHANGING

Our students participate in many types of organizations and they spend, as we have said, more time with mass media than in schools. They have ideas of their own! So have teachers. Popular demands for a different kind of organization from that of the traditional school are heard more and more often. Demands for real participation are heard in most countries; new and more active roles for students are becoming imperative in schools where resources are scarce. Both teachers and students question traditional forms of leadership. Many question the quality of schooling, both internally and externally. More productive schools may be seen as an aspect of increased emphasis on quality of life.

What is happening to schools is what has already happened to many organizations in society: a paradigm shift. People in our organizations are seeking a more meaningful life, more useful roles, increased relevance and a bridge from school to life 'out there'. We are moving towards the 'learning organization', so well described in P. M. Senge's *The Fifth Discipline* (Senge, 1990), and described and analysed as related to schools in our last book on Institutional Development Programs, *Can Schools Learn?* (Dalin and Rust, 1983). Senge calls what is happening 'metanoia' — a shift of mind. It is a process where we grasp the deeper meaning of 'learning'. Through learning we 'reperceive the world and our relationship to it', and 'a learning organization is an organization that continually expands its capacity to create its future' (Senge, 1990, p. 14). This is the central message of the IDP — to help schools 'learn how to learn', to become real learning institutions with capacities for change to create the future.

We see the pressures for change coming from the external environment as well as from the schools themselves. Forces for renewal come in many forms, intensities and qualities. Therefore, they appear quite different from school to school. There is no single recipe for meeting the challenges. Schools, there-

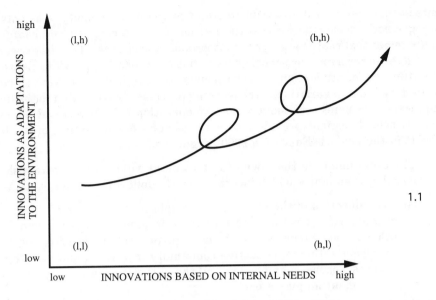

Figure 1.1   *Change as mutual adaptation and development (Dalin, 1978)*

fore, need to cope with both *external demands* and *internal demands* for renewal in a creative development process, as Figure 1.1 illustrates.

Schools cannot be indifferent to many of the fundamental changes in the environment. Some of the responses to these challenges may be reflected in central guidelines, in the curriculum, and regulations. Other environmental challenges have a direct impact in the classroom, for example as events unfold on television, as the local peer group becomes more aggressive, and as parents demand more from schools. Schools will need to deal with a number of these challenges on a continuing basis.

We have also illustrated that as society is changing so are we, the students, teachers and school managers. Our expectations toward our workplace, our roles, toward what learning is all about, to mention a few dimensions, need to find response in the way we organize work in schools.

Many of these challenges, external as well as internal, are in conflict with each other, demand more resources, more competence, leadership and a wholly different method of problem-solving. To us an innovative school is a school that has *learned how to learn*, that has developed the capacities to deal with these challenges in a meaningful way for everyone involved.

## THE SCHOOL AS THE UNIT OF CHANGE

All the forces created by political, economic, social, and cultural forces in society, new policies and administrative measures decided by school authorities, and the aspirations of people within a school, meet in one place: the school.

Policy aspirations can only materialize in the individual school. These forces and policies are interpreted differently because they 'meet' different sets of people, circumstances and conditions. Standard solutions are doomed to fail. They will produce inequality of opportunities. You cannot deal with unequal units in the same way if you want to optimize quality and equity. It is only by taking schools seriously as separate entities within a complex and confusing environment that real changes in the classrooms and the school can be expected.

On the other hand, the school on its own is not capable of providing learning opportunities for students in modern society. Research indicates that as much as 80-90 per cent of variation in the learning outcomes is attributed to the home and local environment. Without a close co-operation with *homes and the community*, schools cannot provide adequate learning opportunities, or as John Abbott in the project 'Education 2000', argues:

> The programme [in the town of Letchworth] would seek to establish a learning community which incorporates the following elements.
>
> (a) The education of the young is the responsibility of whole communities; it is too important to be fragmented. Schools and other formal agencies should play a pivotal role in coordinating provision within an educative community in which young people, parents, teachers, employers and the authorities in local and central government all play a part.
>
> (b) Most learning takes place outside the confines of schools.
>
> (c) Within human communities, however defined, there is an untold wealth of educational opportunity. Informed and involved communities could create learning environments of immense potential.
>
> (d) Information technologies free learning from the constraints of time and place, and with that freedom comes responsibility; young people need considerable support in knowing how to use the potential of open learning.                                                 (Abbott, 1991)

This means that the school needs to 'open up', to 'adapt and develop' (Figure 1.1) together with the homes and the community. However, it begins with the school, and we still see the school as the centre of learning activities and the unit of change.

The local community is vital in another respect. Schools will not survive without alliances, and they need access to new learning opportunities. For too long the schools have been relatively isolated institutions, and they have not benefited from the opportunities that new learning technologies can offer.

## THE SCHOOL AS AN ORGANIZATION

Basically we see the change process as 'mutual adaptation and development', as illustrated in Figure 1.1. Schools, like other organizations, need to cope with both external and internal pressures for change. To understand how schools as organizations cope with the change process IMTEC has adapted four perspectives on organizations into a school organizational model (Figure 1.2).

We see the school as an organization where there is a *mutual interdependency* among the five variables: environment, values, structure, human relations and strategies. When we describe the relationships as interdependent,

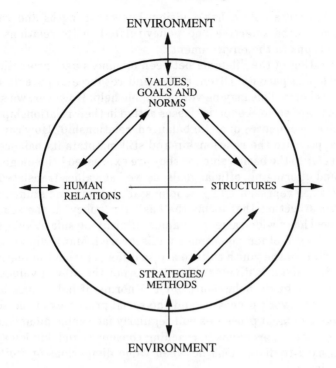

**ENVIRONMENT**

Figure 1.2 *The school as an organization (Dalin, 1978)*

it does not mean that there is necessarily an automatic or linear dependency. In some cases it may be that a change in one part of the organization has direct consequences for another subsystem. In other cases it may be that other subsystems 'protect' themselves from potential consequences. We know, for example, that some teachers may start a new model of teaching that has major consequences for the role of students. Other teachers may simply ignore it. Again, other schools may be more tightly structured to the effect that such an initiative has to be discussed among all teachers and it may also have consequences for all.

The *environment* is important to all schools. By 'environment' is meant the *administrative* links to school authorities, as well as the many informal links with homes, organizations, institutions and businesses in the community. It is not obvious that the school should 'respond to the demands from the environment'. The school also has a unique role of *defining quality* in relationship to learning. A school always has to address new demands against its own vision and mission. Therefore some fundamental questions remain.

- How 'permeable' should the school be?
- What are the consequences of *openness* and *protection*?
- What can the school do to develop a constructive relationship with the environment?

A productive school has mutual and open relations with the environment. A condition for *mutual* beneficial relations is that the school 'understands itself',

7

e.g. has established a policy, has a vision, knows strengths and weaknesses, and therefore can be *selective* and policy-related in its relations with individuals and groups in the environment.

An illustration of the dilemma between openness and 'protection' may be the relationship to parents. Often, active and resourceful parents offer their assistance to schools. This may be very valuable help. However, we seldom find parents from lower socio-economic classes active in their relationship to schools. What are the consequences of an 'unbalanced' relationship? How can the school accept and appreciate the relationship and still maintain its balance?

*Values* refer to the basic values as they are expressed in ideologies, theories of learning and upbringing, official goals, as well as values translated into daily norms. Values are represented by people: staff, leaders and students. It is the complex value structure that forms the basis for 'policy' at the school level.

Each school has a wide variety of values, often living side by side, sometimes in conflict with each other, sometimes undiscovered. Many will argue that the values and norms of the youth culture are so different from the teacher culture that we can talk about a 'divided school'. It is not the official values and goals of the school that guide behaviour, but the norms of individuals and groups that 'regulate' the work processes and the social processes in the school.

School development processes will regularly face value dilemmas, conflicts over goals and norms, problems in reaching consensus and 'hidden agendas'. It is often also hard to distinguish between value dimensions of a dilemma and conflict over interests.

When the integrated upper secondary school system was developed in Norway in the late 1960s, two different school cultures with different sets of values and norms had to be combined in one organization. Vocational schools and *gymnasiums* have traditionally been quite different types of schools, also in their approach towards teaching and learning. The dilemmas were many. Issues over who should be the new headmaster — the vocational school headmaster or the *gymnasium* headmaster — became a subject for debate. Statistics showed that in most cases the new head came from the *gymnasium*. It created frustration among teachers and heads in the vocational schools. Was it due to a conflict of interests, or a conflict over values and norms?

*Structure* is the dimension that refers to how the school is organized (organigram), how tasks are distributed (work organization), and the formal decision-making structure. The school has an official structure as well as an informal structure. There is no simple 'effective' structure; it depends on a set of factors. Also in relationship to structure, the school faces dilemmas. For example:

- How fixed and how flexible should the structure be to protect against turbulence, while at the same time allowing for change processes to take place?
- How much dependency among teachers is necessary to implement the primary task (e.g. teaching)?
- To what extent does the structure allow for mutual exchange, communication and learning?

- To what extent does the structure allow for co-operation, while at the same time giving room for autonomy?

In a school fully occupied with projects and an active planning and development process, the staff found that the timetable simply did not give opportunities for co-operation. Everyone was always busy. A simple structural change made life much more flexible and enjoyable: the midday break was extended by 30 minutes, allowing for a one-hour break. It created opportunities for meetings and co-operation for everyone. Quite simple, but effective in this case.

*Relations* refers to the internal human relations in a school; among students, teachers, and leaders; in the classrooms; in the playground; and in the staffroom. The quality of an organization is often reflected in the relations among people: between groups, and between the leaders and those who are led. Learning happens through dialogue. It is an important goal for schools to strive towards good human relations. In this area also the school faces dilemmas:

- How can 'membership' really be felt, even when personal values, personality and norms are different from those of the majority?
- How are feelings expressed? Can a school accept all forms of feelings (and their expression)? And how can one be fair? (For example, do we treat boys and girls alike?)
- Do we accept that all members, students as well as leaders, have the right to influence, and how can we deal with unacceptable ways of using influence (by leaders, teachers and students)?
- Does the school have an open and constructive communication process at all levels, or is energy blocked because people do not talk to each other?
- How does the school deal with conflicts and problem-solving?; does it have acceptable procedures and norms or are these *ad hoc* or non-existent?
- Is the school working with its own culture and climate, and are 'process' issues accepted, as well as discussions of content?

*A school faced a fundamental leadership crisis. Over some years the relations between the head and her staff had become unfriendly and hostile. It started with an initiative on the part of the head to supervise instruction in the classrooms. She had had complaints from many parents — particularly related to 3 of the 22 teachers in the school. She did not feel comfortable discussing the issues directly with the three teachers, so she decided to 'deal with all teachers the same way' — and 'quality control' was becoming the top priority of the school district. Teachers proposed 'peer supervision'. However, the head felt strongly that 'quality control' was her responsibility towards parents and the superintendent. . . . One episode after another brought the dialogue to a full stop. . . .*

Human relations issues are vital in any organization. In a learning organization they are critical. That does not mean that a 'problem' in interpersonal relations can necessarily be 'resolved' through human relations training (or similar methods). Also, what appears to be a problem might well be the result of value differences, structural issues, relations to the environment, etc.

*Strategies* refers to the ways in which resources are allocated, and the overall curriculum and teaching-learning strategies in the school. It also relates to leadership, processes of problem-solving, human resource development, decision-making and quality control. It is the role of the leadership to strike a balance between values, structure, relations and the environment. There are issues and dilemmas in this area too; for example:

- To what extent is it desirable to have a common teaching-learning strategy?
- Is the decision-making process clear to everyone involved?
- What are the procedures for delegation?
- Who has the real power to influence decisions?
- To what extent does the school have the necessary competence to provide a quality programme? Is existing competence used, and appreciated?
- Does the school have the necessary resources, are they flexible enough, and does management know how to use resources more flexibly?
- Does the school provide opportunities for school renewal, are there norms and procedures that reward creativity, and does the school learn from new experiences?

Research on 'school effectiveness' makes it clear that *leadership* is one of the most crucial factors determining the quality of schooling. Although the IDP deals with the school as a whole, it is also clear from our practice that we need to work with school leadership, often in parallel with a school development programme.

## Effective leadership

The literature is full of advice on leaders. Many of the slogans related to leadership are hardly empirically based. If they are, the sample of leaders and organizations studied certainly does not allow us to make sweeping generalizations, particularly not generalizations across sectors (e.g. from schools to industry), or even across cultures.

The emerging 'effective schools' literature, primarily developed in North America over the past 10 years, has had an impact on many leadership development programmes. We talk about generalizations such as: an effective principal has a vision, is able to involve teachers and development work, sets standards, provides support and cares for the human side of the organization. Clearly there are several more in-depth studies that become more specific but, however, lose their generalizability. Nevertheless, we can draw on several 'effective school' studies.

We know little about what constitutes an 'effective' leader in a *learning organization*. Even the terms 'effective' or 'productive' do not sound right.

These are concepts from a production paradigm with fairly straightforward goals and lines of authority. Some want schools to become 'production centres', to measure 'learning' as achievement scores (at least in those subjects where it can be measured with some degree of certainty), and to be 'clearer about what schools are for'.

As will be discussed in this book, schools are much more complex organizations than most industrial enterprises, and they need a different kind of leadership to be successful. In this book we shall look particularly at the role of leadership in the 'management of educational change' (Chapters 7, 8 and 9).

## CENTRAL AUTHORITIES AS PARTNERS

What then is the role of external and, in particular, *central* authorities? Clearly, many of the forces in society, briefly sketched above, have an impact on schools in general, and the response from the school system at the *central level* is vital. Many of the changes have implications for the curriculum, for the dimensions of the system, for the way educational resources are allocated and organized, for teacher competence and leadership, and for the relations between the schools and their environment. In fact a number of basic assumptions about schooling in modern society need to be questioned at the national level (see also Chapter 9).

There are good reasons why the dimensions and speed of changes in society are such that only a concerted effort at the *system level* will do. The school systems of the OECD countries have for years tried to meet the challenges at the central level. What have we learned about *policy implementation*?

First, let us look at some of the key assumptions behind a strategy for change that is based on *system initiatives*.

1 System strategies for change (e.g. a new curriculum) assume that a change to be applied in all schools will indeed be seen as an *innovation*. In other words, knowledge exists at the central level, taking into account all the varied conditions of single schools and local school systems that will produce an improvement for all schools (or at least a majority of schools).

2 It is possible to *manage change*, to establish rational goals, to arrive at a consensus understood and accepted throughout the system, and to provide the necessary qualified support for the change process and develop commitment to the desired policy changes.

3 Schools are seen as *targets* for change, and teachers as consumers of new ideas and products. Basically the school is seen as a *delivery mechanism*. It is therefore assumed that schools will *adopt* solutions prepared at the system level.

In a period when educational changes and new products were the same thing (e.g. new curricula, textbooks, media), the efforts of curriculum centres, pedagogical centres, and research and development agencies clearly reflected the research and development (R&D) mode existing in other fields, such as agriculture and even industry. Increasingly these agencies have become more professional in their relationship to schools. However, the three assumptions mentioned above are often still valid. What have we learned from these central efforts?

1  Schools do not adapt. The situation in each school is different. The 'culture of the school' is a dominating factor in the 'implementation process'. In fact, words like 'development' and 'implementation' indicate some sort of linear process, where schools are left to 'implement' something thought out somewhere else. Reality shows that schools seldom adopt 'an innovation', but rather try to adapt to new realities (in which central pressure for change is one factor) (McLaughlin, 1990).

2  New challenges to schooling are not resolved by 'plugging in' a new innovation. That very concept is taken from technology and has very little relevance in schools. Change in schools is a complex political, ideological, social, organizational and personal process. It may be just as relevant to ask what the school does to the innovation (and the innovator) as to ask what the innovation (and the innovator) does to the school (Dalin, 1978). New 'solutions' need to be understood in the context of schools as complex social systems.

3  Resistance to change (in the research literature in the 1970s) is often looked upon as negative, and must be further understood to grasp the dynamics of the change process. Dalin has identified the following barriers to change in schools.

(a)  *Value barriers*, or opposition to a given change process because actors do not *believe* in the values and norms implied in the effort. Education deals with very basic human values. It is seldom a technical matter alone. Some innovators are often more interested in the technical aspects of change than the implied values. This does not help.

(b)  *Power barriers*, or reluctance to engage in the change process because it may alter the power balance in a negative way. Changes in the curriculum are not purely 'professional issues'; they may also alter the relative weight (and thereby resources) among subjects taught. Fusion of schools is another example of change where power plays an important part.

(c)  *Practical barriers*, or uneasiness about getting involved in the change process because of scepticism about the management of the process, are widespread (not only in schools). The change process is often haphazard, decision-making unclear, resources limited, staff development insufficient, and often the process demands more time than envisaged.

(d)  *Psychological barriers*, defined as the reaction when a person is unwilling to engage in the change process, even if that person agrees with the values and norms, does not stand to lose power, and cannot identify practical problems. The reason for this 'rigidity in personality' may be found in past experiences that have been quite unpleasant.

These barriers operate at the *school* level and in a variety of ways. The research literature provides a comprehensive list of 'barriers to change', and good summaries of our present knowledge about the change process (e.g. Huberman and Miles, 1984; Pink, 1989; Fullan, 1991).

4 The efforts of R&D organizations in education have developed considerably since the 1970s. It became clear that a 'product vision' was not the right strategy, and therefore, many of the centres that survived adopted a 'change vision' for their work. If one's goals were real school changes and not the development of products, then there might be a role for new products, but as just one part of an overall change strategy. R&D centres increasingly work with schools or school districts as their clients, with concrete changes as their outcome measures.

5 We have learned a lot about the *external role* in education. Although school systems are highly structured (some would say bureau-cratized), individual schools are loosely coupled. What goes on in the classroom, and what really matters, namely the learning process, cannot be 'managed' from the external environment. From John Goodlad's work in the 1960s to the work of Huberman and Miles in the 1980s, the message is clear: managers cannot mandate what *matters*, they can only *enable outcomes* (McLaughlin, 1990). It is still clear that system management has a role; Huberman and Miles found that it is a combination of pressure and support that matters and, moreover, it is through dialogue and real interaction with the school that the change process takes place.

There is real tension between the perspective of the school as the unit of change and the government's role. In many instances schools may respond more easily to short-term felt needs than to future challenges. The government may see a need to meet future challenges (e.g. the ecology crisis, new technologies) to secure quality (e.g. through an external evaluation of schools), and to secure equality of educational opportunities (e.g. through its financing policies).

## MEETING REAL NEEDS

We know that many attempts to renew schools fail. This may be true for many externally initiated changes, as well as for changes started within the schools. The reasons are many. No single theory can explain the success or failure of innovations. From IMTEC's research on the change process in schools, we find that the following factors (Figure 1.3) are minimum conditions for change (a more detailed discussion can be found in Chapter 2).

### Real needs

Often change processes start with an 'innovative idea' without any clear idea what the needs of the 'client system' are, and how the idea would influence the

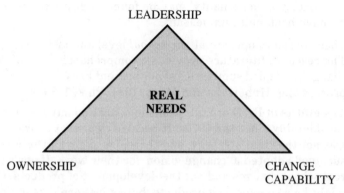

Figure 1.3    *The 'real needs' model (P. Dalin, 1987)*

culture of the school. One of the most difficult processes is to determine the needs, because needs change as the school works with the dilemmas of change. It is necessary to define the 'real needs' of the users at an early stage. However, it is even more important to structure a process of learning throughout the development work to enable the participants to discover their needs for renewal.

## Ownership

This discovery process, or learning process, is complex and cyclic. We often rediscover our values and therefore our real needs. This, however, can best be done if we feel that we are part of the discovery process. We must develop a sense of *ownership* of the ideas and of the process of change. It is a process of gradual confidence in the programme and in the people who work for the changes. It can only be done when the individuals involved trust each other and gradually 'open up' and discuss realities (see Chapter 6).

## Change capacity

The motivation and the involvement of school faculty and staff are not necessarily there as the programme starts, and do not develop automatically. They develop gradually as we open up, trust each other, and feel 'membership' in the group. It is a job for school leadership to develop a sense of ownership. There is, however, one factor that goes with ownership, and that is the competence of the individuals involved. If the teachers and others involved in the change process do not *master* the new practice, it is more difficult for them to develop a sense of ownership. The ability of and possibilities for teachers to master new practice is vital for their motivation and for the success of the learning process. To succeed with change the school has to build its *change capacity*. And this 'change capacity' is basically related to the competence of teachers and other actors; however, it also deals with more structural conditions in the later stage of the process (see Chapter 8). What concerns us is that the organization in society, which more than others should be *a learning organization*, seldom takes its own learning seriously. This, however, has to do with the way the school is organized and the way human resource development is conducted (see Chapter 7).

Mastery has often been seen as a grasp of *technical* skills. To us mastery goes beyond a new technique, a new method or additional information. It is a question of personal growth, a process that questions assumptions, clarifies dilemmas and gives meaning to new data. It is also a question of group learning, to define the learning task as a *joint* activity, to learn from each other, to draw on the strengths of each participant and to develop a common vision.

## Leadership

Leadership is important at all levels: in the classroom, at the school level and at the system level. This leadership, however, does not necessarily need to be formal leadership. As we will see from the leadership discussion in Chapter 7, an informal student leader in a classroom could play a very important role in a development project. A teacher in a collegial group who plays an important informal leadership function may well help the school leadership to develop the necessary attitude of ownership towards a programme. This does not mean, however, that the formal leadership is not important. It means that the formal leadership also needs to integrate with the informal leadership of the school to be able to implement major innovations.

Leadership, understood as change management, needs to be concerned with the way organizational learning is designed, how the process of learning is facilitated, how resources are used for learning, and how learning is organized and evaluated.

The process of discovery — of learning — is complex. As shown in Chapter 2 and throughout this book, discovery depends on a gradual development of a sense of *ownership* among the users towards the ideas and new practice, and it depends on a staff capable of doing what is needed. Teacher mastery of new practice is vital for motivation and for the learning process to take place. Finally, a process needs leadership at all levels: in the classroom, in the school and at the system level.

## CHANGE AS LEARNING

IMTEC's research on the change process in schools has shown that schools differ considerably in their capacity for change, the difference being partly due to their innovation history and partly due to how 'tightly' or 'loosely' coupled the organization is (Dalin, 1986). This is an important part of the 'culture' of the school. The change process will unfold quite differently in:

- fragmented or 'loosely coupled' schools (with or without innovative experiences);
- 'project schools' that have successfully implemented changes in 'projects' in various departments and sections of the school;
- schools that have a common vision, ideology and norms, and are used to coping with change as a learning process throughout the organization; our ideal of a *learning organization*.

# The first cycle: the fragmented school

Fragmented schools are schools that are 'loosely coupled', with little *common* innovative experience among staff, where there is little common understanding of needs, little discussion, and often a norm that each person looks after him- or herself. There are limited initiatives for improvement and renewal; often these initiations are 'hidden' within the one teacher/one classroom context. A fragmented school may well have some classrooms that function well, and with excellent teaching; however, this is often merely coincidental.

In fragmented schools major initiatives for school change will most likely come as the result of pressure from the environment, usually through the local education office or the school inspectorate. Initiatives may also come with a change of leadership; however, they seldom result from a joint staff initiative. Figure 1.4 illustrates this 'first cycle' of development.

As a fragmented school is faced with new challenges from the environment, school management may well use this as an opportunity to change internal practices, and even begin to discuss internal needs for change. It may well be that only a few teachers are 'mobilized'. However, the change may result in 'project learning' and a new climate and norm: that development work is both stimulating and rewarding. It may also lead to reflections over goals and some clarification of needs, at least by a few teachers.

It is not unusual for this type of school to need extensive help, even in such a small-scale effort. The assistance often comes from the district office, and it is most likely 'tied' to a given mandate: to implement some form of man- dated change programme. As the school learns to cope with change, however, it may be evident that other needs should be given priority and can form the basis for a new 'development cycle'.

# The second cycle: the 'project school'

A school that has for some time been involved in innovative projects, where teams of teachers work together, and where the management is involved in the initiation and co-ordination of improvement programmes, will usually have more projects than it can cope with. External demands are taken into account to the extent that they may support already existing initiatives. It is likely that the main drive for change comes from groups of staff and school management.

A major challenge for 'project schools' is to develop *common* goals and norms. Management and other school leadership attempt to mobilize and co-ordinate human and physical resources, and there are fair chances for joint project learn- ing and thereby common reflections of needs and formulations of new goals.

In the 'second cycle of the development' (Figure 1.5) groups of teachers take the initiative, or sometimes the whole school mobilizes time and energy to react to a felt need. The staff involved may try to develop a vision and several projects usually get started. After some time the staff defines new needs as experience is gained. Colleagues are active in the sense that they express their opinions, and they are often consulted even if they are not directly involved. Most often co-operation happens within one subject or within a broader interdisciplinary group.

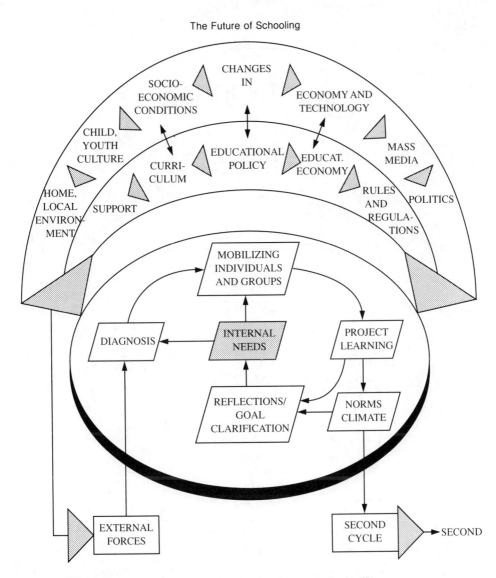

Figure 1.4 *Organizational learning: first cycle (the 'fragmented school')*

The school management of 'project schools' often needs help to restructure, to resolve internal conflicts and dynamics, to work towards *common* projects, and to build co-operation among different and often competing teams of teachers.

## The third cycle: the organic school

The third type of school is often referred to by IMTEC as the 'organic school'. However, it is really a school acting as a *learning organization*; a school that has a development process where most teachers (and often students and parents as well) are involved. Norms are under development, methods and procedures are questioned and modified, and even relationships and behaviour

17

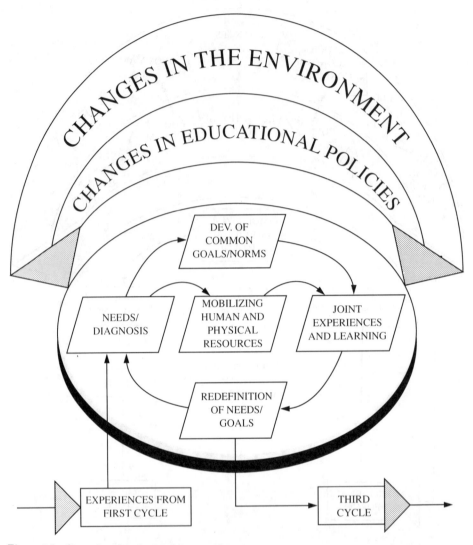

Figure 1.5  *Second cycle: the 'project school'*

are undergoing change. New objectives become generalized and new practices institutionalized (Figure 1.6).

Initiatives for change may come from within the school, as well as from the environment. The school is *open* to improvement, clear about strengths and weaknesses, and has motivation and capacities to cope with improvement processes.

At the end of such a process teachers may tell each other, 'We have reached where we wanted to get to in our development; however, we are still not satisfied. Only at this stage do we really know what we want, and we want to go further.' Then the fourth, the fifth and the sixth cycles in the learning process start, and a continuing development culture will be part of the daily life of schooling.

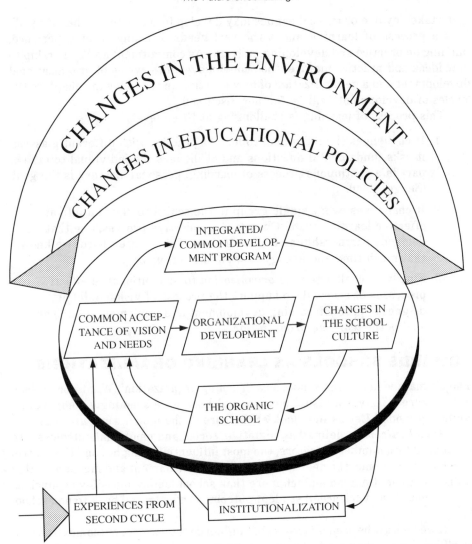

Figure 1.6   *Third cycle: the 'learning organization'*

We see the 'learning organization' as a vision for schools, a goal that will never be fully reached, but a future that is worth striving for. The purpose is to create schools that can better respond to the needs of young people and society in a world that is constantly facing new challenges. The only way schools will survive the future is to become creative learning organizations. The best way students can learn how to live in the future is to experience the life of a 'learning school'.

The renewal process in schools is seldom systematically planned and 'managed'. It is often a process of trial and error. What is first felt as a need later becomes less important, and often one returns to the starting point, asking new (and some of the old) questions. What seems to be an unimportant activity

19

undertaken by one or two colleagues may develop into a concern shared by all. It is a process of learning about the real needs, learning from experience, building on practice and developing mastery. As commitment and ownership to new ideas and practice mature, the school moves into cycles of organizational development and a generalization of new practice. In the following chapters the 'cycles of development' will be further discussed.

This process of learning is challenging at three levels:

1 It challenges the individual to look at practice with different glasses; it asks fundamental questions and challenges the individual to take part in a continuous process of learning: personal mastery is the goal (Senge, 1990).

2 It challenges every single group in the school to develop into an effective learning team. Change is a collective process, one that demands partnership and collaboration. This is often hard; we know that much time and energy is wasted in groups.

3 Finally, it challenges the *organization* to institutionalize effective processes of renewal, to support the process of vision-building, diagnosis, problem-solving development and implementation. The goal is the *learning organization*.

## TOWARDS SCHOOLS AS LEARNING ORGANIZATIONS

The ultimate vision is the school as a 'learning organization'. What does it look like? Figure 1.7 gives a visual picture, which shows a seemingly complex and confusing model! Let us first look at the core of the model, the *outcomes*.

*School outcomes*, defined as cognitive, social, and emotional outcomes, are influenced by a number of factors, the most influential being beyond the control of schools. The home, the peer group, the local environment and media probably influence student outcome much more than school factors (possibly as much as 75 per cent of the variance of student outcome can be traced back to non-school factors).

If we look at the *school factors* that influence total school outcomes (the sum of all learning among students *and* adults in school), we argue as follows.

The *school culture* has a major influence on the quality of opportunities that the school provides for each child. The ethos of the school as a whole and the climate of the individual classroom have a direct bearing upon teaching and learning (Rutter *et al.*, 1979). Studies show that, for example, the culture of the individual classroom is very stable over the years and has a large influence on the academic success of the students (e.g. Gjessing *et al.*, 1988). IDP is concerned about the values and norms that are practised within the school, the structural and the human dimensions, as well as the procedures and processes that regulate daily behaviour.

The *management of change* to us is a fundamental part of the organizational culture and it takes on a particularly important role in a learning organization. For schools to improve they need to organize the improvement process as a continuous undertaking. Teachers who want to learn more are given learning

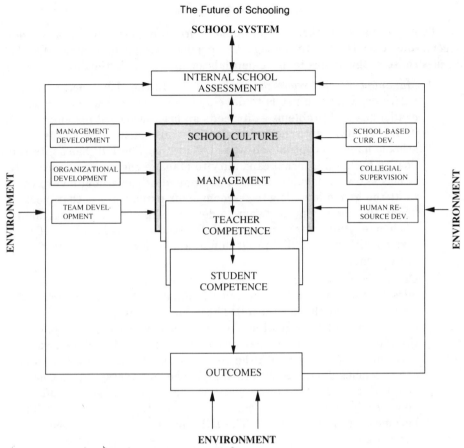

Figure 1.7    *The school as a learning organization*

opportunities, groups that need further growth are supported, the complexities of implementing new practices are dealt with in a professional way and the school is open to further improvement. In other words, the culture accepts the change process as part of the everyday life of a learning process, not as an unusual event.

*Teacher competence* is critical to success. A trademark of a learning organization is *competent staff*, who set high standards for themselves. One of the reasons for joining a school is love of learning. A critical service to teachers (and other adults in the school) is opportunities for learning and personal growth. (We shall discuss this dimension in some detail in Chapter 6.) Needless to say, the key link between policy and implementation is the teacher. His or her mastery becomes the core of a problem-solving school.

*Student competence* is clearly a condition for meaningful school outcomes. Students need to master a number of critical skills, such as thinking skills, problem-solving skills, human relations skills, group dynamic skills, as well as more specific subject matter skills, to become successful students (in terms of outcomes as defined above). We believe that this can best be facilitated in a positive school and classroom climate with an openness for learning and growth, and with highly competent teachers.

There are basically three major support programmes to enable a school to become one that is able to manage the needed change processes. We shall discuss these programmes in more depth later in this book; they are, however:

1   *Management and organizational support*: In the IDP concept the entire organization needs to develop a capacity to deal with new challenges and problems — it needs an organizational development (OD) capacity. Few schools have trained OD consultants and few schools have conceptualized what OD means. The IDP has as its main goal to build an internal capability to manage the change process. It is necessary to develop skills to be applied at the school level as well as at the group level (e.g. classroom). Our experience is that most heads and their deputies want to develop skills in the management of change. Quite often (as we shall illustrate in this book) the IDP carries with it a parallel programme in addition to work with the entire school.

2   *Curriculum and staff development*: Schools are dependent on a mission defined by others, usually a ministry of education (or a similar body at the local level). These authorities define the curriculum and staff qualifications in broad terms. Schools, on the other hand, have to make sense of them — to fit the general curriculum guidelines with the realities and the staff motivation and competencies available. Increasingly, schools understand that local adaptation is already taking place to a fairly high degree — often, however, 'behind the classroom door', and often based on 'deficits'. It becomes a reactive process. The IDP encourages school-based curriculum and staff development that is open and builds on a common vision of what the school is all about. It encourages an open dialogue and the use of peer supervision and other collegial forms of interaction to increase the likelihood of adult learning.

3   *Internal school assessment*: The final element in a 'learning school'. To monitor the process of development and learning, *formative evaluation*, or an internal process of assessment, is essential. Gathering data about key aspects of the organization on a regular basis becomes the yardstick for further growth. It may also provide data for *external* authorities in their efforts to evaluate schools. The purpose of the internal school assessment process is not evaluation, but learning. It is a tool for growth, at the individual and at the organizational level. As discussed throughout this book, schools are clearly dependent on the school *system*, and also need to interact with a number of groups and organizations in their environment. Interaction with the forces in the environment, therefore, is an essential aspect of development.

These elements are to us essential aspects of a learning organization. The purpose of the IDP is to assist a school in its process towards becoming a learning organization. We shall see that schools are quite different in their growth process, and therefore interventions will differ.

# READING THIS BOOK

This is a book for practitioners. This does not mean that it avoids theory; however, the theory is *practice-oriented*. Indeed, the IDP is theory-based as well as empirically based. It has been used in some 1000 schools in Scandinavia, the Netherlands, the UK, North America and Germany. What we want to communicate is a vision of how schools can improve. It is for heads and teachers, for inspectors and support personnel and for the informed citizen.

The book is organized around the *consultant training programme* because this programme is essential in the IDP, and also follows logical 'cycles' in the change process. We will not be able to present fully other major aspects of the IDP (e.g. school leadership development, policy development at the district level, etc.); however, we feel that this approach will give the reader the best practical entry to general strategies for school improvement embedded in the IDP. These are the same strategies that school leaders and others involved in change will have to work with.

The consultant training process is in itself interesting; however, space will not permit a full discussion. It is based on the theory of staff development outlined by Joyce and Showers, using a series of learning activities that combine theory, practice, feedback supervision and intervision, and coaching over an 18-24 month period (each consultant trainee working in pairs with another trainee in a given school and receiving regular supervision) (Joyce and Showers, 1980, 1984). The experiences we present through the cases in this book have been presented and analysed in several seminars over the past few years. They are real; however, they have been modified so that their specific identity is protected.

The entire book is meant to illustrate an approach to developing a school's capacity towards becoming a 'learning organization', a process supported by an external consultant. The impression may arise that the IDP *assumes* the use of external consultancy. This is a misunderstanding. The usual process should be that a school by and large develops its capacity without the use of consultancy.

This book is an *introduction* to the whole issue of school development. A second volume, published by the Landesinstitut für Schule und Weiterbildung (LSW) in North Rhine-Westphalia, in co-operation with IMTEC, Norway, is available (in German). It contains more in-depth studies, cases, reading materials, exercises and some instruments. It is for trained consultants and trainers.

# Chapter 2

## Supporting Institutional Development

*Schools have a long tradition in using external consultants, usually in terms of curriculum or staff development experts from the local authority or college. IDP consultancy is based on the assumption that a dialogue between the school and an external consultant will mobilize the internal resources of the school; however, not by the consultant providing solutions for the school. What does it mean then, in practice, to work as a 'process consultant'? What are the phases in IDP consultancy? How can cultural changes be facilitated?*

The purpose of the IDP is to develop the capacities that we see as essential for the learning organization (see Chapter 1). We see this change process as a learning process that deals with the entire school culture, and our goal is that the single school, as the unit of change, will be able to develop the necessary capabilities.

Many schools, however, are far from being real learning organizations. Many schools that we work with are traditional fragmented schools, with teachers quite isolated in their roles, with little connection among departments and groups and with a very low capacity for joint problem-solving. These schools, and many others, need assistance, and this may take many forms.

*Staff development* has traditionally been cared for by standard courses in universities and college. Increasingly, *in-service training* (school-based) is becoming the norm. Other actors, such as pedagogical centres (e.g. the Netherlands), teachers' centres and even independent organizations (e.g. the UK), are taking over a major part of the in-service market. Traditionally, in-service training has been geared towards subject-based courses for individual teachers. Increasingly such courses are seen as staff development for groups of teachers. Other staff development needs (e.g. linked to the school culture, organizational issues, etc.) are seldom met.

*Management development* has not traditionally been offered to schools. Increasingly, this need is met by either national in-service programmes (e.g. Sweden, North Rhine-Westphalia), or through more locally based university courses. Again this type of course has usually been offered to heads and deputy heads. Now, several courses are geared towards *leadership teams*, and some approaches are also school-based and take the form of management consultancy services.

*Curriculum development* and materials development have traditionally been seen as an important activity for 'support agencies' (administration, pedagogical centres, etc.). Teachers are often used in curriculum development teams, in-service training is usually a part of the activity, and changed curriculum and materials are tangible outcomes. In some countries *school-based* curriculum development is becoming an important supplement to more central initiatives (e.g. Norway, the UK, the Netherlands).

*Evaluation* of the instructional process has often been the task of inspectors, a system of quality control that is also undergoing changes. Traditionally, inspectors observed classroom instruction and supervised the work of the school management. Increasingly, the inspectorate is playing a more supportive role, providing advice, training, and technical expertise (e.g. in building a school-based evaluation system). In so far as teacher training and in-service training are undergoing change, so are the role and tasks of the inspectorate (see Chapter 7). 'Peer supervision' or 'teacher appraisal' systems are being introduced in many countries (Evans and Tomlinson, 1989).

The school has access to expertise and resources at the central and local levels, from public as well as private institutions, from other schools and from more specialized agencies. No doubt, the resources are limited, and quite often the support is not viewed as relevant or of adequate quality. Sometimes the school is not sufficiently aware of its needs, or has difficulties in defining them or in choosing among alternatives. Also, the culture of the school is often opposed to external influences, in particular to external expertise. For many reasons, therefore, some schools do not use external resources.

Schools are supposed to be learning organizations. A productive school culture reflects accepted principles of learning. Adults in schools need also to be learners. Without systematic and continuous learning at the individual, group and organizational levels, schools as learning organizations will not survive. They will be more like prisons than dynamic laboratories of development. It is a strength to invite external resources into a learning process. It may also be a strength to *refuse* 'experts' who come to the school to *sell* expertise, solutions, approaches, or policies.

To take schools seriously is to understand them as learning organizations. This means, among other things, to understand the values and the norms of the school, needs for change, individual and organizational strength and weaknesses, and the norms of learning. To undertake IDP consultancy means to work with the school as an organization; to be sensitive to the culture and its needs for renewal; to respect the right of the school to define its own needs, select strategies for change that suit the school; and to assist the school in the process of change.

IDP consultancy is about another type of resource for schools. It is not about content expertise (e.g. a new method of instruction, a new style of management). An IDP consultant is concerned about the ability of the school to utilize and develop its own resources, to improve the 'problem-solving capability' of the school, and to link the school with the external expertise required (as defined by the school itself).

Organizational learning was defined at three different levels by Argyris and Schön (1974).

1 Learning that deals with the *means* of the school, but does not raise questions about the aims. It is a question about *efficiency* of existing practices, which Argyris and Schön called 'single-loop learning'.

2 Learning that deals both with the aims and the means, that from the experiences of the situation today try to develop a new vision, new objectives and new means (which Argyris and Schön called 'double-loop learning', or what is sometimes called 'restructuring' in American literature).

3 Learning that has as its main objective to 'learn to learn', that helps the school to evaluate its own practice, to jointly develop new objectives and programmes, and helps the school to problem-solve issues and conflicts, and to restructure itself to cope also with future challenges.

The main objective of the IDP is to help the school move towards a 'learning organization', to provide the capacity to meet new challenges from within, or from the environment, in such a way that the real needs of students and staff are met. As a result of the IDP the school will not only establish new practices in given areas, but it will also gain experience and competence that enables it to manage change processes in the future. The school 'learns how to learn'.

## IDP ASSUMPTIONS

During the past 15 years IMTEC has worked with a number of schools in Europe and with about 200 colleagues, who have been trained through the two-year consultant training programme for IDP consultants. During this time we have learned a lot, changed much of what we did in the earlier phases, and reformulated our assumptions, which will be presented in this book. The original assumptions of the IDP are partly valid; however, they have since been modified (Dalin and Rust, 1983). As we see it today, the following assumptions are important in the IDP.

1 *The school as the unit of change*: Those who are going to live with the consequences of the changes, those who feel the pressures for change, and those who need to invest in change are the ones best positioned to carry out change. We have argued above that all forces for change materialize in one place — the school — which is dependent on external support, on policy guidelines and resources. However, reaching desired objectives can only be done in the context of the individual school. External authorities can best be partners to schools, by providing needed support and setting standards.

2 *The school as the motor*: The school must be in charge of the change process. External consultants can and should help only to facilitate the process. Sometimes schools work well without external consultants, and sometimes a 'third party' may be vital for the success of the process. The job of the consultant is to assist in the development of the internal capacity.

*The chairperson of the school's Steering Committee is on the phone: 'Edward, we really liked what you did last week with the staff. The seminar was excellent — and you were very much the key figure'.... 'Oh, I am pleased to hear that you learned a lot'.... 'Now, yes, that is true. In fact the staff has already asked me to book in for a second and third seminar'.... 'I am pleased to hear that you want to work more on these important issues; however, you remember our contract: you know as much as I do about these issues and should be in charge next time'.... 'Yes, I remember, but that is not what the teachers want. They want you, and I do not feel comfortable taking over if that is what the teachers want.'... 'Listen, I see your point, but I think that my job is done at this point — on these issues. Why don't we sit down and plan it together?'... 'Maybe, can you get over here soon?'*

The IDP consultant faces many difficult dilemmas. This is just one: how can he help the school to become an effective motor? What are the behavioural implications for the consultant?

3 *Subjective and objective reality*: Behavioural changes are based on the interpretation of reality as experienced by the participants. There clearly is an *objective* reality; however, it is the *interpretation* of this reality that is essential for the mobilization of energy necessary for the change process. Objective reality, for example the student drop-out rate, staff turnover, achievement scores, budget and budget allocation, will always play a role. More important, however, is *what data mean to the actors*. There might be scarcity of resources, but schools with the same amount of resources cope with it in very different ways. The IDP process attempts to document objective as well as subjective reality, to feed information back to participants at various stages of the process, thereby 'confronting' participant perceptions as part of the learning process. Because the growth of an institution to such an extent is based on *perceptions*, all participants have the right and should be given a real chance to participate.

4 *Change as co-operation*: The objective of the IDP is to strengthen the problem-solving capacity of the school. It may involve practice change at the individual level, changes in values and norms, changes in the way groups and classrooms function, pedagogical changes and more general organizational change. This is not possible without wide participation. Perceptions are formed as people with different views interpret reality and strive towards an understanding of needs, and begin to formulate visions and goals. Co-operation, however, also has its negative undertones.

*The teacher had tried co-operative learning in the classroom and his experience was quite negative. Students talked and*

> *talked; however, very little was produced and it was not at*
> *all clear who was really producing. When the headmaster*
> *suggested more planning time among teachers, his immediate*
> *reaction was negative: it would mean quarrels with teacher X,*
> *the hard work would have to be done by himself and possibly*
> *teacher Y, and besides, many afternoons would be spent*
> *without much by way of positive results.*

Co-operation is important, but it does not mean that all problems can
or should be resolved by co-operative activities. It is not an ideology.
For some work individual contributions are essential. Sometimes a
group effort can do no more than delay the outcomes. Also the
degree of co-operation is dependent on the 'maturity of the school'.
In an early phase, often when a school is 'loosely coupled', forced
co-operation will very often backfire. In fact, to get a development
process started in such schools may be impossible without a high
degree of individual work. Increasingly, however, individuals see
their contributions as part of a whole, as part of common needs, and
therefore that co-operation may be wanted and necessary. Despite
this caution it is necessary to stress the need for *co-operative* learning,
the need for team learning and organizational learning. It is particularly
important in schools, where teachers often work in isolation.

5 *Conflicts as opportunities*: Instead of avoiding conflicts, the IDP *uses*
conflicts as opportunities for understanding the reality of the school,
for raising key issues related to participants' perceptions of reality,
and for exploring ways in which energy 'stored' in conflicts can be
released for the benefit of the school. Conflicts offer opportunities
for learning because they often provide a chance for clarifying issues,
for putting unresolved issues on the table and for helping to
understand another point of view.

> *For a long time I had avoided talking to her. She irritated me*
> *more than I would admit — her way of taking over a meeting,*
> *dominating the agenda and pressing her points. I saw many*
> *colleagues frustrated, and some of us talked about it when she*
> *was not there. I must admit that I had begun to be afraid of*
> *her. It is quite unreal: I am the head and she is just a teacher; I*
> *admit, a very good and respected one. In fact students like her*
> *a lot, and she tends to take popular stands to defend the*
> *students. I simply don't know how to 'regulate' her, and I am*
> *sure we will not get anywhere near a decision on the new*
> *project if she is going to be involved. I just have to confront*
> *her; but how and when?*

Conflicts of a personal nature, conflicts over interests, or conflicts
over values and norms are commonplace in schools. School norms
are quite often to avoid conflicts, and the results are often low
productivity and personal frustrations.

There is another tension that institutions need to live with, namely the tension between reality and the vision. There will always be a distance between the real and the ideal situation; this may cause concern, irritation and tension — a tension which, however, is necessary. In the often slow process of developing a joint vision, the school goes through many phases of trust-building, personal growth, team-building and value clarifications. A vision is more than a statement, it is a value achieved through hard and joint work.

6 *Process values and programme goals*: The IDP is based on a number of values and theories already presented in this chapter and later in this book. The IDP is not value-free. It carries a number of messages that we believe are important for the development of quality schools.

On the other hand, an IDP consultant does not carry with him 'advice' or a new 'policy', or a given 'technology', or a 'solution'. In terms of *what* the school ought to do the consultant respects the right of the school to decide. This does not mean, however, that the consultant is uninterested in or detached from the process of deciding. His or her role is rather to ensure that a clear and productive process of decision-making is developed in the school, that alternatives are considered and that the relevant data are known and understood.

> *It was not popular among many staff, but it became clearer and clearer: this school needed more discipline, not the old type, but certainly more order and respect for time and other people. Would it mean that we had to put more restrictions on the agenda? How could we do that when we had already given both students and teachers so much freedom? How could we convince the students? The consultant asked a question: 'Is it more discipline that is needed or clearer norms and structure?' We went back to the data and found that we indeed enjoyed our freedom and would be willing to pay for it. Could we work with the students to let them develop norms and a structure that would put more order in their lives as well?*

IDP consultancy differs from much of the external consulting practices known to many schools. Quite often such a 'consultant', usually a subject matter expert, a school inspector, or somebody else from the 'system', comes with a 'fixed mandate'. He or she is there, for example, to explain and give advice on the implementation of new curricula decided by the district. It is mainly a question of how the school 'as a consumer' can adapt to new system conditions. Many IDP consultants will also be confronted with such 'system demands' but their role is a different one. In the early phases the IDP consultant will help the school to look at all the external forces and the internal needs that may be relevant in relationship to new demands. It is the role of the school to find an adequate solution, and it is the role of the IDP consultant to facilitate the process to enable the school to find the best possible practice in relationship to new demands (Schein, 1990).

7 *Effectiveness is situational*: Schools are complex social systems. Hundreds of variables intermix in a variety of ways and provide the unique 'picture' of a specific school. The literature is full of advice on what 'effectiveness' means. In the leadership literature, for example, there are many schools of thought and even more advice.

Our experience is that very few general solutions have applications to organizations. Our present knowledge base, our instrumentation and our perspectives are limited. We cannot cope with the complexities in one theory. What seems to be 'effective' in one school is not necessarily effective in another. There are too many variables to take into account to automatically assume that success can be transferred. We believe this is true in the pedagogical arena, as well as in the organizational and management arena. This, of course, does not mean that we cannot learn and should not draw from 'school effectiveness' studies, but that they have to be *adapted* by the school to make a difference.

Most schools are not effective learning organizations. High educational achievement scores (usually the indicator of an 'effective school') are not necessarily the most important indicator of an effective learning organization. Effective leadership, for example, in the former is not necessarily the same as in the latter.

To help the school to develop solutions that function effectively in the context of the school, it is often necessary for the participants to *change perspectives*, to look at the problem in a different way, to 'rediscover' reality. Very often, problem-solving is unable to progress because participants are unable to get away from an established point of view. In this respect different concepts or 'images' of organizations may be useful for a creative learning process (Morgan, 1986).

8 *Freedom of manoeuvre*: The school is part of a hierarchical bureaucracy, and is in many ways restricted in terms of development. Such restrictions may be real; however, often they are simply perceived as barriers to development. So many school leaders are acting as 'civil servants', not as managers, and they have a hard time defining their room of manoeuvre.

> *The project meant a fairly large reallocation of resources in the budget. In fact, if all those computers were to be purchased it would mean spending nearly a full-time teacher salary on a yearly basis. Teachers had proposed to do that since there were two vacant teacher posts anyway, and so far other teachers had organized work so flexibly that there was no problem. The only problem was this: the head really had no authority to use salary money for computers. If the head asked permission, two things would happen: the superintendent would say no, and he*

*would consider shifting those vacancies to other schools that
are in desperate need of more teachers.*

We see external authorities as important partners in school
development. It is essential to understand that effective external
leadership is a combination of relevant *support* and effective
*pressure* (Huberman and Miles, 1984). It is clearly legitimate for
external authorities to set standards and to secure quality as well as
equality of educational opportunity. In this process, however, we
know that considerable space for manoeuvre is vital for schools to
succeed in their role.

9 *Planning and implementation as one process.* The IDP assumes that
participants are involved in the process of change from early
identification of needs until implementation. The traditional division
of labour between *planning* on the one hand and *implementation* on
the other is not functional. The IDP can be described as 'cycles of
learning'; and to be involved, as the needs are originally defined, as
ideas are shaped and tested, is essential for the learning process
and for ownership.

10 *Schools can learn*: Only individuals can learn. They also learn from
organizational life. And they learn together. It is the sum of
individual and collective learning that forms the organization. To us
an effective school is a school that takes its own learning process
seriously.

Teachers and students learn best from behaviour. To learn
through development processes is a type of organizational learning
that helps the school to develop its own problem-solving capability.
It is our experience that we often forget how complicated and
challenging behavioural changes are and how much effort is needed
for an organization to change its behavioural patterns. Not only
does it take a long time, it depends on knowledge, skills and a
trial-and-error phase that is often quite long; and it is dependent on
collegial support over time.

Organizational learning is a concept introduced by Argyris and Schön (1978).
The starting point is the basic idea that institutions are central 'learning centres' in today's society. Much of daily learning takes place in institutions. On the
other hand, institutions are also undergoing a learning process (Türk, 1989). The
learning effect that human resource development attempts to represent
benefits not only the individual but also the entire organization. Türk is particularly concerned about how the organizational structures should 'facilitate and
not hinder the learning processes'. This is also the concern of the IDP.

Is the IDP about organizational development, or something else? Is it about
action learning or action research? Is it systematic problem-solving? Is it
planned change? These questions cannot be answered easily. The IDP draws
from the theory and practice of several development traditions; however, it
forms a unique set of principles and practices that focus organizational learning

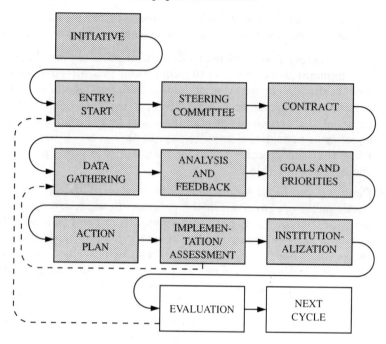

Figure 2.1  *Linear process description*

in schools. The IDP is an approach to development that is tailor-made to schools as learning organizations.

## THE IDP PROCESS

This book outlines and analyses how the IDP process works. We illustrate a process where the school interacts with an IDP consultant, since this gives a comprehensive picture of the process. We will see that the process in most schools has some common elements. However, it is practised differently in each school simply because the school is the unit for change, and therefore the contextual factors are critical for the application of the IDP. This is particularly true as far as the use of an external consultant is concerned. Several schools, in fact, work with the IDP without the use of consultancy. We outline the general steps that are usually taken in the IDP process.

The process can at first be seen as a linear set of activities that fall into several concrete steps, as outlined in Figure 2.1.

### Initiation and entry

Schools engage in development work for many reasons. It may start with a felt 'problem', but it does not have to. Some very successful schools want to further develop their organization and take initiatives to *avoid* problems. In any case, there exists, often, a very vague but felt need for change. We find that this early 'warning' or indicator is essential; however, we know that 'the school' will expand and modify its needs as participants engage in the process. An IDP consultant finds him- or herself engaged in three different types of processes in this cycle.

1 *Understanding* the need for change and trying to feed back to the client his/her perceptions.

2 *Building a relationship* with the client, exploring roles, expected tasks, commitments, and the potential for a productive relationship.

3 *Establishing a contract* with the client that will clarify who the client is, what the role of the consultant should be, and what resources and time will be committed to the process.

## Joint analysis and diagnosis

As 'the school' (now usually represented by an internal steering committee) starts to work on the tasks with the consultant, a number of issues are usually put forward. Again, the consultant is 'recycling', helping the school to obtain a deeper understanding of needs and gradually developing the relationship. Also, it may already be clear that the contract needs modifications. In this cycle the consultant usually assists in some specific tasks.

*Formulating areas of concern*, or issues that seem critical to the further development of the school. This is usually a brainstorming list of issues, thoroughly discussed in the Steering Committee. On the basis of this understanding several steps are taken:

*Data-gathering*: either the gathering and analysis of existing data, and/or the gathering of new data by the use of standard and/or tailor-made instruments. It is the Steering Committee which decides what data to gather. This process leads into:

*Data analysis*, which is always done *jointly* within the Steering Committee. Often the consultant plays a facilitating role. Usually this process leads into:

*Data feedback and a dialogue*, with all participants (e.g. all teachers) helping everyone to get an understanding of the data, and analysing what it means to them. Data alone do not matter. It is participants' perceptions of the data that have meaning. This is the first instance when participants begin *jointly* to realize the 'gap' between the way things are and what is desired. It may well create tension; however, it also creates an opportunity to mobilize energy for renewal.

This is a process that helps participants to think *systematically*, rather than in terms of isolated phenomena, episodes or issues. The use of alternative 'images', testing data from many sources, helps the participants to *discover* the dynamics of the organization.

## Goal-setting

Goal-setting is the school's ability to formulate its intentions and establish alternatives, and is the essential part of this cycle. The analysis of data usually clarifies a number of issues. It is essential in this part of the process to facilitate a creative process that helps the school to formulate its visions and goals. Several activities play an important part in this cycle.

> *Setting priorities* among many alternatives is difficult. The consultant helps the school to formulate problem statements, and thereby sorts out a *meaning* from the mass of data available.

> *Value clarification* is a process that takes place throughout the entire process. However, at this stage it is particularly important since the school will have to decide what to do. The IDP is not a consensus seeking process. Values need to be *negotiated*; sometimes consensus is developed, and in other situations the school decides to live with several sets of values.

> *Action planning* involves transforming intentions into concrete plans that can be realized in the school. A number of 'project planning' techniques and delegation of work to task forces is the normal pattern in this cycle.

## Testing and evaluation

To transform plans into reality, the school will usually pilot some of the project ideas and give an opportunity to some teachers and students to try new practices. In other cases the nature of the change itself is comprehensive and systemic, implying that all participants have to change (e.g. changing into a new work organization). During this cycle the role of the consultant may change, and the following activities are central.

> *Training* in areas such as project management, evaluation and group development (e.g. team building) is a common activity. It may also be necessary to give specific training in content-specific areas (e.g. the use of computer simulations in mathematics). Such training is given by others besides the IDP consultant, who sees his or her role as linking the school with needed external resources.

> *Monitoring and evaluation* of the implementation of new projects is essential ('formative' evaluation), both because the effects are not obvious, and also because often only a few of the teachers participate in project implementation in the first phase. The consultant assists the school when needed, in the design of a monitoring and evaluation process, and helps to feed data from implementation back to participants and non-participants.

## Generalization and institutionalization

The piloting usually goes through several cycles with increasingly more teachers and students involved. This means more staff training, often materials development and other types of support (see Chapter 3). At some stage the school will have to routinize the change effort and make it a 'normal part' of the school. Several activities are essential:

*Evaluation* of a 'summative' nature, as the school tries to establish the value of new practice. It is essential that the evaluation is done properly (in particular if there is disagreement to begin with). The discussion over evaluation data might well bring forward a deeper understanding of needs and set the stage for a renewed experiment or totally different pilot schemes.

*Structural adjustments*, or changes in the way the school is organized, the formulation of new procedures and the modification of norms and rules may be important.

*Resource allocations*, or at least re-allocation of existing resources, is often an essential part of routinization of new practice. Schools seldom have many free resources; usually it is a question of time allocation of subjects and activities.

*Staff development*, or helping staff not yet involved to gain the necessary skills for new practice, is now essential because new practice is compulsory. Usually the school can use its own staff in this process since it has gained considerable experience during the project period.

*Consultant withdrawal* may happen at any time; however, at this stage it is essential to consider the termination of the consultant-school relationship. Has the school achieved what it set out to do? Has it gained experience and does it have the capacity to deal with new challenges? If not, in what areas of work does it still want to consider further assistance?

It is important to understand that these activities do not happen in a linear way, one after the other. The activities may appear at different times in the process; they can appear several times in different ways and in different intensity. The process is, by its nature, cyclic. While one works formally with data-gathering and analysis of data, for example, this activity also gives good possibilities for team development. In different phases of a project, staff development must have a high priority, and evaluation can, on the other hand, give a chance to raise new questions that again may modify the programme. School development is a complex and comprehensive learning process where changes in the school culture are central (see Chapter 5).

These concrete steps are important because they provide the *capacity-building opportunities* in institutional development. Through these steps the school is increasingly involved in complex learning processes — if the activities involve the entire school. Figure 2.2 illustrates the relationships between the concrete action steps in a typical IDP process (see right-hand column) and the processes that are critical for institutionalization. The figure provides an illustration of learning outcomes of the process.

1 It helps the school to use alternative perspectives and systems thinking on what are experienced as 'problems', and thereby it is in a

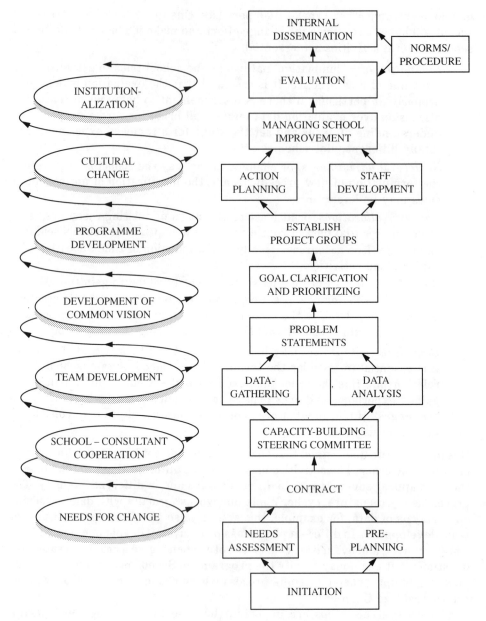

Figure 2.2 *The IDP process.*

better position to clarify its real needs (a process that will often reappear as the institutional learning process matures).

2 It models a working relationship built on trust, through the co-operation between the school (often the Steering Committee) and the consultant. To function well this relationship must reflect a dialogue based on trust and norms of openness and clarity.

3  It builds learning teams, first through the work in the Steering Committee, later in work groups, and finally in the regular work groups of the school. Again the Steering Committee work is seen as a model; individuals from this group also learn to master group work and are often used as moderators in other learning teams in the school.

4  It helps to develop common values, visions and norms. It seldom *starts* the process; it is rather to be seen as a consequence of trust-building, ownership to the process and personal and team learning.

5  It helps the school to improve programmes and operations in the school, these being the concrete outcomes of a series of 'projects' and, often, preliminary concrete outcomes of the first phase of the IDP. Although such projects are important, they are only seen as a component of the institutional development process.

6  It helps change the school culture, by practising new behaviour, by joint work in teams, by staff development and collegial supervision. It is the most complex part of the IDP, it is not straightforward, it cannot be 'engineered'; it is a late stage in a process that has involved the entire school.

7  Finally, it helps the school to institutionalize new problem-solving behaviour, through the intensive learning process that has taken place at all levels throughout the entire development period.

As we now turn to the individual phases and activities within the IDP we need to repeat: it is not a blueprint that fits all schools. It is not a linear process where one step follows the other. It takes many turns, the cycles are often repeated, and some processes are much more important in some schools than in others.

# Chapter 3

# Initiation

*'Aller Anfang ist schwer', the Germans say. 'Well started means half way through', is an old Norwegian saying. What type of school will ask for consultancy? What do we mean by 'consultancy'. How is it possible to understand the 'real needs of the school'? Schools, like other organizations, learn; what does such a learning process look like? How do we proceed when a school seeks assistance in a development programme? How can we get partipants to shift perspectives?*

In Chapter 1 we have presented the 'mutual adaptation and development' perspective of educational innovations. Innovations are the result of a creative dialogue among forces within the school and in the environment.

A change process may start *within* the school: with the ideas of one teacher, as the result of a discussion among staff, as an initiative by students or parents; or *outside* the school, as challenges presented in a new local or national curriculum, as an expert proposal, or as the result of major socio-economic changes in the local environment. And these are only a few examples!

Wherever the process of change is initiated, it needs to be understood and integrated as a task by all those concerned within a school. The long and often difficult process of adaptation, development and implementation needs to be managed by the individual school. How does 'the school' get to the point where it identifies with the need to change existing practices? In Chapter 1 we described three different categories of schools, and their characteristics in terms of their capacity for change. These have different capacities to manage change; they approach change challenges differently, and they can best be described as representing three *cycles of development*, a process by which the school is involving more and more teachers and students, and where learning from the projects is gradually shared, forming a new culture.

To initiate change is often difficult. An internal proposal may be seen as criticism of existing practices or may raise questions of power and conflicts. A proposal from the government might be seen as irrelevant and unrealistic. Some expert proposals may be experienced as unrelated to what really goes on in the school, and so on. Wherever initiation comes from, it raises *process questions*. The first meeting concerning a proposal, the style and atmosphere of intervention, may well be important for the further development of a programme.

An Institutional Development Program (IDP) consultant will seldom *initiate* a programme. He or she would more likely be called to the school as one or several proposals for change are discussed. It is often when school management needs a different perspective to handle a change proposal, or when particular skills are needed, that a consultant is called in. In the following we describe and discuss what happens as the school works with a proposal and draws on an IDP consultant.

# THE NEEDS OF THE SCHOOL AS THE STARTING POINT

To have 'real needs' as the starting point for school development is not unproblematic, not least because the 'needs' are often diffuse and therefore difficult to express clearly. Something that on the surface can be seen as a 'need' can over a period of time become much less important than the more underlying needs that were not formulated or even felt from the beginning. One of the most important tasks of the school leadership and the IDP consultant in the entry phase is therefore to help the school to identify and express the needs for development and change.

The consultant will, during 'entry', ask a number of questions aimed at clarification of needs. He or she is not always sure how the answers should be interpreted, but will try to make a first assessment of the situation. The entry phase and the 'diagnostic phase' may therefore overlap. Also, the consultant goes through an important learning process. He or she tries to learn as much as possible about the partners without fixing him- or herself on particular interpretations. An open, listening and questioning attitude is important.

The more or less clearly formulated or felt needs, as these are expressed by the participants, must always be taken seriously, even if they, as far as the consultant is concerned, seem peripheral. In the first meetings it is probably more important than ever to be open, listening and trying to interpret what is being said and what is being done. Every item can be an important detail for later diagnosis. Some schools wish to start modestly and to discuss fairly straightforward issues and problems, such as how one can develop norms of punctuality for both students and teachers. Other schools do not want to start a process that deals with the entire school. They would rather make fairly limited changes, for example questions connected with introductory courses. Some teachers are so concerned about the problems and the unpleasantness that they think are associated with a comprehensive school development programme that they do not even want to start with small steps. Others feel that they need time to prepare themselves. Some express a need for more competence; others want to work straight away to improve the co-operation of the staff, while yet others might express a need for better leadership.

Such wishes and felt needs are something all participants and the consultant will have to register and take into account. Many school cultures are not open enough even to discuss problems, and believe that problems should be dealt with internally. This indicates that the entry phase is not always easy. Quite often the problems are not dealt with, they are often swept under the carpet, and they may hurt much more at a later stage. We know from our practice in private enterprises that willingness to cope with issues is much more common; it is not only allowed, but quite vital that both strong and weak parts of the organization be identified and worked with, often in co-operation with external consultants. This more constructive attitude towards improvement is gradually also penetrating the public sector, as our experience from the Netherlands and Scandinavia indicates.

While individual needs may be important, the IDP is basically concerned with the needs of the school as an organization and the needs in different groups and departments of the school. This does not mean, however, that management and the consultant should set aside individual wishes and needs. These are important for the individuals, and at times also important for the school. Sometimes needs are connected with the head, who quite often is the person who asks for assistance. It is important to take individual needs seriously and look upon them in relation to organizational needs.

Some needs can be connected to smaller groups in the staff, e.g. co-operation problems in a teacher team. Such needs can, to a greater or lesser degree, be prioritized; it all depends on how relevant they are for the situation as a whole. If such problems are blocking further development, to deal with them here and now may be one important step to get further ahead in the school development process. The same is true for needs that may look relatively minor to begin with but, if taken seriously, may be the incentive to move towards a more comprehensive school development programme. The fact that the consultant may be able to deal directly with a felt problem could be the first step in the development of trust which is the basis for a co-operative programme.

The basic principle for the IDP, however, should not be lost: the entire school and all its different functions need to be dealt with in a comprehensive school development process. The chances are clearly that what is expressed as an important need when a consultant deals with one or two members of the staff may look quite different when other groups express their interest. It is important to listen to all points of view, including those of the students. It is often a question of alternative perspectives on the work of the school. To assess individual needs in relation to school needs is a very important task of the school management and the IDP consultant. If this succeeds, it provides a good basis for the beginning of a school development programme.

To discover and assess the most important needs in one or more groups, and at the same time appreciate the comprehensive needs of a school as an organization, is an impossible task in the entry phase. We know, however, that what are seen as needs will change over time as we learn more about the school as an organization, and therefore the task in the early phases is to recognize the various needs and be open for modification and change as the development process unfolds. This is a recognition of the fact that needs are not static and cannot be decided once and for all. They change as needs are satisfied. There is a social dynamic in the development of needs, also within an organization, as we have tried to illustrate in Figures 1.4-1.6. Some needs can come from within, the so-called internal needs, or the starting point may be outside the school as an organization.

We shall now, in some detail, describe how an external consultant may become involved with the school in an institutional improvement effort. This description would be fairly typical for the 'IDP entry' in a school, and may happen in any one of the three types of schools as described above. It should be clear, however, that many schools prefer to work *without* an external

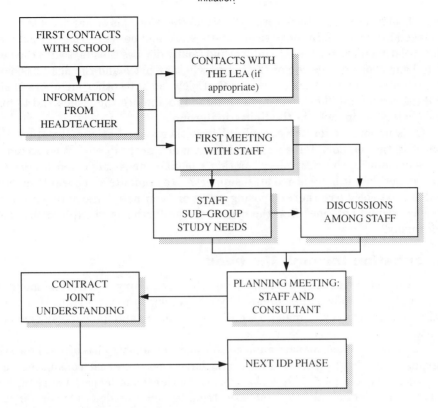

Figure 3.1  *Contact and contract phase*

consultant. Many of the same processes will still take place, often initiated and led by the school management (Figure 3.1).

The first contact of a consultant with a school may happen by chance. For example, a consultant meets a staff member, or the head contacts him or her to ask for a discussion. Some of the basic issues may be taken up as early as during this first discussion. The consultant will inform those involved in the discussion about his or her competence and way of working. The partners at the school inform the consultant about the school, what the development needs are and also what they would like to discuss further with an external consultant. Usually the head or a representative of school management participates in this first contact meeting.

## The first orientation to the head

The attitude of the head is one critical factor in the development process. Full support from the head may create a positive working climate and also encourage hesitant staff members to put time and work into development efforts. On the other hand, if the head expresses scepticism and hesitation, he or she may also get support from other sceptical colleagues. It is therefore important that the head is from the outset positively inclined, and wishes to support the effort. The early discussion with the school leader is therefore of vital importance. Often the school leader is the initiator anyway and therefore his or her acceptance can be taken for granted. In those cases where staff members or even students take the initiative there is a need to inform and finally discuss the ideas with the head. A full and broad discussion of the issues will take place and the head has every opportunity to express his or her point of view, as have other members of staff and the consultant. The meeting is designed to explore the issues and to build good relationships within the 'initiation group'.

It is important for the consultant to gather some basic information. How broad is the support for a school development programme? Who asked for 'development' in the first place? Is this a management-supported programme idea and/or does it have broad staff support? Are students and parents involved and in what role? Are there opposing views or eventually alternative proposals to what should be done? Can the consultant go further and explore the issues informally?

## Information through the head

If the contact is basically with the head at the beginning of a development project, it should also be supplemented by contact with the total staff. If this does not take place the result may be scepticism, rumours and unnecessary negative attitudes.

Experience from 'management consultancy' in industry has often shown that labour unions have been sceptical, and have seen external consultancy as a 'management strategy'. This we have also experienced in schools where the head was the only contact person, who later tried to 'sell' the idea to his or her staff. In order to avoid such a situation it is important to have informal discussions with different representatives of the staff and sometimes also with students.

Sometimes a broad information meeting is organized, or other meetings where there is a chance for an open and informal discussion, and a chance for the consultant to learn more about the school and for the staff to get acquainted with the consultant.

Since those who are sceptical will usually be represented in these first discussions, it is important that the arguments against a change programme (worries and opposition) are taken seriously, assessed and thoroughly discussed in an acceptable way. Scepticism is not only acceptable but wanted. Also, those who are usually against school development should be encouraged to express clearly their opinion, without having to defend themselves because they may have a different point of view. At the end of such meetings some time could be spent on looking at a possible next step, for example a conference where all teachers and other relevant partners are brought together.

## Information conference with the whole staff

In the first meeting between the consultant and the staff, a full discussion of the development project idea and the possible consultancy will be presented and discussed. The meeting is usually led by the head and the consultant is an invited guest who should have at least half an hour to present him- or herself and his or her work.

The starting point is obviously the ideas deriving from the school (e.g. from the school leadership) about what needs to be done. Following such a presentation the consultant has an opportunity clearly to present the IDP, the approach to development work and the consultancy that may be used in the process. In the discussion that will follow it is normal to encounter both positive and negative points of view, scepticism, criticism and barriers against the development process being suggested. It is the task of the consultant to listen to all arguments in the most objective way possible. His or her task is to make it clear to all participants that different opinions are needed, necessary and normal in any development process. Even in this first meeting it is possible to clarify viewpoints and to get a better understanding of how the staff assesses its needs, and possible also for the consultant to represent a different attitude in a discussion that will be experienced as constructive.

## The Steering Committee

It is essential that the development process is anchored in the school from the first moment; in most cases, in the staff, who usually take on most of the burden of development work. Therefore one should elect a Steering Committee as early as during the informational conference. Such a group may include earlier contact persons, but it could also consist of a committee recently elected by the teachers' conference or the school board, should the project include students, parents and others. What is important is that the Steering Committee represents the different points of view in the school, and also that the leadership of the school is represented. We do not think such a Steering Committee should be any larger than eight persons (see Chapter 6).

The task of the Steering Committee is, as the name indicates, to lead the IDP process. The Steering Committee is not a part of the formal school management structure. It is a *temporary group* that may exist as long as the project evolves, usually one or two years, or at least as long as it is necessary to assist in the implementation of the programme. The Steering Committee is in other words a 'temporary system' or a project organization that is delegated the responsibility to plan and implement a school development programme.

The second option is for the school management to lead the development process. This is recommended in many cultures, including most schools in North America. The Scandinavian experience tells us that the temporary group system, where all parties are represented in the Steering Committee, is a stronger mechanism. This does not mean that the school management is not represented; indeed, it may well have representatives on the Steering Committee. If a temporary project organization where all parties are represented is set up, whether a programme should be implemented or not will not become an issue between the management group on the one side and the staff on the other. It becomes a joint undertaking where all parties can express their opinions, and everyone has to carry the burden of development. As discussed in later chapters, it may well be important for the school management to take over responsibility at a given time in the process (see Chapter 7).

# A WRITTEN CONTRACT

As the staff decide to involve themselves in a comprehensive school development programme this becomes a high priority in terms of the daily work of the
school. Even if the *school* takes such a decision, it does not necessarily mean that
all teachers or the majority of teachers actually participate in the work. To a
large extent this depends on the nature of the change programme and also on
the phasing of the work. In most cases we recommend that at least two-thirds
of the staff are positive about a development programme and are willing to participate. It is also important that the minority which is against the programme
is fully informed and is involved as much as possible in the discussion of the
effects of the programme.

When the staff have decided to undertake an IDP this is done in writing,
e.g. in the form of a contract or an exchange of letters. We recommend written
contracts because expectations change gradually over time, and it is important
to have a starting point to go back to. Precisely because we know that the work
itself will clarify new needs and also a need to revise the contract, it is important
that something is expressed in writing from the beginning. This does not
preclude the possibility of rewriting the contract as one learns through the
process. This would also help the school management to clarify expectations
and to take an active role in the reformulation work. This places pressure on the
school to take the initiative and to become the driving force in the IDP. In such
an exchange the responsibilities, roles and norms for the work need to be
clarified. Even if the contract needs to be as concrete as possible, when it comes
to the needs that the school would like to work with, it should also be open to
adjustments and modifications following joint formative evaluations in the
process.

To elect a Steering Committee and to sign a written contract is for most
schools a new experience that may be frightening and may create certain prob-
ems. Teachers may ask themselves: 'What can we now expect? We do not want
to be drawn into unnecessary conflict situations! Hopefully people from the
outside will not think that our school has such serious problems that we need
someone from the outside to help to clarify them! Hopefully the consultant is
really competent to take on the work and not a theoretician without practical
experience of the classroom!' These and many other cautious notes are heard in
most cases in the entry phase.

It is important that one does not wait too long before writing a contract. Too
long a time when nothing is really decided may well increase anxiety and may
create an impossible climate for work. To avoid such unnecessary anxiety a contract may have formulations that take up the following:

- what needs the process will work with, and how the work will be
  done (norms),
- what joint expectations the parties have,
- what we expect in terms of workload,
- who has the responsibility for what activities and decisions,
- norms of participation,

- the time perspective,
- the ultimate vision of the IDP: the school as a learning organization.

It is important that the contract is clear but not too detailed. Excessively detailed contracts may well regulate the activities, whereas the development process can actually take place through those surprises and learning that will occur in development work.

## A SPECIFIC SCHOOL CASE STUDY

This case study is taken from a primary school in Bochum, Germany. The school is in an urban area where there are many workers and immigrants. The school has 18 classes and there are 19 teachers, many of them part-time. From a consultant's daily log:

> The headmaster had told the local education director that 'the school' was interested in participating in a district-wide development programme to test out the new curricula. To be exact it was actually the headmaster personally who was interested in the project. The following phases took place:
>
> 6 July 1987: A discussion is held between the consultant and the headmaster and a few teachers. Together they assessed the tasks that would be undertaken, the process, the time dimension, the costs, the possibility of having a Steering Committee and the need for an external consultant. The representatives of the school were quite interested and positive; however, they felt a bit unsure about the idea of a Steering Committee. The reason was the following: the teachers involved wanted concrete help to practise the new curriculum guidelines, and they did not see this as a joint task for the staff. They saw it rather as a task for a few involved teachers who would actually do the work. It was also said that it was necessary to think about the colleagues who were sceptical and withdrawn and did not want to participate. They might feel threatened by a structure such as a Steering Committee that might be formed at a later time. At the end of the meeting it was decided to present the project to the whole staff, and to leave the decision about the Steering Committee for the time being.
>
> 15 September 1987: The consultant has a conference with the entire staff. The entire curriculum guidelines programme initiated by the local education authority, the concrete project ideas and the role of the consultant were discussed. Several examples were given of what the school could do in concrete terms and how these tasks could be handled. A discussion took place about resources, both professional and physical, that the school would need to use. At this stage of the meeting a brainstorming session was held, along with some structuring and reflection. The feedback at the end of the conference ended in a decision to meet again soon.
>
> 22 October 1987: The school has invited a representative of the local education authority. This was a consequence of the meeting on 15

September and was an initiative from the staff. The purpose of the meeting was to give the representative of the LEA the staff's perception about the resources needed for the agreed development process. A number of arguments were raised because the staff felt that the material and human resource conditions were inadequate, had negative consequences for instruction, and would not help in the development process. The staff wanted more resources should the curriculum be changed in the desired direction.

5 November 1987: The consultant had his second conference with the staff. A long discussion took place about the next steps. It was agreed to concentrate on a theme on the lines of 'how can we rearrange the worktable to better implement individualized instruction as intended by the new curriculum?'. Agreement was reached about a new joint conference regarding this theme. Towards the end of the meeting the group formulated more precise objectives and project activities, the role of the consultant was clarified, and a nearly unanimous vote to create a Steering Committee was taken. The election of the Steering Committee was postponed until the next day because there was disagreement about who should participate.

The consultant made the following comments concerning the conference on 5 November:

It was pretty clear that the staff was divided in terms of what functions the Steering Committee should have. One comment was: 'The different positions must be represented in the group.' Another said: 'The Steering Committee should include not only those who are interested in the new curriculum, but also those who are sceptical about the whole thing.' This comment led to a very emotional and tough discussion that blocked most constructive discussion. Four female teachers had said they were willing to participate in the group. Mr D was proposed, but he refrained with the rationale that his point of view was already represented. Instead he proposed Mrs X, who, however, rejected the proposal for the same reason. When the staff could get no further, I proposed that the Steering Committee could be elected the next day and that the election should be secret.

The Steering Committee was elected the next day, but a written contract had still not been agreed upon, and the consultant had not pressed for it either. They worked from a verbal agreement, namely that the development programme, broadly speaking, should continue and that the Steering Committee should prepare the next conference with the staff.

We did not choose this case study as a model case, but to illustrate some of the pragmatic and often detailed issues that the consultant needs to deal with as the rather cumbersome process of development gets started.

# THE STEERING COMMITTEE AND THE CLIENT SYSTEM

We are moving towards an agreement between a 'partner' or a 'client' and a consultant. One of the most important questions in the entry phase is therefore:

## Who is the 'client'?

Before we answer this question it is important to underline that the concept 'client' is somewhat problematic. It is an old concept that gives us associations with therapy as well as with legal practice. A client (Latin: *cliens*) in ancient Rome was not a free citizen, but a dependant who was in a situation of dependency upon a patrician or patron who defended the person against arbitrary persecution and misery. There are two reasons why we have decided to use the term 'client'. First, it is a concept that is traditional in international consulting practice and therefore is accepted in the professional community. Secondly, and at least in the early entry phase, some of the original meaning has some relevance: the school management and the staff are at this point of the process not totally free and independent, in the sense that to some extent they need the help of a consultant to advance further in the process. This dependency will, however, cease to exist during the development process. The best indicator that the IDP has been successful is that the consultant is not needed and the school is able to manage its own process of development.

With this definition of the term 'client' as a basis we turn to Edgar Schein (1990), who distinguished between four types of clients who may represent a 'client system'.

1  *Contact clients*: Those persons who are involved in the early entry phase, or those persons that the consultant deals with first. The contact clients would normally connect the consultant with the part of the client system that they see as having special responsibility or needs (e.g. the head).

2  *Transitional clients*: Transitional clients may for some time be in the centre of the development process as the work concentrates on their needs. One example would be a teacher group who would like to work together on an interdisciplinary project. After a period of preparation it is discovered that the project has links and connections to a more general problem of curriculum relevance. The process now calls for all teachers to be involved, who then are the:

3  *Primary clients*: The primary client that the consultant usually works with is a representative group of all staff and the school management group, namely the Steering Committee. This committee is a key mechanism for the IDP process. This group, however, is a temporary group that does not represent itself, but basically the entire school and also the:

4  *Ultimate client*: The ultimate client is usually the student body. The IDP has changes in school outcomes as the ultimate goal (Figure 1.4). The goal of the learning organization is to better cope with the

rapidly changing demands and to provide students with a more relevant and quality-based learning process.

The broader the client population, the more likely it is that it will contain conflicts of interest. Sometimes the client system is defined to include parents, the local community and other groups associated with the school. In those cases, if the Steering Committee is composed of all major interest groups conflict resolution will be part of the agenda for that group and for the consultant.

In some German schools that we have worked with the head traditionally has a stronger hierarchical position than in other countries, at least more hierarchical than in the Netherlands and Scandinavia. When the school leader discovers that it is the entire *school* and not the head who is the driving force in the IDP, and when he or she discovers that the head might well be a member of the Steering Committee, but not necessarily the chairperson of that committee, quite often some difficult role changes take place. The head has to redefine his or her role, which sometimes may create anxiety and with the consequence that he or she feels drawn into a development process that is not 'under control'. Our consultants in some of the German IDP schools have taken considerable time to work with the school leadership to define a role in the IDP that he or she can live with.

On the other hand, we also have experience from schools where the other members of the Steering Committee are concerned that the consultant 'is on the head's side', as they often see the consultant walking in and out of the head's office! In fact, the Steering Committee may well come into the same position *vis-à-vis* the entire staff, namely that the consultant works for the Steering Committee and not for the staff. Two issues combine in these illustrations: a change process may alter the power balance and therefore the interests in the school, and, secondly, the consultant has to be very clear and direct about his or her behaviour to avoid the misunderstanding that he or she serves a particular person or group. In fact, we are beginning to see the need for a definition of the consultant role.

To avoid unnecessary emotional reactions and unnecessary conflict situations, the issues are therefore taken up with all clients at a very early stage. We prefer to have a role definition written down in a contract; however, often it is a verbal agreement. Usually the agreement is that the consultant works for the entire Steering Committee and does not work with individuals or subgroups of that committee without the understanding of the group, and that the Steering Committee is responsible for the work with the ultimate clients (namely the entire staff and/or the students).

Such a definition does not preclude a consultant from working with the entire staff; however, the responsibilities should be clear: the consultant works for the Steering Committee while the Steering Committee has an ultimate responsibility for the development programme in the entire school. An alternative definition is possible, but it needs to be *clear*. During the development process the consultant may well see the need to work directly with one or several persons or subgroups of the Steering Committee. This is then agreed upon and a parallel consultant-client relationship may evolve. This happens often, for example *vis-à-vis* school management who may have a need to become more deeply involved in the process. This is fully acceptable if, again, it is agreed upon with the primary client, namely the Steering Committee.

## IS THE SCHOOL READY?

In a particular case we discovered that the consultant had to convince staff that they ought to go into an IDP. It was clear to the consultant that the school needed a more comprehensive programme than the one it had suggested; however, no one in the staff knew what an IDP was all about. There is a real information problem here: one cannot learn about an IDP without *doing it*. It is like trying to drive a car; one does not get very far with theoretical information sessions! We have often chosen a method in between: working in the early entry phase with the contact group using organizational development skills and techniques, for example problem-solving, planning, norm-building and goal-setting. We try to involve the contact client as much as possible, to be alert to what happens in the group, to give adequate feedback and discuss progress, and thereby indirectly to allow the group to 'get to know' IDP work.

When would a school actually be 'ready' to start an IDP? Schmuck and Runkel (1985) illustrate the dilemma: the best time to go into a school is when there is a certain psychological readiness within the staff. This readiness is usually present in staff when open communication is common, when co-operation is accepted, when the school leadership accepts change and innovation (or at least does not work against meaningful renewal), when the staff have a general perception of where they want to go, and when staff can look back on successful experiences with educational change processes. The problem is, however, that such schools probably need an IDP less than most schools! Such conditions are those which we find in schools that could do very well without any external assistance.

We do not have a definite answer to the question of 'readiness'. We find that the readiness issue is related to the 'maturity of the school' issue that we raised at the beginning of this chapter. If we work with a very 'fragmented' school our expectations should not be the same as when working with a 'project school'. The fragmented school will have to go through several processes of building cohesion in its staff. Individual projects may be the norm for some time, school management may well go through a separate development cycle, and slowly the school culture will have to be modified to accept a broader development approach. In 'project schools' that have some successful experiences with innovations, where there are interested smaller groups working with school improvement programmes, the chances of building a comprehensive school improvement programme are very real. It would, however, take considerable time also in these schools to prepare the staff for 'joint ventures'.

'One step at a time' may be a rule that one could apply. To take as a starting point that one will only work with the 'entire school' would leave the schools most in need outside the IDP framework. Such an attempt in a very fragmented school would most likely not succeed, the process would be blocked, and the school might be left further away from improvement than before. What the entry strategy is, therefore, becomes a *tactical* question. It should be clear from the outset that the IDP is concerned with the entire school. It should, however, also be clear that the consultant is ready to start anywhere in the organization that can be seen as a leverage point for change.

## THE ROLE OF THE CONSULTANT

A consultant has to some extent a 'maieutic' role. The term 'maieutic' comes from the Greek and can be translated as 'the art of delivery' (pertaining to midwifery). It illustrates the method Socrates used in order to get his students to understand a problem. In the same way that Socrates played ignorant, and with a number of questions helped the students themselves to think and thereby develop their own internal control, the consultant is helping the client to use his or her own ideas and experiences in the process, thereby enabling him or her to experience the process as his or her own.

In a successful IDP school there is considerable similarity between an ideal school leader's role and the consultant's role. An experienced school leader would usually not push his or her own ideas and initiatives to the forefront and give him- or herself credit. An experienced school leader would rather be a good listener, give credit to those who put forward good ideas, give support to proposals that will develop the school further, give individual teachers a chance to show initiative, and try to help his colleagues to gain 'ownership' of the school improvement programme. Of course there are clear differences between the consultant's role and the head's role. For example, the head is in charge and takes decisions, while the consultant does not. The head might well benefit from observing and discussing with the consultant how ownership may be developed.

Consultant roles have been discussed many times in the professional literature (Block, 1981; Kubr, 1986; Lippitt and Lippitt, 1986). Different roles, different functions, and an increasingly larger 'repertoire' of techniques are presented. Kubr distinguishes, in principle, between two basic roles: the *resource* role and the *process* role. The resource role is in other contexts often known as the expert or content role. Although there are situations in an IDP where a resource role can be played, it is usually problematic, as it can easily assume the mantle of guardianship expert power (Illich), where the initiative stays more with the experts than with the client. An IDP has as its main objective to facilitate a learning process that qualifies the 'client' to manage his or her own development process. This basic perception of the consultant role is usually called the process role (Schein, 1990). The main orientation of this role is not to use the expertise of the consultant to *resolve* the client's problems. The purpose is to help the client him- or herself to get a broader and deeper understanding of the dilemmas and issues involved and to release the organizational resources available to resolve the problems. In a problem-solving phase the client may well choose to work with a 'resource consultant'. Expertise is needed at many stages of the process. It is, however, the client who ultimately decides what course of action to take.

What functions may a consultant play in an IDP? As we have seen, the main orientation is a process role. However, many functions can be performed to facilitate the process. The roles may be those of

- a *teacher*, who explains ideas, reports facts and refers to knowledge and literature;
- a *trainer*, who diagnoses training needs and often leads exercises in helping to develop skills;
- a *data gatherer*, who gathers needed information for problem-solving;
- a *'linker'*, who connects the school with other schools, teachers or leaders who may be able to assist;
- a *model*, who helps the school to see how new functions and tasks can be accomplished, e.g. how one can deal with surprises and conflicts;
- a *third party* in conflict situations, who is able to deal directly with conflicts without hurting, able to bring parties together and also give support when this is necessary;
- a *'pusher'*, one who reminds the participants of the agreement, one who is able to release the necessary energy to get the process going, but who does *not* take over the leadership;
- an *'ombudsman'*, who represents ideas and interests that have been voiced in the process, but which easily get forgotten among many other issues;
- a *'supporter'*, who can give psychological support when needed, who can give encouragement to the client and who can help to focus the job when necessary;
- a *'designer'*, who is able to help participants to develop strategies and learning situations that help the groups to find their own solutions;
- a *'researcher'*, who may be able to interpret data, analyse situations and episodes and report back to participants;
- a *'facilitator'*, who is able to listen, gather data, report back 'here and now', and help participants to refocus and improve the process.

Whatever the consultant does, it has to be experienced by participants as *assistance* (Schein, 1990). The consultant cannot relieve clients of their problems, only give assistance so that the clients can themselves resolve them. 'The consultant can help the client to master the problems, but shall never move the problems to his own shoulders' (Schein, 1990). Regardless of what functions a consultant may have, he or she has to live within an accepted professional and ethical code. Clarity about role expectations, openness about limitations, mutual understanding of the contract and norms of confidentiality are essential (Kubr, 1986; Lippitt and Lippitt, 1987).

# CHANGING PERSPECTIVES

The IDP consultant will usually not play an expert role; however, he or she is still an expert, namely an expert on the school improvement process. As an expert in this area, the consultant must have basic knowledge and skills in the change process and knowledge about the school as an organization.

The consultant helps the participants to see the issues from different perspectives; he or she has intervention skills, diagnostic skills, and an ability to structure complex sets of data. The consultant is *not* offering advice about what the school ought to do (content), but he or she may give advice to the school on how to *proceed*.

School improvement processes are very complex, and there are researchers who will say that the school is one of the most complicated social organizations in existence. To believe that it is possible to understand the entire process of change through one organizational or one change theory is naive. The school as a social system today, as generations ago, consists mainly of individuals, and their ideas and perceptions about what a school ought to be. To only a very minor degree, compared to other organizations, is the school dependent on technology or the market. The 'product' is what happens in the personality of every individual involved: learning. This is the main reason why we feel that to reduce the school improvement process to a question of technology is premature and possibly damaging to the school.

> *The consultant's first contact with the school gave him the impression that the school had mainly technological difficulties, i.e. needs that could be met fairly straightforwardly. It was said that the school needed technical assistance to develop the necessary material to teach the new curriculum. When the Steering Committee discussed this, and the consultant suggested bringing some expertise in on the subject, it was soon discovered that a power problem was blocking the work situation. The female teachers of the school were quite interested in the new curriculum; most of them were indeed very interested. This school, however, had a headmaster with fairly patriarchal traits who had made this issue a main priority of his own, and he wanted some very particular pedagogical experts to teach his staff how to implement the new curriculum. This was not to the liking of the staff, and they became very sceptical about the whole idea of getting involved in the school improvement effort. The consultant was not aware of these underlying problems and he was soon identified as 'the headmaster's man'. The consultant felt that the situation was blocked. He therefore avoided any behaviour that could be interpreted as 'advocacy' of the new curriculum, or as taking any stand in terms of the content of the school improvement effort. He tried to listen to what happened in the group and he soon discovered that the power problem and the leadership problem was the 'real need' at the time, which had to be dealt with before any curriculum implementation could take place.*

The above case description illustrates that within a given context, technological, political, cultural and professional elements work together and interrelate in a complex and often surprising way. Work started in one area alone may soon be blocked if the consultant and the client are not aware of how the 'problem' is connected with other aspects of the situation and the organization.

One way of looking at the different aspects of a situation is to use different perspectives as we analyse a situation. Systematic variation in the analytical perspective will help both the client and the consultant to understand the situation (Corbett and Rossmann, 1989). To change the analytical perspective helps us to understand more of a situation. We have found the four perspectives of Bolman and Deal (1984) to correspond very closely to the IMTEC organizational model (see Chapter 1) and we have attempted to add some 'school cultural dimensions' to the Bolman and Deal perspectives.

## The structural perspective

The structural perspective looks at the division of labour, specialization and differentiation, at hierarchies and positions, organizations, organigrams and economy, the way the school accomplishes its tasks, clarity in the goal structure and technological efficiency. The structure is usually illustrated through organigrams, where roles and dependencies and linkages in formal structure are also clarified. This perspective also illustrates how the tasks are distributed, how work is done, degrees of dependencies among teachers, among students and between the school and the environment, and degree of autonomy and co-operation in the daily work.

## The political perspective

The political perspective focuses on the way power and influence are distributed in the school; it looks at authority and control, at the way resources are distributed and used, and at potential conflicts of interest in the school. This perspective has recently been further strengthened by what has been called 'micro-politics' (Küpper and Ortmann, 1988). Micro-politics is concerned with the often hidden power and influence structures among people (use of humour, favouritism, etc.), such as attempts to gain support from outside (political parties, church organizations), to use the 'opportunities', to be seen at the right places, to have 'popular viewpoints' in the right situation, to make oneself indispensable, to adapt oneself (e.g. have the right manners for the right situation, avoid taboo topics and dress in the correct manner), to place oneself in a favourable position (e.g. put oneself at the centre of attention, spread hero stories about oneself, talk down others, control the information and let others experience dependency). At the more macro level in schools the political perspective is concerned with equality and opportunity, with career prospects, with participation (e.g. boys and girls), and with special favours being given to individuals and groups.

## The human relations perspective

With the human relations perspective the attention is on individual needs. The working climate and personal style will be at the focus of attention. The basic assumption is that if the individual has a good time, it is also good for the organization. Therefore, issues like group membership, the way feelings are expressed, the way individuals and groups work together, the way problems and conflicts are resolved, and how co-operation in general is experienced are the focus of attention. In particular, in schools the interaction between teachers and students is essential, the assumption being that when teachers and students work well and closely together, it will benefit all, and benefit student learning.

## The symbolic perspective

The symbolic perspective discovers myths, rituals and ceremonies that may be as important as goals, power and technology. This perspective often sees organizations as circus, theatre or drama, where plays are initiated, histories told and plays performed. Intuition and fantasy are regarded highly; less important are technology and rationality. Lack of clarity, ambivalence and ambiguity are emphasized. Bolman and Deal (1984) say: 'Problems develop when the actors play their roles badly, when symbols lose their importance and rituals their power.' It may be important to look at the school's history, its rituals, its traditions and its daily norms. Jokes in an organization, as well as those things one does not speak about, may be as important as the official curriculum, and the characteristics of the teaching force as important as their roles.

In the entry phase the consultant sees and hears many things, but his or her observations are dependent on which perspectives are being used. One of the most important conditions for a consultant to discover is his or her own perspectives. To improve the ability to understand by using different organizational perspectives is part of organizational learning, which is at the heart of the IDP process.

The school also needs to discover the perspectives and assumptions commonly used in a particular school. 'Confrontations' with other perspectives, other 'mental models', are needed to test our own assumptions; otherwise we may become prisoners of our own mental models, the structures we live and work in, and the approach we take. Quite often an external resource, such as a process consultant, may be needed to initiate the process (Deal and Kennedy, 1982).

# Chapter 4

# Joint Diagnosis

*All schools have strengths and weaknesses. How clear are staff and students about the characteristics of their school? Often managers and teachers have a particular 'problem' or a particular task they would like to resolve. Often we find that other issues block the solution, because 'everything hangs together'. How do we diagnose a school as an organization? What advantages does it have to use organizational surveys, and what are the advantages of less comprehensive approaches? When is it appropriate to use a certain method for data gathering, analysis and a dialogue? How can we at the same time be open and yet treat data confidentially in our work?*

*As the consultant was driving from the meeting with the headmaster a number of thoughts went through his mind. What could the problems be in the school? The headmaster had been rather vague. The Steering Committee seemed to be divided. The brainstorming session showed that there were a number of issues that the teachers wanted to take up.*

*It really didn't make much sense at the moment. How should we proceed? Was it at all possible to get a picture of what the school was all about? How could the consultant try to ensure that it was not only the active and vocal teachers who had a say?*

*The two consultants were well prepared for the meeting, they thought. In their bag were the results of the staff questionnaire. The analysis was pretty obvious, they thought. . . . Coming to the meeting of the Steering Committee and showing the data, however, did not produce clarity. In fact, the analysis presented by one of the consultants started off a very heated debate and the meeting ended inconclusively. . . .*

*It was a very tough day for the headmaster. . . . The whole staff had just completed two days of analysing the school, on the basis of the work of several task forces. The survey results fed back to the staff were clearly critical of his leadership style. If it had not been for the supportive climate that his colleagues and the consultant had helped to develop over the last year, he would have considered quitting the job. Now, he felt accepted; however, he knew he had a big job to do. . . .*

These are just a few examples from IDP practice that illustrate a few dimensions of the process of diagnosis. It is a complex and demanding process for everyone involved.

# A DEFINITION OF JOINT DIAGNOSIS

Diagnosis, in and of itself, is difficult. If you put the word 'joint' in front of 'diagnosis' it increases the complexity of the process. If we attempt a definition, joint diagnosis is

> a process where all actors affected by the change process are involved in the definition of the issues, in searching for relevant data, in conceptualizing and understanding the data and in creating, as far as possible, a common understanding of *what is involved, who* is involved, what *causes* the situation, what *kind of issues* are at stake and what the actors *want to do about it.*

The objective of joint diagnosis is to mobilize for impovement based on a real understanding of needs. The purpose of diagnosis is not to attain *consensus*. It may well be that the school is divided. Joint diagnosis is not a process by which reality is blurred or difficulties ironed out. To effect it is to deal with reality with open eyes; to stay with this reality and do something productive about it. Moreover, it is not the consultant who should be able to do something about it; it is the school. One major objective, therefore, during diagnosis is to improve the capabilities of the school for managing the change process (see Chapter 7).

# THE CONSULTANT ROLE IN JOINT DIAGNOSIS

The role of the consultant in this process is *not to act as an expert* on solutions. It is not his or her task to tell the school 'what the problems are', or to 'design the future'. Nor is he or she a 'doctor' either. The reasons why the consultant's role is *not* to provide a diagnosis for the school are based on our understanding of how social systems change. The best guarantee for an improvement in a situation is that those involved discover the problems and dilemmas, and jointly mobilize energy to resolve them. The role of the consultant is to facilitate a process that enables the school itself to make a joint diagnosis.

What then is the role of the IDP consultant in this process? He or she is a person who *facilitates learning* in the organization. He or she knows that real data may be threatening to some, but also that anxiety should not hinder the learning process; that conflicts can be opportunities for learning, if they are processed well.

The consultant is concerned with two types of diagnostic processes. In close co-operation with the school (usually the Steering Committee or the entire faculty) the consultant (a) helps to bring relevant data into the process of analysis, looks at different interpretations, sounds out different groups or individuals with particular interests, and (b) helps the school to arrive at *pictures of itself*. By the term 'data' we mean any information in the rational as well as the symbolic reality, regardless of whether this information exists in quantitative form or not, whether it is quantifiable or not. Data, therefore, could be a number, a document, a verbal or written statement, a complicated text, a motto or a myth, a name or an episode. Usually in this process it is a question of identifying strengths and weaknesses of the school as the participants see them. The data in and of themselves do not matter much. It is the meaning that participants give to the data that matters.

The diagnostic process is also concerned with the capacity the school has to manage the needed development processes. School leaders are not used to the concept of managing change. Schools are relatively stable organizations. The skills needed to plan and implement changes, the problem-solving skills needed, the group development processes and the processes of assessment are examples of areas that the school needs to master.

Many development projects do not succeed, not because the school personnel do not know their strengths and weaknesses, but because they do not know *what to do*. They do not have sufficient experience in going through change processes. Consequently, they fail. Problems become too demanding and the process fades away.

The consultant helps the school to understand what it needs to be doing to arrive successfully at the goals set for the change programme. The consultant, therefore, is as interested in the implementation process as in the goals. He or she is concerned that the schools actually will be able to achieve these goals. The school needs to be ready for the challenges of changing practice. It needs to be concerned about its own capacity to manage change; it needs to 'learn how to learn'. To structure the process in such a way that it maximizes the opportunities for organizational learning is, therefore, an important task at this early stage.

## THE PROCESS OF ORGANIZATIONAL LEARNING

In a typical IDP process the *entry phase* has provided ample opportunity for discussing 'the problems'. Typically, managers, teachers, students and parents may have volunteered to talk about the school. These 'signals' are clearly important. They often give consultants early 'warnings', help them to see some of the interests involved, make them sensitive to potential conflicts and help them to get acquainted with the people concerned.

As consultants see and listen they learn. Their first rule is to be sensitive to the environment in which they work: 'What is he *really* trying to tell me . . . why are only two persons speaking up in this meeting . . . why is the headmaster so open with me and so closed with his teachers?'

Consultants learn from what is said, and from what is not said. They learn through non-verbal behaviour. They learn from the ways the school is organized, and from the physical appearance of the school.

Being sensitive is not the same as engaging in diagnosis. In making a diagnosis consultants put values on their observations; they make judgements. There is always a danger that they might do this intuitively. It is hard to see something one dislikes without making judgements. Their job is not to make judgements, but to help the school to make judgements about its own practice.

The consultant's job is that of a *pedagogue*, a person who helps other persons to learn. The first rule is to base judgements on reliable information. What kind of data do I have? From where do I have the data? Are they reliable? Have they been counter-checked? What is the sample that I draw my data from?

We see immediately that it is potentially dangerous to rely on volunteered verbal data. Who dares to talk to a stranger anyway? Are those most vocal in a meeting necessarily representative? Do all participants really *participate*? Do the withdrawn persons represent a different point of view?

Organizational learning is dependent on reliable data from a representative group of persons. What is 'representative' depends on who the client is and what kinds of issues are at stake. We find that many clients are afraid of information, particularly from groups they see as representing different views:

> It was hard to get the Steering Committee to agree to conduct a 'climate survey' among students. Teachers fully agreed that classroom discipline was a problem in many classes; however, they felt that a survey among the teachers would be sufficient. After all, they would know what the problems were. Involving students would only disrupt an already difficult situation. . . . The consultant tried to convince the Steering Committee that they might miss some very important information that might help them to resolve the issues, but with little success. . . . It was only when they analysed who would be involved to improve the present situation that they realized that students could potentially have a very important role in changing the school.

*Who* is involved in providing data is partly a question of obtaining relevant, representative and reliable information. But it is more. It is also a question of mobilizing energy for change. If we realize that some actors need to be deeply involved in the change process we also realize that their perceptions of the issues are important.

The purpose of the IDP is *organizational learning*. Diagnosis is not an end in and of itself. It is an important step towards learning. It helps us to be clearer about ourselves and about others. It does not mean that we necessarily agree with others, but we can begin to understand and to see the school from the point of view of others.

The IDP helps us to *listen* and to *see*. We begin to understand that others may have a different understanding of the same phenomena. We also realize that others may have a different interpretation of the same data. We begin to see our own problems in sorting out facts from interpretations. We also begin to realize that it may be hard to change perspectives. Let us look at a teacher's report in an IDP school:

> It was a tough session for the headmaster. The data really showed that he did not lead the school as we [the teachers] wanted. I was really satisfied that we finally had some concrete facts to put on the table. Finally, we could tell him what we felt. . . . It was not until my own students had a session about my teaching that I started to reflect on how the headmaster must have felt during our session with him. I can tell you that I was deeply hurt when my students told me what they felt about my teaching. It really did hurt me. I think about it often. . . . Actually I have started to look at our headmaster in a somewhat different light . . .

Organizational learning deals with our feelings as well (Watzlawick *et al.*, 1967). We begin to see some of the emotional and ethical implications of change. We no longer avoid unpleasant confrontations. We need to see reality from different perspectives. But we are there to help each other. The IDP is concerned with the climate for change. Does the school have a climate that fosters organizational learning? The consultant acts regularly as a 'process consultant', helping the Steering Committee as well as other groups involved to establish norms for the process and to support individuals in their learning process.

## THE NEED FOR A THEORETICAL BASE IN DIAGNOSIS

One cannot look at everything in an organization. It is too complex. Also, one cannot *do* everything; a *strategy for intervention* needs to be developed. In both cases — trying to analyse an organization, and trying to *change* an organization — a theoretical base is needed.

Our first theoretical assumption in diagnosis is that 'everything is linked together', the world does not consist of a number of separate, unrelated forces. Therefore we must think systemically, and we must think together, because only a joint picture will give us all the pieces in the puzzle, and also because the synergy effect is important. We experience that the total is more than the sum of the parts. We also experience feedback, we see the chances for personal growth, and we begin to discover the possibilities in a 'learning organization'.

Many organizational development activities are quite pragmatic in nature; they lack a theoretical base. In Chapter 1 we outlined IMTEC's theories of the school as an organization and the change process. We also discussed the assumptions behind the IDP which integrate our organizational perspectives and our change perspectives.

Clients often come to a consultant with a 'problem' (see 'Scenarios' below). The consultant will listen to the information given and will work seriously to understand and to help the client to resolve 'the problem'. Since, however, the IDP is based on a theory of schools as organizations and also based on a theory of change, what appears to be 'the problem' might well be looked upon as part of a more complex issue.

We need a *systemic* diagnostic perspective. It is not easy to understand causes and effects in an organization, in particular when causes and effects are separated in time (and often place). Senge calls this the classical 'learning disability' of organizations (Senge, 1990). Today's problems often come from yesterday's solutions, and if we do not take care the cure may be worse than the disease. This is one reason why the IDP consultant's job in this phase is to help participants to *understand* the school as an organization in a systemic way.

We know that 'everything is linked together'; we build our perspective on an open systems model and realize that what happens in a given subpart of the school may well be linked in some way or another to other subparts or issues. Often persons become scapegoats, and complex issues are reduced to isolated 'problems'. Complexities are nearly always reduced, simply because we can seldom grasp the complexities (or do not want to listen to alternative views).

To accept the given 'problem', however, making clear that the IDP is based on *theories* and that therefore the 'problem' has to be seen in a systemic perspective, is in our view taking the client seriously. To accept only the 'problem' and try to resolve it often leads to a superficial treatment and the school is no better off.

The theoretically based change process has, however, some pitfalls, if it is not taken seriously. The IDP assumes that the *client* must understand and decide, and that the consultant is only a *facilitator*. How does this relate to a theoretical base? The dilemma is that a theory often 'takes over', affecting the perspectives, the kind of data gathered, the diagnostic approach and the solutions proposed. This is, after all, the purpose of using a theory as a base for analysis. In fact, we all use a 'theory', often not clear to ourselves. For the client to be in charge he or she must not only see and understand the theory, but accept it as the basis for the work.

It is part of the pedagogical role of the consultant to help the school to see the relationships among issues and organizational subparts. This can be done in a very practical way:

> We all knew that something was wrong in teacher Klein's classroom. In fact students complained, also parents had complained to the headmaster. We all 'knew', but no one talked to Mr Klein about it. We did not know what to do. Our climate was not open enough. We were afraid of hurting each other, and even if we did take it up with Mr Klein, what could we do? We had very few possibilities of really helping him — or the students. The headmaster himself had disciplinary problems in his classroom. He and Mr Klein did not work well together. In fact Mr Klein had become more and more isolated, although he was not the only teacher with problems in his class.

What is the 'problem'? Who is influenced by the situation? What causes the problem? What kind of problem is it? What is our goal, if we want to intervene?

These are the basic issues related to the diagnosis. It becomes quite obvious that even if Mr Klein needs help, here and now, it will not change the more basic problems in the school. We need to look at the organizational issues with a theoretical base and we need a change strategy, based on a change theory.

## THREE SCENARIOS

Schools approach the development process in a variety of ways. The IDP works with many different kinds of development strategies. In this section we illustrate three different scenarios that we have learned from IDP practice covering the most typical situations.

### The problem focus

In most cases a consultant is contacted by a representative of a school because the school has a concrete problem. It is often the head who calls, and he or she feels that an 'outside person', may be helpful 'in this particular situation'. The mandate is, to begin with, fairly limited; come and help us to resolve this problem! Figure 4.1 illustrates the process in this scenario.

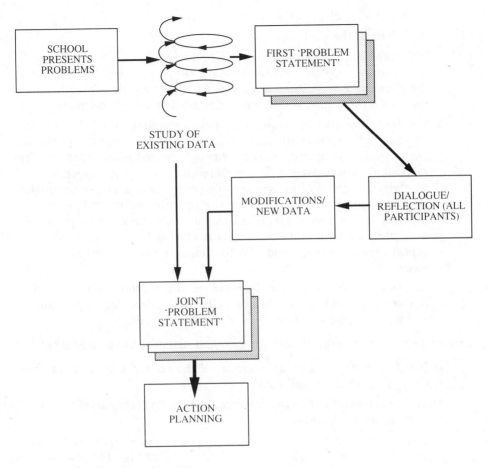

Figure 4.1 *Problem-focused analysis*

The scenario illustrates a process by which the 'problem' as stated by the school is reformulated in a dialectic process. A school may have problems with 'discipline' (e.g. values and norms), with an increasing drop-out rate, with the internal climate (e.g. co-operation among staff), or other 'concrete' problems that need to be resolved. The following process may unfold.

1 The school approaches a consultant with a 'problem' and assumes that data that already exist form an adequate base to work from. The consultant accepts the job on the condition that he or she can work with all available data and the participants in the process.

2 He or she uses existing data, looks at reliability issues: the sample, the types of data missing and alternative interpretations of the data.

3 The consultant works with the 'primary client' and comes up with one or several 'problem statements', that include:

(a) Who is affected by the problem?

(b) What causes the problem?

(c) What kind of problem is it?

(d) What do the goals seem to be?

This 'problem statement' is clearly *tentative*. It builds on existing data and discussions with the primary client only (e.g. the head or the Steering Committee). If agreed, each participant takes time off to reflect on the issues and to write down his or her concerns.

4 The tentative problem statement is then discussed thoroughly with all those who may be affected by the problem. Usually the picture is challenged, new perspectives are brought in and often other problem statements are produced. These statements have the support of a much larger group of individuals. The consultant may use techniques such as 'cognitive maps', creative and open brainstorming, value clarification exercises, etc. Often this dialogue needs to be repeated several times with other participants. During the dialogue new aspects are discovered and new participants become potentially relevant.

5 On the basis of a shared understanding of the problem(s) a development plan is designed (usually by the Steering Committee), and we move into other phases of the IDP process.

This process is not unproblematic. However, it also has some strengths:

- It is fairly easy to gain acceptance for the scenario, building on the client's perspective and data.
- The development of *trust*, essential at this stage, is easier than in more complex designs.
- The school works with very concrete problems that are experienced as difficult. There is therefore *energy* to go through the process.
- It is based on the resources of the school and therefore is not expensive.
- It avoids the negative feelings often connected with formal organizational surveys (see below).

The process also has some weaknesses:

- The consultant depends totally on the initial understanding of the primary client.
- There is little control over the quality of data gathered (question of reliability).
- There is a possibility of the consultant's being *used* by someone to promote a given understanding of the situation.
- The database is often limited, and too limited to arrive at a comprehensive understanding of the situation.
- The inadequacies often become clearer at a later stage.

# The task focus

In other situations a representative of the school will contact a consultant because he or she wants to strengthen the school in relation to certain accepted objectives:

> *The ministry had issued new curriculum guidelines. It was now up to the individual school to find ways of changing practice to meet with the new objectives. Schools had some resources, they could plan the implementation themselves, and seek, if needed, external assistance. Where could they find a consultant who could act as a resource person for curriculum development?*

In these cases the school personnel know that there are many obstacles to development. They are usually aware of the fact that to change practices, procedures and rules is not always easy. They have experiences of innovations that have not been implemented. And so they seek advice. These are situations where the school does not necessarily have a 'problem'. The school is faced with new challenges, and personnel may benefit from external assistance, perhaps from persons with specific experiences in the area. If the school decides to involve a consultant, the process shown in Figure 4.2 may occur.

The school does not necessarily have a 'problem'. It may have a *challenge* or a *developmental* task. The school may be looking for an expert and/or a process helper. Both may be required, and this point needs to be clarified during the first phase (entry). During the 'diagnostic phase' the following scenario is illustrative.

1  The starting point is the task definition of the school. The consultant starts with several informal discussions within the school. The tasks are usually set either by external authorities (accepted and/or adapted by the school), by the management of the school or by the staff. The tasks are somehow taken for granted. The question is usually not *why* change, but *how* to change, to reach the desired objectives.

2  During these informal discussions a number of issues are clarified: how accepted the objectives are, how ready the school is for a change in the desired direction, who would be affected, what the stumbling blocks may be, and so on. In fact, the client and the consultant may arrive at a comprehensive problem statement (where the objective is the original request or a modified statement).

3  The Steering Committee and the consultant now engage a wider group of participants (whoever is affected) in the process of developing an acceptable problem statement. This could take time and could involve a series of meetings and several groups.

    It is essential at this point to assess how widely the objectives are shared, how committed participants would be to work on the development tasks and what the barriers might be. Large faculties are usually organized into smaller groups of five to eight participants, and various micro-designs help to develop some shared problem statements.

63

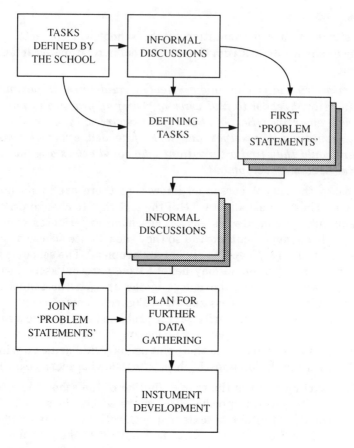

Figure 4.2   *Task-focused analysis*

4   Usually the process includes some plan for further investigations, instrument development, data-gathering and analysis (and we are following a path that we shall describe more fully in the third scenario).

Our experience with this scenario is, again, that it has strengths and weaknesses. On the positive side:

- It is an approach that allows the consultant and the school to get to know each other, and therefore gives opportunities for building trust.
- It often resolves several problems in the process simply by involving the actors in a series of discussions.
- It is tailor-made to the individual school and therefore there is a good chance for selected personnel to develop ownership.
- It is less threatening than formal organizational surveys.

On the negative side:

- The consultant is often 'stuck' with an expert role and may have difficulties working with the process.

- It is often a 'search in the dark', and hard for the consultant really to get a grasp of the issues.

- It is hard to 'control the sample', because the most vocal often provide most of the information; and to ensure 'full coverage' takes much time.

- There is ample opportunity for manipulating the data, and the Steering Committee (and the consultant) may well overlook important issues.

## The institutional focus

The 'client school' wants to 'take its own temperature', look at its work in a more comprehensive way than usual, to assess a variety of factors that contribute to learning, and to be open for several paths toward development. The school may not have a 'problem', but is struggling with a wide range of issues that need to be looked into. This approach to diagnosis starts with a formal *organizational survey*. Figure 4.3 illustrates this scenario. There are several starting points: 'We want to improve our practice', or 'For some time we have felt the need to reconsider what we are doing', or ,'We want to develop a clearer vision for our school' or 'We need a more comprehensive understanding of what we are all about, to be able to improve'.

Such a broad orientation to diagnosis is, in our experience, characteristic of what we have called 'project schools' and 'problem-solving schools' (see Chapter 1). With such a broad starting point the school wants to have an overview of the most critical aspects of school life. The school wishes to understand the situation as it is (real), and as one would like it to be (ideal), and to document the needs and problems, the strong as well as the weaker sides of the organization. If the school wishes to start with such a broad overview, the typical process is:

1  The Steering Committee goes through the organizational diagnostic instrument, for example the IMTEC 'GIL instrument',[1] discusses modifications, decides on the adapted version for the school and administers the instrument (usually for all participants within a time frame of 1-2 hours). The consultant (or the Steering Committee) codes the data and presents all data in a readable fashion. All participants are guaranteed full anonymity. GIL comes with a computer program that enables the school to code and present the data according to a number of options.

2  The GIL may illustrate a number of possible 'problem situations' or areas that indicate distance between what is desired and what is

---

[1] IMTEC has developed several diagnostic instruments, the most comprehensive being the *'Guide to Institutional Learning'* (GIL), which has been used in a number of schools in many countries in Europe, North America, Asia and Africa.

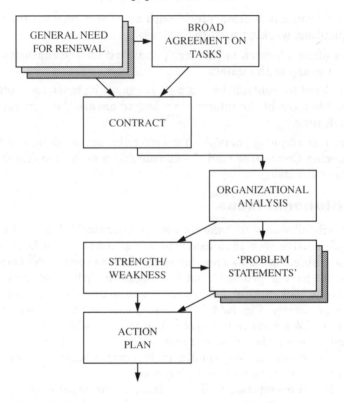

Figure 4.3   *The institutional focus*

actually taking place (see the section about the GIL below). Usually
the GIL provides a fairly comprehensive set of such 'problem
situations'.

3  Either the Steering Committee or the entire faculty now develops
a few 'problem statements' (see above). These will usually be
challenged by alternative perspectives. They need to be checked
and rechecked before the meaning is clear and/or accepted by the
participants (there may of course be divergences). Again there are a
number of micro-designs possible by which shared problem
statements may be arrived at.

4  On the basis of these statements an action planning process starts
that will lead to a 'development plan' (see Chapter 5).

This approach also has its strengths:

• It is theory-based and provides a comprehensive assessment.
• It provides a broad database and gives all actors a chance to provide
  data on an equity basis.
• It documents strengths and weaknesses of the school. Individuals do
  not need to stick their neck out to put sensitive data on the table.

- The GIL is linked closely to our open systems model and it is possible to draw tentative inferences among variables, for discussions with the client system (see the GIL presentation below).
- It provides a fairly clear method of diagnosis that can be mastered by the client and the consultant. Data-gathering takes about 1½ hours.
- It is relatively inexpensive (as the consultant will spend less time gathering data).

It also has its weaknesses:

- Many would say it is a 'large net for small fish'. It certainly should not be used uncritically. There is no need for an organizational survey to resolve fairly limited issues.
- The amount of data from a comprehensive survey like the GIL may well be overwhelming if not presented well.
- The GIL also documents quite sensitive areas (e.g. leadership). It documents areas that may well be avoided with another approach (it is not always 'right' to unveil everything).
- It does depend on a trained consultant in certain phases of the process.

Organizational surveys are commonly used for different purposes, and they should be differentiated. Some companies regularly conduct standardized opinion surveys, often with a representative sample of employees. The purpose is to 'take the temperature'. This use of surveys often produces suspicion and misunderstanding, and it does not develop the ownership or produce the energy needed for change.

To be effective, organizational surveys need to be used with the purpose of *renewal* of the organization. It is the *school* (and not a researcher) that owns the data and decides how to deal with it. Often the process itself leads to the development of new objectives that are met by a development programme. This is the typical IDP process.

## THE GUIDE TO INSTITUTIONAL LEARNING (GIL)

The GIL is an organizational survey constructed to reflect the perspectives of organizations as they are built into the 'organizational model', discussed in Chapter 1. We understand an organization as the interplay of a variety of factors related to five main dimensions:

1 values and norms,
2 structures,
3 human relations,
4 strategies, and
5 the environment.

Within each of these dimensions there are several subcategories of data that we see as essential to consider as we study the school as an open system. The GIL instrument is a *discrepancy* instrument, allowing participants to use a Lickert scale of 'real' dimensions (how it is today) and 'ideal' dimensions (how I would like it to be). The discrepancy can also be seen as a way of operationalizing the 'needs'.

The main dimensions of the GIL are as follows. The GIL is designed so that every item is connected to a dimension, a subcategory or a variable in the conceptual framework that was outlined in Chapter 1. The data are reported in the form of profiles which correspond generally to a variable of one of the organizational dimensions. These profiles may be described as follows:

## Values, beliefs, goals

The discrepancies in values and similarities of participants are explored in this profile. Although some attention is given to fundamental beliefs (*Weltanschauung*), the major focus of the profile is devoted to the organizational goals and tasks. We stress here that it is important to explore values and beliefs, not because there should necessarily be consensus among members and between members of an organization, but because it is important for them to understand what these values and beliefs are, and to find ways in which institutional members can live with them and/or modify them.

Because institutional development is crucial, certain items in this profile address, specifically, the issue of change and institution members' beliefs about change.

Teaching and learning are the dominant activities in school, and this profile provides participants with an opportunity to assess the importance of various possible instructional aims. There is no end to the attempts of ministries and school boards to define such aims, but ultimately a school staff (sometimes also parents and students) must clarify its own instructional aims and the priorities various institutional members give to these aims if the aims are to become a functional part of the life of the school.

## Instructional practices

The instructional modes of teachers are of central concern. We do not assume that one teaching or learning style is better than another. In fact, evidence is clear-cut that differing styles have different effects, and their value can only be assessed contextually. This profile helps clarify what they do and what they feel it is important to do. It is also critical to assess the gap between teacher and student perspective and preferences.

## Institutional climate

This profile helps clarify the morale and general atmosphere of the institution. The level of satisfaction, support, trust, flexibility and competitiveness is assessed, as well as the degree to which individual participants feel they are a vital part of the organizational process. This includes a measure of their own commitment to the institution as a humane, pleasant place to live and work.

## Norms and expectations

Any institution possesses informal norms and expectations or a code of 'do's' and 'don'ts' which defines appropriate and inappropriate behaviour. They are not written and are therefore only learned by experience in the institution. This profile raises questions which should help institution members clarify certain dimensions of this code, and it also provides information which could be of potential help in altering the code in some productive manner, if they so choose.

## Leadership

Two leadership variables are assessed in this profile. The first looks at the managing capability of leaders, the ability to maximize different capabilities and to co-ordinate competing interests. The second looks at leadership style as reflected in dichotomous continua such as flexible-rigid, people-oriented and/or task-oriented, innovative-traditional and enthusiastic-reserved.

## Decision-making strategies

Institutions establish certain styles for dealing with problem situations. An institution should be clear about how decisions are made and who makes them. This profile is intended to help institutional members reflect on the scope of the database they use in making decisions, the frequency with which they make important decisions, and the degree to which staff confront or avoid problem situations.

## Influence and control

Human relations include the informal influence and power structure of groups and individuals in and outside the institution, such as parent groups, teacher unions and central authorities. This profile allows institution members to assess the perceived degree of influence of these groups on their own work, and it also allows them to assess the degree of influence they personally possess regarding their own work and regarding aspects of the institution as a whole.

## Degree of institutional change

It is crucial to obtain a measure of the perceived change which has taken place in the whole school (the work units and the individual realms) in order to understand the judgements of individuals pertaining to other profiles. This profile allows participants to indicate the change which has taken place in these spheres during the recent past.

## Task and time structure

In this profile, we assess the workload, schedules, routines and relative time given to tasks and activities by school personnel. One of the major difficulties with 'loosely coupled' organizations such as schools is that the same persons perform a multitude of different roles. The critical point of reference in this profile is the relative amount of time individuals devote and would like to devote to

69

these tasks. We do not imply that one arrangement is better than another, but we do feel that because all personnel engage in so many activities, theoretically it is possible to establish a better fit between tasks and the individual preferences than typically exists.

## Incentive and reward structure

An institution must balance forces for the status quo and change in such a manner that some stability is maintained during the renewal process. The reward structure can serve both as a stabilizer and as a force for change. There are two ways to look at incentives and rewards. The first is to assess the factors which the institution and broader school system deem important. The second is more personal in that each individual sets priorities and finds fulfilment in different ways. Both approaches are included in this profile.

Each of the above 10 profiles has a number of data forms, which are intended to facilitate data feedback and comparisons. Figure 4.4 gives an example of one profile listed above.

## ANALYSIS AND DATA FEEDBACK

For illustrative purposes we have selected part of the sub-scale that we call the 'decision-making process', which contains a total of 23 items. We have illustrated the first nine items of a school faculty where 41 teachers responded as shown in Figure 4.4. The third item says 'individuals or smaller groups act on their own as they wish'. Forty-one teachers answered this item. When they assessed the real situation, one chose the value 5 (never), while seven preferred the value 1 (always). Of the other participants, six chose the value 4, 17 the value 2 and 10 the middle value 3. As far as the ideal situation is concerned, the frequencies were somewhat different, which led to a discrepancy in the middle values (between real and ideal) of a total of 1.41 points of the scale. In general a discrepancy of more than one scale-point is fairly major, and it should lead at least to a discussion if it illustrates an issue that needs attention. Item number 7 in our example, 'Individuals and groups fight to pursue their own interests', shows a discrepancy of 2.05 scale-points. The frequencies show that 35 teachers feel that this behaviour is one that is practised too often. Only two persons in the staff feel this is an ideal situation. Here we find a major discrepancy between 'real' and 'ideal', and probably a point for further discussion. The answers to item 3 underline this point.

The preliminary assessment of GIL results usually starts among the members of the Steering Committee, who sometimes even do the data-coding and summations themselves, eventually with the use of a computer-assisted program.

As the Steering Committee goes through the data from all 10 GIL 'profiles', a picture of strengths and weaknesses will begin to emerge that enables the Steering Committee to come up with a number of potential problem statements. They will also find a number of 'horizontal linkages'; that is, what is discovered in one profile may be supported by another.

From all the profiles the first tentative interpretations will be formulated

Indicate
a) How your school approaches problems (REAL)
b) How you feel your school should have approached the problems (IDEAL)

| | -(1)- | -(2)- | -(3)- | -(4)- | -(5)- | -(6)- | -(7)- | -(8)- | -(9)- |
|---|---|---|---|---|---|---|---|---|---|
| 5 | -/3 | 1/11 | 1/13 | -/7 | 2/2 | 3/1 | -/12 | 2/2 | 2/3 |
| 4 | 9/7 | 7/14 | 6/19 | 7/18 | 12/9 | 6/4 | 3/15 | 8/1 | 2/2 |
| 3 | 17/14 | 13/7 | 10/3 | 14/7 | 16/12 | 16/4 | 3/12 | 15/3 | 15/5 |
| 2 | 14/12 | 16/4 | 17/2 | 14/4 | 8/10 | 14/17 | 19/1 | 15/11 | 19/11 |
| 1 | 1/5 | 4/5 | 7/4 | 5/4 | 3/7 | 2/15 | 16/1 | 1/24 | 2/19 |
| Δ | 0.05 | 0.90 | 1.41 | 0.93 | 0.32 | 0.32 | 0.85 | 2.05 | 0.60 |

ANSWER FREQUENCIES (1-5)
(REAL/IDEAL)

DIFFERENCE IN THE MEAN VALUES

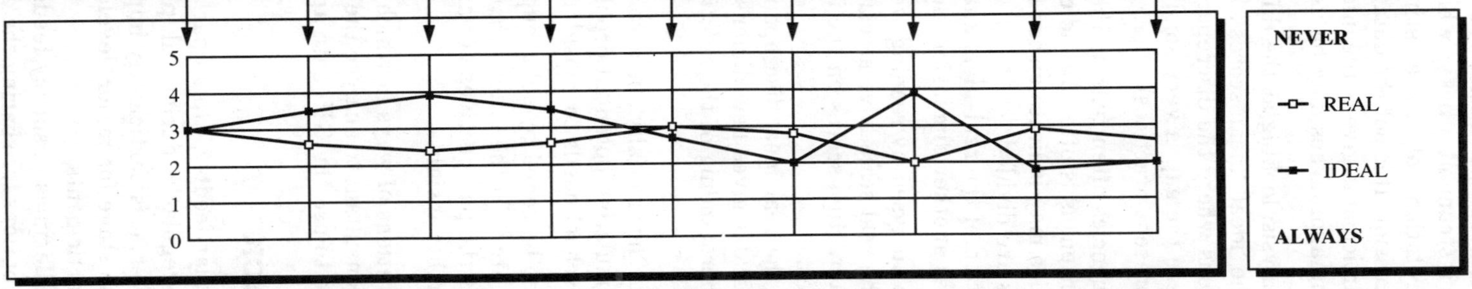

NEVER
—□— REAL
—■— IDEAL
ALWAYS

| 1 | 2 | 3 | 4 | 5 | 6 | 7 | 8 | 9 |
|---|---|---|---|---|---|---|---|---|
| The staff deny that problems exist. | The staff discuss without finding solutions. | Individuals and small groups act on their own as they see fit. | The management receive proposals from staff; however, they use them only if they agree. | Teacher groups with different interests negotiate to get a solution. | The management and staff work through the problems together. | Individuals and groups fight for their own interests. | It is quite clear who is responsible for what. | The management separate the less important issues from important ones. |

Figure 4.4 GIL results (from the 'decision-making process')

and discussed. The consultant will assist the Steering Committee in under-standing the way the instrument works, while the Steering Committee is responsible for interpretations of the existing data. The GIL instrument provides a basis for discussion. It is not the data themselves that are important, but the *meaning* that participants give to the information. In analysis of the GIL instrument the following approaches may be used.

1 Discrepancy analysis; looking at the differences in scores between the 'real' and the 'ideal' 'mean scores'. It may well be of interest to look at dimensions where the discrepancies are large, as well as dimensions where the gap is very small (where participants are satisfied with present practices).

2 Analysing frequencies often tells us the degree of consensus on a given issue. Consensus is often an indicator of *readiness* to act. Large frequencies may indicate either that an issue either is unclear or that opinions are divided.

   A combination of the real-ideal analysis and the frequency analysis provides another dimension and new insights.

3 The GIL is also analysed by reading 'vertically'. Those items that score high on the real scale have a relatively high priority and/or are seen as important. High scores on the ideal scale are indications of desired activities.

   Combining the real-ideal discrepancy scores with the high/low scores on both scales gives new dimensions to the analysis. It provides an understanding of the *relative* importance of the various scores.

4 Reading the GIL 'horizontally', or across the 10 subscales, provides the data for formulating potential problem statements, or at least issues that the school needs to consider.

5 The GIL can also be coded by subgroups (e.g. groups of students, administrators, etc.). To the extent that the Steering Committee is concerned about the perspectives of various *groups* these data might well provide further insights.

These are simply illustrations of ways in which the GIL data can be analysed. It is not the job of the consultant to analyse the GIL. His or her job is to assist the Steering Committee to use the GIL data appropriately for analysis.

## SURVEY FEEDBACK

In the IDP process regular feedback to all participants is essential. Feedback of information occurs regularly during all phases of consultation. In the diagnostic phase, however, it is particularly important because the understan-ding of the data sets the stage for major development projects that may well have implications for participants.

There are several dilemmas in survey feedback, and the consultant needs to consider a number of options for sharing the data with the faculty (and other participants). Since organizational surveys usually produce an overload of information, one of the issues is how to present the data in a meaningful way, without subtracting important information. In general the following dilemmas are observed.

1 How can data be available to all without producing overload and confusion? This is often handled by the Steering Committee 'reducing' data to a given set of main issues (which works if there is genuine trust between the Steering Committee and the participants). There are different models and practices of reducing data overload; however, they are often resented because the staff want maximum influence on data interpretation.

2 How does one balance the need for confidentially with making data available to all? People are not identified directly in the GIL (with the exception of the head, under certain conditions), but in small schools it may still be possible to 'interpret' the GIL and guess some relationships. It is essential for the process that individuals feel that confidentiality is respected. During the dialogue when participants make sense of the data, a number of critical issues and sensitive topics would be discussed. Only through active and professional work with the group is it possible to arrive at satisfactory understanding.

   At this stage, but also earlier, it is important to discuss the norms for the learning process that the school improvement requires. 'How open can I be? What happens if I tell the others what kinds of problems I have with my class? Can I trust that confidential information will not be related to others outside the group?' Conscious effort to develop openness is a precondition for participants to discuss their own strengths and weaknesses.

3 To get 'inside' the data takes time. Since time is scarce it may produce anxiety or frustration if the data are not fully understood. Since we know that it is not the data that are important, but the meaning we give to the data, this frustration must be dealt with. Time for reflection, time for illustrations, role plays and simulations often represents *time-saving*.

4 'Ownership' is essential in the IDP. In some cases there might be a conflict between the Steering Committee making the decisions and the faculty or management who wants to be involved in the act. Schools are not familiar with 'temporary systems', or 'adhocracy', as we may call the Steering Committee. Clear rules and norms need to be developed for the decision-making process.

5 To be effective, the dialogue must be authentic and direct. At the same time it is important that it does not damage human relationships or hurt individuals unnecessarily. We have to realize that facing data might hurt. How do we deal with this? What is the support structure to deal with personal development within the IDP?

It often becomes necessary to provide assistance to individuals parallel with the work with groups.

6 The relationship between the Steering Committee and the consultant must be clear, and is decided by the Steering Committee. However, in this phase it is often the case that the consultant acts as an expert on organizational surveys (and on the GIL in particular). Experts may well 'take over', and the norms must therefore be clarified and checked throughout the process of diagnosis.

7 The analysis must be theory-related and clear, and at the same time practical and relevant. Participants must feel that 'this is my school'. Theory-imposed interpretations do not work. It is when participants illustrate an issue, and a theoretical perspective might help to give the illustration *meaning*, that it works.

8 During the diagnostic phase there is often an issue of balance between the *content* and the *process* issues. The school is often more concerned with getting the 'right diagnosis', and less often sees the importance of dealing with the issue of *relationships*. Since the consultant knows that process issues must be dealt with to create the climate for change and developing the necessary ownership, his or her job is to help the Steering Committee to see the importance of both dimensions (content and process).

We have stressed several times in this chapter that the IDP builds on joint diagnosis where the consultant is given a facilitating role, and where participants are encouraged to interpret the existing data and put them into a meaningful context. To go through the different GIL profiles jointly helps to create the necessary psychological readiness to do something about it.

It is the users who have the relevant experience to enable them to understand what the information really means. The most important validation of data is the joint assessment that takes place through what we call 'communicative group work'.

Only when the users are drawn actively into the diagnostic process can they develop a sense of ownership towards the tasks ahead. This attitude and practice is crucial to the success of the school improvement processes. That some or all members are drawn actively into the process does not necessarily mean consensus, but that serious co-operative work gives a better chance for understanding and for building trust (French and Bell, 1990).

## ALTERNATIVES TO THE GIL

There are good reasons for using the GIL instrument to provide a broad basis for diagnosis and dialogue, but we also use other techniques. We seldom use the GIL in small schools (e.g. those with fewer than 10 teachers), to ensure that anonymity is guaranteed. As discussed above, we do not use the GIL if the school has a defined 'problem' or 'task'. Quite often, however, the GIL is being used in these schools one or two years after a specific development programme has been started.

In many schools there are several teachers who hesitate to fill out the questionnaire. There may be suspicion or anxiety that the information will be misused. There may also be anxiety that problems may be uncovered that have been swept under the carpet for years. There are a number of reasons why questionnaires should not be used. We therefore often try different methods, some of which are presented in the following section.

## Self-study

This method was first presented by Friedrich Glasl (1975) at the Dutch Institute for Organizational Development. With the help of a self-study, the participants can identify and give priority to important problem areas. The self-study throws light on the immediate and felt problems and makes it possible to develop a list of priorities from a set of agreed-upon criteria.

This method makes it possible for participants to portray their own school, on the basis of analysis formulated in teams. This method too builds on a questionnaire, but this time a questionnaire developed by the school itself. It can be changed following the needs expressed by the participants without disturbing the quality of the items. The self-study builds on the following four principles:

1  *Openness*: Goals and methods of work are openly discussed among participants to avoid any form of manipulation.

2  *Tailor-made questionnaire*: Each school develops its own variance of a questionnaire. It is tailor-made to the school and the situation and the dilemmas that the school is trying to resolve. Even though an instrument is developed from scratch, or is basically an adaption of an old instrument (GIL could be the starting point), it develops ownership and a questionnaire that is experienced as tailor-made.

3  *Self-study*: Although quite often a consultant will function as a facilitator, it is important that the staff are in charge. To develop their own tools is an important motivational factor for the staff.

4  *Concrete steps*: The self-study can be divided into fairly clear phases that are distinguishable from each other. It is to some extent a linear process, therefore more easily understood, and also helps participants to know 'where they are'.

Compared to the often fairly unsystematic attempts at a pedagogical debate among staff, the self-study has a number of strategic advantages. As the step-by-step model in Figure 4.5 illustrates, the pedagogical debate does not end in the air, as is often the case. Here it ends in concrete proposals for activities that may lead into a school improvement progamme. To start a self-study also implies that the staff are further committed and are concerned that it will lead to results. A self-study represents a project that is assumed to lead to concrete results.

One of the most important phases of self-study, as in other methods we have presented in this chapter, is the feedback process. The results of the questionnaire may give participants a picture of the school within the area of investigation that might help them to formulate a plan of action. As with other

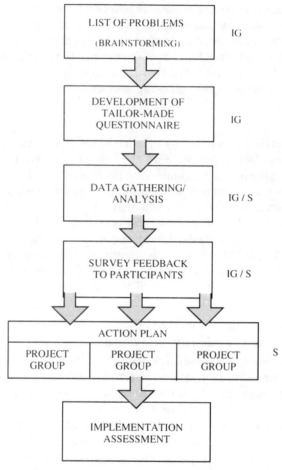

Figure 4.5   *Self-investigation. IG = initiation group, S = staff.*

methods, self-analysis also has its problems. If the various participants are fairly
one-dimensional and fixed in their way of looking at the school, the information
from the self-study will not provide alternative perspectives. The innovation
potential of the project is therefore in question or has at least been reduced.
Because self-analysis may well have a limited potential, it is important that
the consultant assists the school in looking at the data from alternative
perspectives.

## A pedagogical account

This is a method that our German partners at the Landesinstitut für Schule
und Weiterbildung in North Rhine-Westphalia have developed (Buchen, 1986;
LSW, 1988), and it has three phases:

1  to become aware and conscious about the *implicit* school programme,
2  to review critically the existing school programme, and
3  to further develop the school programme.

The starting point of the first phase is that within each school there exists some form of 'implicit school programme'. This could be based on the school's specific 'traditions'; a school might have a particular emphasis on, for example, 'aesthetic subjects', or it might have a particular 'profile', a particular 'façade'. that it would like to emphasize to give the outside world a particular picture of itself. To make the implicit explicit, as clear and understandable as possible, the staff decide to go through a 'pedagogical accountancy'.

When the staff go 'carefully through the accounts' they are not talking about their objectives or wishes, but the actual activities that are observable, and that can be said to characterize the school. Every staff member is therefore asked to answer the following question: 'What activities have, in your opinion, been important and influential in our school programme?'

A brainstorming process then helps to make the existing, but not yet explicit, school programme more open and conscious. To express it in writing also makes it visible. The results of the brainstorming meeting are systematically structured from criteria decided upon by the staff. This process usually starts a lively, but not necessarily very pedagogical-oriented, debate among the staff. Figure 4.6 shows the different phases in this process.

To move away from the implicit school programme and the co-operation needed to systemize and make it more explicit, some hours' group work is needed during which the real pedagogical situation in the school is assessed. Teachers try to assess where the school stands pedagogically and organizationally on the basis of what has been discussed. The purpose is to clarify the existing and the future goals and at the same time set up some principles for the further development of the school.

The discussion, now with its basis in the explicit school programme, helps to clarify the opinions and the nuances in attitudes among the staff. In addition, the dialogue itself helps to clarify other points of view, and it usually also makes it clear that further consensus about the pedagogical programme is necessary for a joint effort to be successful.

There is a danger with the starting point in 'our profile' that the discussion will not be deep enough, that the relationship between the content of the school programme and the pedagogical guidelines in the curriculum is not sufficiently clear and discussed, so that the discussion becomes very pragmatic and superficial. To avoid this we have developed a matrix to help analyse the existing school programme critically. With the assistance of this tool participants will have to look at the more basic ideas: have the principles of the curriculum been taken care of, and is the pedagogical practice in harmony with national goals?

This analysis of existing practices, as they are expected to be, gives an opportunity to understand what the pedagogical practice of the school really is. At the same time it provides a starting point for a potential development programme. It also gives an opportunity to refocus earlier traditions in the school, to modify them or to drop them. Such processes of accountancy should be done on a regular basis, because the school programme is not static, but will always be related to a context and to objectives. The discussion can obviously help to formulate new objectives for the future work of the school. This could lead to new priorities and a school development programme.

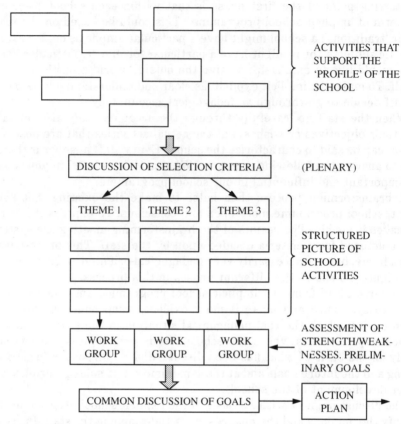

Figure 4.6   *From an implicit to an explicit programme*

The third and last phase of this process is to help participants understand their school in pedagogical terms, and to formulate new and modified objectives for the school on the basis of their experience. Again brainstorming and structured analysis are used; however, the priority setting in this phase has another dimension, as it is now focused on further development.

It is possible for the school to go further into the development process without the use of a consultant. It is our experience, however, that schools fairly quickly and superficially finish their 'critical assessment phase' and try to go into action planning. This transition from diagnosis to action is critical in any school improvement process and therefore considerable space is needed to discuss it (see Chapter 5).

We have attempted, in this chapter, to show that in the different phases the school has different needs and a different readiness in terms of analysis of its own practice. The starting point differs. What are seen as needs may differ widely. It is the task of the consultant, in co-operation with the school, to find a strategy that helps the school go through a process that releases energy and creates openness, and that mobilizes participants for the real work of development.

Diagnosis is an exercise in getting to understand realities better. It is also the beginning of a dream — of something better; it begins to create a vision, and to realize the tension between the 'real' and 'ideal'. It is an exercise in active listening; there is room for both discussion and dialogue, and it is the beginning of a *joint* vision. It is something we may do together.

In this chapter we have shown some of the approaches and instruments that are used in IDP schools. During the first few years the IDP was, to a large extent, related to an organizational survey approach. Our experiences led to a considerable expansion of this perspective. We are now much more concerned about finding an approach that is suited to the readiness of a particular school, that opens up areas for further development and that secures a process of change, rather than about a full and comprehensive understanding of the school. We have learned that a joint diagnostic process is a learning process over the entire programme period.

# Chapter 5

# From Goals to Activities

*What are the characteristics of pedagogical objectives compared to objectives in other sectors of society? What are the implications of these characteristics for the school improvement process? Can a school be 'managed by objectives'? Why is it necessary to understand and control the means as well as the goals? What are desirable objectives, or what is a 'good school', and who can and should determine that? How can a school proceed to be able to clarify and develop its goals? How can a staff agree on goals? How do we get from goals to activities? What factors are important when we want to set priorities among a number of desired goals?*

The connection between analysis and activities is a complicated process in school improvement. Goals do not follow automatically from a diagnosis. And furthermore, the means or the activities cannot easily be deduced from the goals. Figure 5.1 illustrates the discontinuity that exists in this process.

Since the activities cannot easily be deduced from the diagnosis and the goals, there is a disconnection in the rationality of the process. From our own practice we know that the connection between the diagnostic phase and activities over goals is a very problematic one, because both ambiguity about the goals and conflicts about the means are natural phenomena in any organization (see also Beckhard and Harris, 1987).

## THE DILEMMAS

Insecurity and conflicts can be better handled when we know the reasons *why*. Insecurity and conflicts in this phase are related to the fact that activities do not automatically follow diagnosis. The relationship is rather asymmetric: the diagnosis is one side of the process. Even if it is typically difficult and takes time, it is in principle possible to agree on a diagnosis through the IDP. An equally clear proposal for a solution is much more difficult to agree upon.

We take the example of a lower secondary school that we have worked with. This school had a very authoritarian headmaster who had little room for ideas from staff members. The diagnosis here was unanimous, and the headmaster himself agreed. But what would it mean? Should the headmaster be advised to take individual therapy? Should instead the staff be drawn more actively into the decision-making process? Should the whole staff and the headmaster together go through 'group dynamics' sessions? Would the school function more productively if the headmaster were to change his leadership style? A number of ideas were proposed. Were they realistic? Who can take such

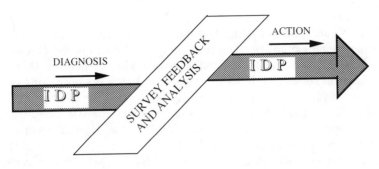

Figure 5.1 *From diagnosis to action*

decisions? What would happen if the headmaster did not agree? Whose interests would be served by the various proposals? The decision about a given solution to a problem does not depend only on the diagnosis, but on a number of factors related to the problem, to the school and to the environment. It is when we have to choose a concrete strategy that we realize the need for a broad understanding of the school as an organization. We then begin to understand that what is identified as a 'problem' is part of a much bigger whole. We also realize that we need to be much clearer about the goals, and the goals are somewhere between the analysis and the activity. The specific goals would therefore determine *what we choose* and *where* the activity should take place. Therefore, at this stage the goal determination process is a very important one in the school improvement process. This, however, we only discover when we are forced to make a decision. Goals can only be operational when we understand that they have consequences for our lives.

## THE CHARACTERISTICS OF PEDAGOGICAL OBJECTIVES

To attain a formulation of pedagogical objectives is a complicated process. Pedagogical objectives are in several ways different from objectives in other sectors of society. Pedagogical objectives are *reflective*, and they are often the target of disagreements and contradictions (cf. Klafki, 1989). Objectives formulated in an industrial organization are, on the other hand, much clearer; they are, for example, related to winning bigger shares of the market and to earning more money. Even health and social organizations may have clearer objectives, where numbers and indicators are available that can be helpful for action planning. It could, for example, be a goal to have at least one practising medical doctor for every 1000 inhabitants, or a given number of square feet of living space per person.

The most important educational objective is upbringing for the child's coming of age, an objective that includes the ability to act responsibly. The lack of this kind of maturity is, according to Immanuel Kant (he talks about '*Unmündigkeit*' in his 'Was ist Aufklärung?' of 1783 (Kant, 1923)), a person's inability to think and act on his own.

If one takes this definition seriously, it means that one cannot teach a student 'self-reliance'. If a person is told to think and to be responsible, one would in that same instant make him *dependent*. The meaning of self-reliance and independence cannot be taught, it can only be discussed and understood through reflection. A group of students or staff can involve themselves in such a process of reflection; however, this is probably the only thing that can be done. As individuals we all act differently from what we are told. To measure what self-reliance and independence is is therefore questionable. Comprehensive pedagogical objectives cannot be completely operationalized or quantified. The rather discouraging discussion about curriculum taxonomy and the debate around educational technology at the beginning of the 1970s provided ample examples! The 'management by objectives' bandwagon today is another example of a misunderstood belief in rationality. Immanuel Kant deliberately *only* formulated the objective 'negatively'; he talked about what *dependency* meant, rather than trying to define what independence was. The moment a comprehensive objective is operationalized, it becomes *unimportant* or *not valid*.

Pedagogical objectives are not free from 'contradictions', and the real choice of objectives actually happens in the classroom. Pedagogical objectives are not straightforward; they need reflection, a continuous comparison and assessment. No one but the person who knows the *student*, the context around the student and the learning situation can in reality decide the objectives. It is in the classroom that the objectives of the school are prioritized, because only in the classroom is there such a close connection between objectives and means. To give one example: most national curricula demand that each individual student is taken care of and is able to develop his or her attitudes and skills to the optimum. The objective is that the teacher will have to take care of the high-ability students, as well as those who have less ability in a particular subject. Any form of pedagogical activity (since resources are limited) implies *a choice*. A teacher who concentrates his or her energy on certain students is in danger of neglecting others, at least to a certain degree, even if that teacher uses the most modern methods of instruction and the students as a resource. We have often tried to hide these contradictions in our anxiety to give due weight to the principle of equality of opportunity. A term such as 'differentiation within the class' is an expression that indicates that *all* students will be taken care of. All practising teachers know that they have choices, and thereby are faced with dilemmas. To specifically help some students' development may well hurt that of others. This is a continuous dilemma for which the individual teacher must find a balanced solution, where the 'objectives' very seldom give any form of guidance.

Both school management and staff need to take pedagogical realities into account, as when the discussion is on how far one can involve others when decisions about objectives are made. It is not a question of dictating given objectives for all! The process is rather, in joint session, to arrive at objectives that can be shared voluntarily. Our experience is that it makes little sense to try to deduct such goals from nationally decided objectives, or even from pedagogical theories (Meyer, 1972). Only through serious common analysis of the reality of the school can the students and teachers realistically set the objectives.

This discussion has one purpose: to show that to clarify a goal, and then to plan the activities to meet these goals, is not a technological problem, but a very complicated pedagogical and social process.

## GOAL CLARIFICATION: WHAT IS A GOOD SCHOOL?

In recent years a number of attempts have been made to clarify the objectives of schools through empirical research. Since the late 1970s one part of educational research, called 'effective schools research', has used empirical research methods to answer the question: 'What is a good school?' (Reynolds and Cuttance, 1992).

This debate started when some British and American research reports about 'effective schools' were presented. An important contribution was the early study by Rutter *et al.* (1979) about the effectiveness of secondary schools in London. Of particular interest was Rutter's description and analysis of what we call the 'ethos' of the school: 'the cumulative effect of the different factors in the school-situation seems to be much larger than the influence of any single factor.' It is likely that, from interaction between different context factors, a given 'ethos' is developed; a basic norm that determines values, attitudes and behavioural pattern characteristics for the school as a whole (p. 211). This 'ethos' has also been investigated by other researchers (Mortimore *et al.*, 1988) and it is documented to be an important school quality, independent of the socio-economic levels of the student group. The 'ethos of the school' was soon accepted as an 'empirically based indicator' of an 'effective school'.

The discussion of what is 'an effective school' has been very much on the research agenda in the USA since the late 1970s. The starting point in the USA has been rather narrow, namely how the school can be more 'productive'. The research design and methods have been fairly similar, and the goals have been to identify what characterized the so-called 'effective schools'. 'Effectiveness' basically meant student achievement results in certain basic subjects.

If one looks at the various characteristics of 'effective schools' that the different studies have come up with, one finds a number of differences. There are also, however, several common traits. In 1982 Edmonds presented a summary of the main characteristics as documented in the 'effective schools' studies. He presented five main characteristics, and these have been cited since in a number of countries. An 'effective school':

- has a school leader with leadership qualities, particularly interested in instructional leadership;
- gives priority to instruction in the central basic concepts and has less concern for other school activities;
- has a challenging learning-oriented atmosphere, helping each individual to 'stretch' him- or herself;
- has teachers who require that each individual student gives his or her best and reaches at least a minimum level of achievement; and
- has a climate where learning progress is recognized and controlled (Edmonds, 1982).

Such a list of characteristics of 'effective schools', deduced from different

83

empirical investigations, is still doubtful. Discussion of these results in relation to comprehensive school research in Germany and in the UK has proven that there are no simple and indisputable research-based criteria for school quality. Most of those who have done research in this area have primarily been concerned with student achievement. The question of better educational opportunities for all, a very important objective in most school systems in the Western hemisphere, has often been neglected. Also, questions related to the climate of the school have often been neglected. These examples should make it clear that empirical research cannot give a complete answer to what the objectives of the school ought to be.

In addition there is little distinction in the 'effective schools' literature between analysis and assessment. The empirically proven characteristics of 'effectiveness' are quite often used as a yardstick for quality. What a 'good school' is, is a *value question*. What *leads to* a good school is an *empirical question*. As long as we know what we mean by a good school, we can map what factors seem to be related to such practice, and what leads us to a 'good school'.

The criteria for school quality have been subject to critical assessment by several British and American researchers in recent years. Good and Brophy (1986) show in a major study that most researchers in the USA have limited the concept of school policy to 'school effectiveness', and again this concept has been very narrowly defined as student achievement in some basic subjects. To Good and Brophy, school quality is more than student achievement, and student achievement is more than what the researchers so far have defined. As far as these researchers are concerned, what so far has been done is only to measure the achievement results in one or two basic subjects at one or two levels of the school system.

A number of research reports (e.g. Brookover *et al.*, 1979; Rutter *et al.*, 1979) use a much broader definition of quality, where school climate or the school 'ethos' is included too. These more difficult studies, however, are no less problematic than the more limited effectiveness studies. On the one hand is the possibility that the 'school climate', and thereby also the 'pedagogy', is being instrumentalized. A better climate could easily be understood only as a *means* to achieve effectiveness and better student results, which would imply that the intrinsic value of good human relations and social learning was being overlooked. On the other hand, it is easy to get into an impossible argument concerning what causes what. Will a positive climate create better possibilities for learning, or are better learning results a necessary condition for a better climate? Or is there any relationship at all?

We are also concerned about the sampling procedures for most of these studies, namely to choose 'good schools', and to use only student achievement results as criteria. Then the task is to describe and analyse the achievement criteria empirically and relate any independent factors to these criteria (Purkey and Smith, 1983).

Empirical studies cannot give us any answers to the question of school quality. What is a good school is not an empirical question. Empirical research represents the *descriptive* elements of the issue, while the question about school quality is the *normative*. 'Quality can always be better' is one of the conclusions in an OECD report (1989, p. 135), but this report has forgotten that quality is a theory — and a value-loaded concept.

The German educational tradition has tried to resolve the dilemmas around objectives by establishment of a *Bildungsideal*, an ideal for the upbringing of young people. Bohnsack (1989) has recently brought this into the discussion. Even if such an approach expands the horizon it cannot resolve the basic dilemma, namely that what constitutes a 'good school' is dependent on the values and interests of those who discuss it. An alternative school, for example the Rudolf Steiner school, has a *Bildungsideal* different from that of a typical British primary school or a German *Gymnasium*. Empirical research with the goal of establishing criteria for good schools cannot replace the clarification of goals at the individual school. Whatever theoreticians or empirical researchers may say, it is not looked upon as either important or valid at a given school, either for the staff, the students or the parents. It is our experience that in the individual school it is only the experienced 'real needs' that count, and it is against these experiences that clarification of goals has to happen. In addition, whatever goals are established, they need to be *owned* by the school, so that energy can be mobilized to work towards them.

When this is said, we must also add that research related to 'good schools' has given us important information. The concept of 'school culture' today has a central place in the debate, although it has been used in school research for a long time. Its importance for school improvement processes was described and documented in the early 1970s (e.g. Sarason, 1971). In the Rutter study the following is said about the culture of the school: 'The main trend in what we have found underlines the fact that it is not only how the individual student is treated that has important consequences; also the general social climate or the "ethos" that characterizes the school as a social organization is of importance' (Rutter *et al.*, 1979). Rutter *et al.* conclude that the results would be better if the staff agreed about norms and values; and that in schools where the work was planned as a co-operative effort, the attendance rate was better and the discipline problems fewer and less serious. They also found that where teachers co-operated within such a system of norms, a very good work climate was developed that had positive consequences for instruction. Rutter also reported that 'ad hoc co-operation had little sense, and only verbal understanding about goals and norms does not lead to results'. It is ongoing co-operative work that gradually changes the school culture, and has an impact on the qualities of the school.

It is not possible to establish objectives for a 'good school' in advance, either from empirical research, or from a given educational theory. Such an *a priori* definition will usually lead to alienation in relation to the goals or to a process where the teachers agree superficially, but in practice do not put energy into the task. The real goals for the pedagogical work (within the overall objectives set by society) are that it is only the school itself, and primarily the staff, which can decide; first through clarification of goals, and thereby through a process where consensus is reached. The meaning of a 'good school', however, only the school itself can decide, try out, assess and reformulate.

It should therefore be obvious, when we think about the characteristics of the pedagogical objectives, that 'management by objectives' as a strategy for schools cannot be realized, at least not in the traditional definition of this concept. This concept has as one of its basic elements to separate objectives from means, to define objectives at a high level of the hierarchy and to delegate the means to the 'implementors' and thereby mostly be concerned about evaluating the 'outcomes'. It is quite likely that this governance system will lead to an unproductive control activity, to less communication between management and teachers, and to a preoccupation with the least important pedagogical activities.

On the other hand, any organization should assess its own practice against valid research. It is part of the development of the school culture (see also Chapter 6). Can staff learn from effective schools research? Haenisch (1989) proposes that staff, in relation to a given research result, try to answer the following types of questions: 'What have we done in this respect in our school? To what extent are we able to do what is proposed? Will a change in practice also have negative side effects?' 'In this way the staff will be able to discover where its own strengths and weaknesses are. It is also likely that the staff will see that there are different routes to improvement and there are also things that one will not be able to accomplish' (Haenisch, 1989).

To use effective schools research as a starting point to clarify goals at the individual school, as Haenisch proposes, is probably a very useful approach. We also know that discussions over objectives are something most school staffs show a tendency to avoid, partly because it leads to conflicts and to few practical results. In this chapter we propose some methods to improve such a discussion.

In Chapter 4 we discussed the GIL instrument which provides important information for a goal clarification process. The GIL itself in fact represents a complex and differentiated goal system. But here also we find the asymmetry between analysis and action. It is possible to say that one can clarify, to a large extent, the objectives of the school by comparing the 'real' items with the 'ideal' items. Where the discrepancy is largest, the chances that there is a need for change are very real. To clarify such discrepancies, through a serious dialogue where also the concepts are clarified, is an opportunity for staff to give meaning to the data. There is, however, no automatic relationship between such discrepancies and desired objectives. A few examples of exercises that might encourage the staff to move further are given below.

## EXERCISE IN GOAL IDENTIFICATION

This example is related to the debate about good schools, and therefore we call this process 'What is a good school?' (Figure 5.2).

On the basis of discussions in the school of what a good school is, debates on the basis of research on the same theme, and co-operation with a number of teachers, 87 items that can be seen as indicators of a good school have been developed (e.g. 'management and teachers discuss the values of the school'). A number of items look similar; however, they have different meanings. Combinations of different items will give different 'sums' and therefore different 'profiles'.

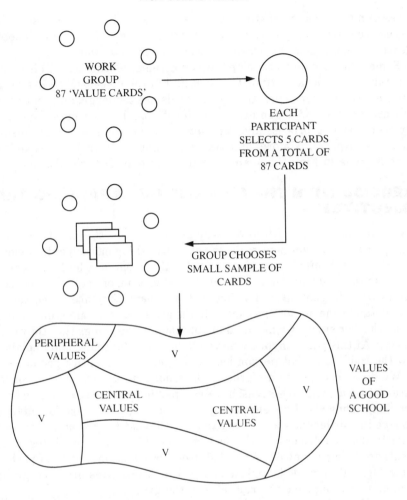

Figure 5.2 *The exercise: 'What is a good school?'*

The exercise starts with individuals, taking their time, choosing a small number of items (written on cards) that for the individual give a totally acceptable picture of a 'good school' as he or she wishes the school to be. Anyone might write additional items on cards if there is no item in the 87 items that represents a particular point of view. In the next phase a small group agrees on a small number of items that as a whole represent an acceptable picture of the 'good school' for that group. In these discussions it is vital that each participant clarify what he or she means with the various items. Often we find that a different item, or a new one, better represents the nuances in the values and goals that a person would like. Through this discussion clarification of goals gradually takes place, and each individual gets to know his or her own goals better, as well as those of the others.

This exercise can also be performed with the opposite starting point in that the question could be 'What is an unproductive school?'. The answers one arrives at may be as interesting as those one gets when the discussion has the first, positive starting point. The last version can also be used in schools, and at least one can reach agreement on what the staff *do not want*.

Some schools want to develop their own items from scratch. This is possible, but it takes considerable time. One will find in the discussions in small groups that often the discrepancies among the cards are too large, and that additional cards are needed for a number of clarifications. This process, however, is a very good learning process and is recommended if the school has considerable time at its disposal. A more 'artistic' expression of central values and related values is given in Figure 5.3, an example from one IDP schools.

## EXERCISE WITH THE PURPOSE OF EXPANDING THE OBJECTIVES

This is another, quite different example that uses the creative energy of participants to discover new goals. We start by asking participants to close their eyes and for 3-5 minutes to picture in detail a room or a building where they would like to learn something or provide instruction, or that they see as a good place to work in general. Following such a 'dream' they are asked to describe this in detail to one person they select in the group. At the same time they should assess whether such a room would enable them to do things that they could not do today. At this point anyone who would like to volunteer could explain and/or draw the room that that person has envisaged for the entire group.

We discovered that this process does not lead to any precise concepts in relations to goals and objectives; however, participants are expanding their way of thinking. They use different perspectives on goals. They are forced to use the language in a different way as compared with what they would normally do in the fairly abstract discussion of objectives, and this means that different aspects of goals are being reviewed. We found to our satisfaction that most participants have a 'dream' or a 'pedagogical vision' which often inspires the group, and which may also improve the relations in the group.

## HOW TO REACH GOAL AGREEMENT

An important question in school improvement is how one gets from a fairly general understanding of a vision and objectives to concrete and, even more important, jointly binding goals. The answer to this question is: the goals are clarified by the means! To make this answer reasonable, we need again to illustrate the relationship between goals and means.

The classical, bureaucratic model of organizations and as the various forms of objectives-driven management systems separate goals and means. As we practise IDP, goals and means are inseparable.

The relationship between goals and means is disputable within various research theories. There are at least two more or less opposite theoretical propositions: the representatives of 'hermeneutically' oriented research stress goals rather than the means (Horkheimer, 1967). The goal perspective plays such an important role that, at least at times, one is reminded of the Jesuit physician: 'The end justifies the means.' Theodor Litt (n.d.) has, as a warning against

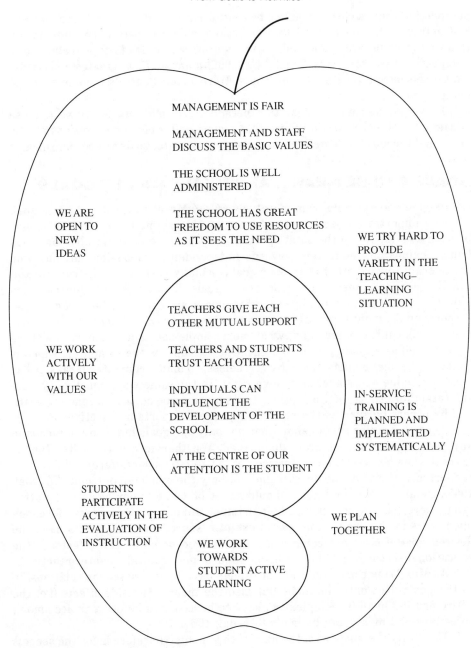

Figure 5.3  *The value profile of a school*

one-sided goal orientation, said: 'Indifference in relationship to the means is the same as unfaithfulness towards the purpose.' The objectives in this case then mean *nothing*. As an answer to this, Max Weber has said: 'To want something mobilizes the ability to master the means' (Weber, 1956).

Supporters of the second orientation in the analytical-empirical research perspective show a clear tendency to concentrate the discussion on the means. Not only does this lead to a situation where in-depth analysis and interpretation of the goals are neglected; in the worst case it leads to a technocratic perspective that, following Schelsky's (1965) point of view, creates a situation where the means determine the goals. Here value neutrality dominates the perspective.

However, neither of these two perspectives holds up when we analyse pedagogical objectives. We realize that means under certain conditions can be goals, and thereby value-defined, and also the opposite: goals can become means.

## GOALS CAN BE MEANS, AND MEANS CAN BE GOALS

Let us give one example from moral education. Moral education can be a goal, even an important objective of value in its own right. It can, however, also be seen as a means to the total upbringing of 'mature and ethically conscious human beings', an education towards independent, responsible citizens who are tolerant toward others, etc. Any goal is usually part of a goal structure and can be seen as a means towards other goals. The same example can also illustrate that it is not unimportant what means are used to achieve a goal (e.g. corporal punishment is probably no longer accepted as a means to achieve moral education!). On the other hand, what most people see as a means may well be experienced as a goal in its own right. One example is the computer, which is a means to achieve many goals. Nevertheless, to many 'computer freaks' it has become a value and a goal in its own right. In the same way, punctuality, consideration for others, or work ethics could by some be seen as secondary goals, and by others be seen as the ultimate and most important objectives.

These examples should show that not only the goals but also the means in any pedagogical process are value-loaded. We therefore agree with Gunnar Myrdal when he says: 'The means are not in value-terms indifferent. Values are connected with the whole process and not only the expected outcome' (Myrdal, 1965). He also shows that goals should never be looked upon as an end station in a process, but only as a part, albeit an important one, of the process. If we look upon goals in this way, a successful use of resources not only could have the desired goal effects, but could also have desired or undesired effects; in the educational sector it could even bring about a pedagogical 'counter-reaction'.

As Max Weber has said, the side-effects have to be assessed in relationship to the goals. Not only the goals but also the means, the side-effects (i.e. the entire process in all its complexity), have to be assessed before a choice among objectives and means can be made (Myrdal, 1965).

To 'clarify the goals with the help of the means' therefore is for the schools to clarify what means are available to reach desired objectives and to assess potential side-effects. At this point goals become realistic. As the staff begins to see the connections between goals and means, they move from goal clarification to goal consensus. One can also see this from a very pragmatic point of view: since goals and means are in many ways interchangeable, and the goal-means relation functions 'both ways', it is not sufficient to determine the goals at the theoretical level alone. The means must be considered at the same time. Our experience is that to clarify the goals through the means has a facilitating effect on the discussion of the staff. It is much easier to talk about the means than to discuss the goals in a vacuum, because these are often seen as value-loaded, ideologically anchored and therefore also conflict-loaded.

As the school has now come to a point where there is consensus about the goals and the means, it goes further into action planning.

## THE FLOW CHART: THE BACKBONE OF ACTION PLANNING

To further clarify the relationship between goals and means we use flow charts that are developed jointly. The flow chart is the first step towards a 'project model' (see Chapter 7), and represents a joint planning technique. Here we use visualization techniques to illustrate the logical sequence of activities and relationships among tasks.

The starting point for such planning is the most comprehensive list of all tasks and activities that participants can think of. The various subcomponents should be split into detailed steps, according to timing, to give the best possible overview of the type and the amount of work in the various subcomponents of a project.

It is vital that the flow chart is a result of group work, where, for example, 'action cards' can be used. The ideas are gathered through brainstorming and written down on action cards. Here we follow two rules:

1 On these cards we do not write wishes or goals, but rather concrete activities and tasks, i.e. we are talking about 'action cards'.

2 The timing will be marked from left to right on a wall chart that is large enough for all the activities and tasks to be listed on the one piece of paper.

There are various visualization techniques, such as colours, arrows, etc., the importance being that there is an easy-to-understand code that helps every participant to understand what type of activity is being talked about and at what time it needs to be accomplished. The flow chart should be able to help us to analyse and take decisions about:

- which activity must be completed before another activity can be started;
- activities that, from a timing point of view, can run parallel;
- whether there are sufficient resources for parallel activities;
- the time when important decisions need to be made for further development of a project; and
- if the activities are in harmony with project goals.

To illustrate what a flow chart looks like, we give an example from one of the schools we have worked with (Figure 5.4).

This is an example of the planning of an interdisciplinary project. Such a flow chart can be developed by a small group of people within 3-4 hours. It is

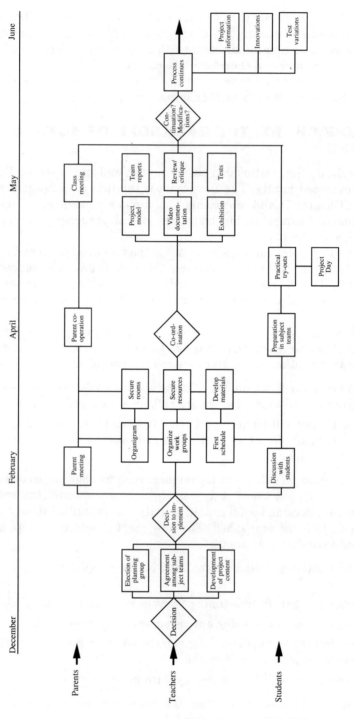

**Figure 5.4** *Project flow chart*

not developed in detail: the various tasks could be divided further, the connections could be better marked, the exact timing of activities could be added, and the names of responsible persons are not yet written up. When a flow chart is developed, however, it is not the perfection and the details that are most important. The most important aspect of a flow chart is that it brings people together through transforming the goal into concrete activities in such a way that it is experienced as a joint project. In the first analysis flow charts are a result of an internal common planning process. To visualize and document what is going to happen, flow charts function as an instrument to help participants reach the desired objectives. They are developed to illustrate how the practical activities are connected with the goals, and at the same time give a clear and consequent visualization for the staff. It is also possible to deduce what human and material resources are necessary at what time, what goals one is looking for and how one's own work is related to others' work. When staff work with flow charts it is necessary to clarify what resources the school has, to plan what pedagogical assumptions are implicit in the project (see Chapter 6).

The advantages of flow charts at this stage of the process are:

1 The development of a flow chart is relatively easy and does not require much knowledge and skill.

2 The various project steps need to be rethought, i.e. the project needs to be carefully thought through in advance.

3 Each task needs to be clarified, both in terms of time and practical implementation and what human and material resources are needed.

4 The co-operative work needed to develop this instrument may contribute to communication and further co-operation and also to the effect that everyone knows what to do and therefore has more self-control in the project.

5 The technical, professional and personal bottlenecks are easier to see and will, because they are discovered early, be tackled more easily.

6 One can fairly easily identify at any time where one is in the implementation of a project.

## SETTING PRIORITIES

When goals and means are clarified, it is easier to deal with the question of priorities. When one has a flow chart where all activities are clearly demonstrated, this is a much better basis for decisions about priorities than if one were only looking at different goals on an abstract level. In Figure 5.5 we have tried to illustrate the road from goal clarification to action planning.

The process starts with a clarification of the general and comprehensive goals of the school. Here one can use the GIL instrument and also some of the proposed activities mentioned above. Sometimes it may also be important to do some exercises that will expand the horizon or the goal perspective, as this may give a better understanding of new goals. Most likely, however, one already has too many goals and cannot deal fully with all of them, and therefore

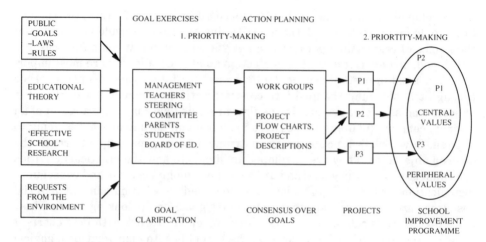

Figure 5.5  *From goals to action*

some discussion of priorities must take place. It is possible to make the first decision about priorities right after an exercise like 'what is a good school?'.

A consultant can facilitate this process and help to clarify the often difficult decisions involved in setting priorities. He or she can raise questions such as:

- What would worry you most if you were the one to implement this project?
- If you were given 20 per cent more time and resources, what would you strengthen in the project?
- If you had to live with 20 per cent less time and resources, what would you have to cut?

Such questions help the participant to take a stand, to identify what is important for him or her, and to clarify this for the others.

It is likely that the staff will find it is beyond their capacity to realize as many as four goals during a school year. In such a situation it is probably wise to take several decisions about priorities, for example to decide how to start and how to take a decision about one project that would be given priority and should be the beginning of a programme. Foltz *et al.* (1974) have some experiences to share in this respect. They say that action planning should start where:

- the dissatisfaction with the existing situation is clearest, or in an area where participants feel that they have a strength and can build on that;
- where results can be reached in a fairly short time, e.g. within the school year;
- where one is reasonably sure to reach results;
- where visible results can be expected.

We see this pragmatic list as particularly important in an early development phase, where school improvement is often met with scepticism (e.g. in 'fragmented schools').

It is important that all four criteria are taken into consideration. How one goes into the process of prioritizing is also important.

1  It must correspond with the wishes of the majority of the staff.
2  It should at least be tolerated by all, even by those who have not given the project their full support.

Therefore it is best not to start with too big a programme or with very sensitive problems, and one should also avoid small and unimportant projects. The school improvement project should have as its goal to involve the entire school. This could easily be seen as a contradiction in terms. How is it possible to combine both? The best advice is to implement every project consciously and at the same time remind participants about the joint diagnosis and the common goals that are the basis for the activities. 'Connecting' what may be seen as fairly small initiatives with a broader and important objective very often helps both participants and non-participants to see the meaning.

## THE CONSULTANT ROLE

This is a phase of the IDP where consultants can play a useful facilitating role. Goal clarification and goal consensus processes are complicated and will often lead to conflicts. It is important that the consultant does not get personally involved in the discussion of content or decisions about goals and priorities. It is the responsibility of the school to clarify the goals. Few schools have themselves engaged in discussions about objectives. Teachers often talk to each other about problems in the classroom, about curriculum, instructional methods and means; however, they seldom discuss goals. Teachers often withdraw from ideological discussions. Therefore it is important to give a hand and support the process:

- to clarify the characteristics of the pedagogical objectives;
- to give information about procedures for goal clarification, something that demands a good deal of sensitivity;
- to work closely with the Steering Committee, where these exercises probably need to take place first; and
- to demonstrate how the process can be implemented and give coaching along the way.

The consultant also has the role of representing a critical view if the participants attempt to implement too much of a 'perfect' and often linear mechanical process. In one IDP school the headmaster got the idea that flow charts could more easily and more efficiently be done on a computer, which would give him the 'correct' network plans. This is a typical but basic misunderstanding. A network plan can be made by one staff member. This would be an action plan that this person alone had responsibility for, and it would probably not be accepted as something owned by the entire school. In this case, therefore, the consultant had to explain to the headmaster that it was not necessarily perfection that was important, but a joint undertaking which is often complicated and less linear, but which builds commitment to implementation.

# Chapter 6

# Changing the School Culture

*What do we mean by 'the culture of the school'? What are the characteristics of the school culture and the way the organization functions? Do schools face new challenges today that might question the relevance of traditional school values and cultural norms? How is it possible to change the school culture at the classroom level, at the school level among teachers and school leaders, and among teachers and students? How can more basic values and norms be changed in an organization?*

The Institutional Development Program (IDP) is built on a number of assumptions about schools as organizations, about the way changes happen in schools and about the way adults and young people learn. The IDP also has long-range goals for schools: to move the school culture towards a *learning culture*, a culture that is able to respond to the needs of students and adults, taking both external and internal needs into account (Chapter 1).

The IDP goes through several stages. At this stage of the IDP process, the school is moving into action, to realize some of its priority goals through pilot projects. A Steering Committee is responsible, and most likely several project groups work on desired projects. Does this mean that the school is *changing*? It does mean that the school is doing something new, but *not* necessarily that the school as an organization is changing. To replace one practice with a new one may simply mean to replace one rigidity with another. For the school to change in the way it functions, it has to change its *culture* (Dalin and Rust, 1983; Schmuck and Runkel, 1985).

Although the IDP assumes that the school is the unit of change, it does not mean that we assume that the change process starts at the organizational level. Changes in the culture of an organization start with *people*: the way we think and act, alone and together. The IDP assumes two parallel strategies that need to be worked on simultaneously:

1 Changes at the *individual level*, by helping the individual teacher to overcome those aspects of the school culture that hinder the teacher's personal growth and learning and the development of a new teacher role.

2 Changes at the *group and inter-group level* to enable individuals to function together, within operational work units (e.g. a subject team) and across work units (e.g. across departments).

This chapter deals with these two basic change strategies. They are very much a part of what the Steering Committee and the consultant are working on at this stage of the process, as several teachers and the leadership team are coping with new challenges in one or several projects. In this chapter we reflect on one essential dilemma: What do we mean when we say a school is changing its culture?

## THE CONCEPT OF CULTURE

Organizations are different. What we experience as the 'way things are' in an organization, the written and unwritten rules that regulate behaviour, the stories and the 'myths' of what an organization has achieved, the standards and the values set for its members — these and many other aspects of organizations differ.

A car factory is different from a kindergarten! A school is different from a hospital (although many would argue that there are similarities). What is also increasingly recognized is that schools differ among themselves, although schools are also *similar* in many important ways. In fact, the 'ethos' of schools may differ widely (Sarason, 1974; Arfwedson and Lundman, 1983; Little, 1989; Rosenholtz, 1989). As discussed earlier in this book, one of the important dimensions of the diagnostic process in the IDP is to clarify values and norms, and how daily practices are related to the perceived values. Our perspective is that the 'school culture' is a complex phenomenon, and we would agree with Hodgkinson that it 'appears' at three different levels (Hodgkinson, 1983):

1 *The transrational level*: where values are conceived as metaphysical, based on beliefs, ethical code and moral insights.

2 *The rational level*: where values are seen and grounded within a social context of norms, customs, expectations and standards, and depend on collective justification.

3 *The subrational level*: where values are experienced as personal preferences and feelings; they are rooted in emotion, are basic, direct, affective and behaviouristic in character. They are basically asocial and amoral.

We find that few schools are clear about their values at the transrational level. Except for some private schools (e.g. Waldorf schools, Montessori schools), few schools have a clear message at this level. At the rational level, however, most schools show clear values through their stated objectives, their norms, rules and regulations, curriculum, daily practices, customs and ceremonies. As we analyse values in practice, we find that the subrational level in many schools plays a very important role, not least because the school is not used to expressing itself clearly at the rational level, and because of the power that individual teachers have (because a high degree of autonomy). Personal preferences have a tendency to play an important role.

Values and norms appear at the individual level, the group level (e.g. classroom), the organizational level (i.e. school level), the subculture level (i.e. schools versus other organizations), and the society level (Hodgkinson calls this the 'ethos' level).

This definition of culture makes it clear that individuals and their relations are a very important determinant of what constitutes a 'school culture'. It therefore becomes critical to influence the culture at the individual and group level, if we wish to finally attempt to change the school culture.

## CHALLENGES TO THE SCHOOL CULTURE

Why is it important at this stage to be concerned about norms and values or the concept of culture? We see it as important for several reasons. First, the present school culture should be able to meet the challenges of modern society. Second, we should know what parts of the school culture may *hinder* meaningful and desirable changes. Some examples of changes in society, and in our views on learning, that have major implications for the school culture are given below.

The *nature of the learning task* is changing. Many schools are still organized as bureaucracies, characterized by departmentalization, separate subjects and departments, teacher independence (and often as a consequence teacher isolation), a heavy concentration on cognitive development and a focus on individual achievement alone. This form of organization and these perspectives on learning are now being challenged; in other words, a culture that reflects stability, predictability and a hierarchy of decision-making is being challenged.

Increasingly, learning is seen in a broader context as personal growth; the development of social skills as well as cognitive development. Group work and group development are seen to be as important as individual achievement. A problem orientation is given increased weight in the curriculum, the relationship between theory and practice is stressed, the need to involve parents and the community actively in the learning process is understood, and a learning strategy that more closely resembles the way we learn in practical day-to-day life is being rediscovered.

All these are just examples of trends that have already been important for some years, and that illustrate the need to understand and deal with the relationships and interconnections in the school, among subjects, among individuals and learning groups, and between the school and the environment. As the school begins to accept its responsibility for learning in broader terms, the need to communicate and negotiate values and norms becomes obvious. For many schools such an emphasis would mean a drastic change in the culture of schooling.

The *student population* is changing. What James Coleman (1987) calls 'social capital' has been dramatically reduced over a period of twenty years, particularly in the large cities. His research shows that the self-concept of students and their attitudes to learning and to work are changing and showing a negative trend, in particular in the larger cities. Media researchers warn about the negative effects on children's concentration of heavy use of video and television (Postman, 1987). Increasing numbers of broken homes and a more horizontal society (with less interaction between the young and the adults) are also factors changing today's youth culture.

Clearly, there are also many positive sides to today's youth culture. Many young people are actively involved in sports activities, leisure activities, religious groups and community clubs. Some are fighting for the rights of others, the environment, international causes and social issues. However, as we analyse what different age groups among the young generation use their time for, we find large differences in opportunities (Volanen, 1987).

The development of a healthy school culture that also provides optimal learning conditions for youth with low social capital will be even more difficult in the years ahead. The concerns about equality of opportunities in a society with an increasing number of unemployed youth cannot be dealt with unless major changes in school and youth policies take place.

The *norms of organizational life* are changing in our societies. Decisions taken without the involvement of key actors, and not shared among those who are concerned, are increasingly questioned. Hierarchical forms of leadership are challenged. People want more out of their professional lives and their careers. How can a school culture develop a healthy climate where students' needs (in a broad sense of the term) and teachers' professional and career needs are taken into account? What type of organization is a productive learning organization? What is a productive school culture? To recognize the learning needs of teachers would be a major change in culture for many schools.

The *value of group work* is increasingly recognized, not only because group work is essential to reach personal and social objectives, but also because group work is becoming such an important element of everyday life and work (Senge, 1990). There are individual gains, as well as organizational gains (Nadler *et al.*, 1979). The methods and technology of effective group work are well known and should be accessible to teachers and students. The value of being able to work both with the 'production tasks' (content of the group task) and with the 'hidden curriculum' (the values, norms and processes that regulate behaviours in group) is that it helps us to understand the value of working with groups to learn problem-solving behaviours, as well as the values and needs required in a problem-solving school. Many schools do stress co-operative work as part of their culture; however, we find that many schools and particularly secondary schools have some way to go before this is an accepted part of the school culture.

Many schools see these and other changes in the context of schooling, and are working hard to creatively meet these challenges. Other schools are bound to traditions and norms that make it hard to adapt and meet new challenges. Old values and norms have usually set traditions in the school that are hard to change. *Culture*, in other words, plays a significant role as a determinant of change.

In our discussion of change theory in Chapter 1 we argued that many teachers are against a given change project because of value barriers and power barriers (Dalin, 1978). We find that many change agents (external or internal to the school) argue for a given project at a technical level ('This project can help us to become more productive ...'), or at an altruistic level ('This project is good for kids ...'). Very few projects are analysed in relation to the school culture as it appears in its complexity in a given school. In our view most projects will have value or norm implications and power implications (certain parts of the school culture will gain or lose).

We have briefly mentioned a few changes that may be a challenge to the traditional school culture. We could have used other well-known examples, such as the rapid development of technology, the role of women in organizations, or the use of students as a resource in the classroom. Our purpose at this stage has been to show that external developments as well as internal needs raise questions about the traditional school culture.

## CHARACTERISTICS OF THE SCHOOL AS AN ORGANIZATION

It is very hard to describe a culture. What we can see is how people in an organization are *behaving*. In our attempt to understand how a school culture functions, we try to understand the characteristics of the school as an organization, knowing that although there are similarities among schools, they also differ in how they cope with some of these factors. To be able to work with the culture of schools, we need to understand it better. One way is to study the characteristics of schools as organizations.

Is it possible in some way to characterize the school as an organization? Several authors have tried. We are not convinced that schools are *that* different from many other organizations. We would like to think of differences in terms of *degree* rather than as *absolutes*. In characterizing elements of the school organization that distinguish schools from many other organizations, we would note the following.

### Pedagogical goals

Several authors have described pedagogical goals as diffuse and often difficult to measure. We see another dimension as of particular importance: pedagogical goals are never fully reached, they cannot be clearly pointed at, they 'talk back' and can best be understood in a dialectical process of reflection. Clearly there are also parts of the goal structure that can be 'isolated', 'measured' and valued (e.g. cognitive goals in mathematics). They will always, however, be only part of the 'goal structure', and sometimes they may not even be very important, in particular in a long-term perspective. In other words, pedagogical goals are complex, they can never be fully reached, they are long term, and they are hard to measure and value (Rolff, 1991).

### The process of learning

This process happens within us. It is a complex maturation process; we learn gradually and it is very much an individual process, where every learner finds his or her strategy and tries to adapt to whatever teaching strategy the school offers. Although some subparts of the teaching process may be standardized and even dealt with through technology, the higher-level learning goals can only be met by human reflection and interaction tailor-made to the needs of the individual learner.

A reaction to these first two factors is to shy away from any standardized way of testing and 'quality control', simply because it will never be able to grasp the complexity of the learning process, it may divert teaching into meaningless activities, and it may be harmful to individual learning needs.

The dilemmas that the school is faced with are complex. How can the school be seen as credible if it cannot demonstrate its 'productivity' in a meaningful way? How can that be done without simply measuring only the easy and often lower-level learning goals? How can one better separate different types of learning goals on the one hand, and different types of evaluation and quality control on the other? How can a more productive relationship be developed between the school-based internal assessment process and the external process of quality control (see Chapters 7 and 8)?

## Standard practices

The teaching-learning process is complex. Research on teaching is a relatively new science. It is probably true to say that much research has not been particularly *practice-related*, and many teachers have gained a fairly negative picture of what research can do for the improvement of teaching. This has probably led to an 'anti-intellectual norm' in relationship to one's own profession. Teachers therefore have fallen back to an easy position: it is only I as a practitioner and my colleagues who know what is best for the children. The tendency for most teachers, therefore, is to rely on traditional, secure and 'standard' instructional practices. When we also know that many teachers to a large extent are autonomous in their role (see below) it is obvious that the chances for real innovation in relation to the daily task of teaching and learning are fairly limited.

## The autonomous teacher

Although teacher co-operation is increasing in most school systems, and the traditional classroom organization is gradually being replaced by a more flexible organization, the norm in most countries (and in particular in secondary schools) is the traditional one teacher-one classroom organization. The learning organizational structure is still dominated by single subjects, individual 'desk learning' and individual teaching (Lortie, 1975; Goodlad, 1983; Little, 1989). For certain learning tasks this is indeed an effective organization of work, for others it is not. It is when the learning task calls for a more integrated work organization, and the school continues its traditional forms of teaching, that the school, the teacher and the student have problems.

Teachers are not used to collegial 'co-operation', simply because it has not been necessary. In fact, much co-operation has been very ineffective and has resulted in even more isolation. As a starting point: to share professional thinking with other adults is simply not always part of the school culture.

Flinders (1988) argues that teachers often work actively to secure individual time 'to be able to get the work done', often because they see co-operation as a waste of time, and as taking energy away from the main tasks. Although we argue that co-operation is important for many integrated tasks in today's society, and also for integrated tasks in schools, we must not replace one rigidity with another! Individual work-time is essential for solid preparation, for some follow-up work, and for further studies and reflection.

Rolff (1991) argues that the 'autonomous teacher' is caused by a conflict between, on the one hand, the expectation that the teacher is a *functionary* in the school system accountable to achieve certain goals (controlled by the school authorities), and on the other hand the fact that there are no general answers regarding good teaching. Although the teacher has a general knowledge of teaching, each student is indeed a unique 'case'. The teacher will therefore protect him- or herself by being in control of his or her classroom environment. Since, also, all professions strive towards professional autonomy, the route towards isolation behind the classroom door is easy to take. The teacher, in other words, moves towards a semi-autonomous role (Rolff, 1991).

## The mechanistic organization

Groups in schools are seldom put together because they are the optimal work organizations! A class of students — the most important learning group in the school — is simply a random group of individuals of the same age. The 'production leader' — the teacher — has not usually been trained for the classroom management role. Seldom, therefore, do schools see their task as being to develop groups as effective work units. Since the personal incentives, as discussed above, tend to favour the one teacher-one classroom organization, this all leads to a 'loosely coupled' system. The school too often becomes the sum of a large number of autonomous activities.

The sum of the last two factors may well be that the quality and the productivity of each classroom occur *by chance*, at least if no effective internal assessment process is working. There is research evidence to document that the particular learning group which a student by chance happens to belong to, and where he or she is part of a particular learning climate, is one of the strongest single factors that influence the learning opportunities for a child (e.g. Gjessing *et al.*, 1988). In some school systems, e.g. in Scandinavian schools, many heads do not see it as their task to supervise instruction, few teachers have been trained for a leadership role in the classroom and little is done to find the most suitable learning group for each child. There are strong arguments that such a 'loosely coupled' system in fact *determines* the learning opportunities for children.

## The lack of incentives

Teachers in most schools may continue with their classroom teaching, and not care too much about collegial co-operation (not to mention co-operation with students), without serious consequences. On the contrary, most teachers see planning work and group work as an extra burden that comes on top of all their other tasks. And those who take a lead will often feel that there is little support for their efforts. Also, teachers who have tried alternatives in their teaching know that it is not always effective, that much effort is needed, and that rewards are rare.

# VALUES AND NORMS OF THE IDP PROCESS

This chapter is concerned with the way the school culture may be changed. Here it is not trivial what the values and norms of the *change strategy* are. We go back briefly to the assumptions underlining the IDP:

1 The school is the unit of change and it is responsible for its own development. The real needs of students and teachers as they try to cope with external demands and internal pressures for change can best be understood and met by a mature school organization.

2 In this process *ownership* is necessary. Those who carry out the hard work of change also need to feel motivated and involved in the process. This can best be achieved as the different perspectives of teachers are taken into account, as co-operation is learned and conflicts used as opportunities for learning and growth.

3 What is 'best' for schools in a given area can best be judged by those teachers who are responsible for the learning outcomes of the students, because these teachers are provided with alternative views, challenges from external authorities, data from research, knowledge about alternative practices and time spent in analysing strengths and weaknesses of the school. This does not, however, imply that the teachers alone are the best judge. They, like others, will have to be 'confronted' with other views, with alternative 'mental models' (Senge, 1990), in a productive dialogue with others within and outside the school, to be able to make good decisions.

4 The change process is a *learning process*, dependent on practical experiences, feedback and dialogue, and mobilization of a steadily growing number of participants. In this process the learning needs of teachers need to be taken seriously. To create a new vision means to *discover*, to use a different *perspective*, to learn.

5 The school is an 'open system'; changes in one part of the organization often have consequences for other parts of the school. Change processes must be understood as systemic processes. A change process, therefore, alters not only technical aspects of the school (e.g. a structural dimension), but also the way people relate, and the norms and values that regulate behaviour. The school leadership has an important role in developing visions and balancing organizational forces.

The IDP takes teachers and school leaders seriously as professionals working in a highly complex job. It builds on the assumption that institutional learning is an ongoing and important process for both the young and the adult. It assumes a culture that is open and willing to learn also from the environment. It is a process building on a systemic understanding of the change process with emphasis on a systematic, co-ordinated and managed process. In other words, the IDP is a *challenge* to many traditional school cultures.

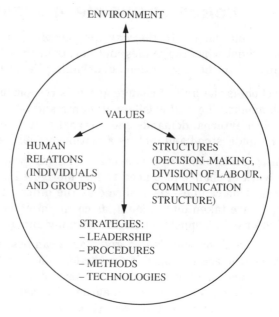

Figure 6.1    *Values and organizational behaviour*

## VALUES AND ORGANIZATIONAL BEHAVIOUR

We now move a step further and analyse how the schools' values and norms influence other important aspects of the school (Figure 6.1). We use the IMTEC model of the school as an organization to illustrate what these values may mean in organizational terms (see the IMTEC organizational model, Chapter 1).

### School values and 'relationships'

The nature of human relationships is at the centre of attention in a school development programme.

If ownership of the change process and co-operation among teachers are to be achieved, basic communication built on trust and openness throughout the school is vital. The IDP has in the long term higher-order learning as an objective. For these learning processes trust and safety are essential.

If the school is to be 'in charge', it needs to mobilize energy and motivation. If it is to learn to live with change in an ongoing learning process, the roles of learners — adults and children — have to be redefined. It is also clear from IDP experiences that not only the formal leadership of the school, but also the informal leadership (among teachers and students as well) need to be fully utilized to achieve good results. In other words, the new learning organization asks for major changes in norms and values that have a direct impact on human relationships.

## School values and 'structures'

It may not be so clear how the structures of the organization will have to change. It becomes clearer when we remind ourselves of how we define 'structure': decision-making structure, task structure and communication structure. There can be no successful IDP process without full participation by all relevant parties in the decision-making process. Schools with hierarchical traditions have a particularly long way to go. New challenges often call for additional tasks and redefinition of tasks. Schools with a fairly rigid differentiation of tasks will have a particularly difficult job ahead. Change processes also call for active and productive communication lines horizontally and vertically. Schools with a fairly 'fragmented structure', with isolated teachers and isolated work units, will have a particularly difficult job. IDP values, in other words, would have a major impact on 'structures' (Marx, 1990).

## School values and 'strategies'

To what extent do IDP values have consequences for the way the school tries to respond to internal and external demands, through its procedures, methods, teaching-learning strategies, technologies and leadership? In fact it is the very nature of the IDP process we are talking about. We believe schools need to build up their evaluation and needs assessment process, be sensitive to the needs of students and parents, to have procedures to deal with these needs, practise methods of problem-solving that reflect the values of the school, and define and practise leadership that fits the needs of the school. We do not advocate a particular leadership style. Effectiveness in leadership is, in our view, situational. However, sensitivity about the needs for leadership and ability to deliver what is needed is essential. In other words, the IDP also challenges the way school management traditionally approaches development tasks.

## School values and the 'environment'

Schools are increasingly facing changes and challenges from the environment. Mass media, changes in the youth culture and changes in the home environment challenge traditional forms of schooling. New government regulations, budgetary problems and new curriculum requirements put schools under pressure to change. Major changes in the use of technology question methods and practices in the school. The school, although it is the unit of change, is not an island on its own. It is responsible and accountable to parents, the school board and society. It must report and defend its own decisions, and in some countries where the market regulates school attendance, it must also market its own services. The IDP advocates that to survive schools need to take these demands seriously, and meet these demands in a constructive dialogue to develop innovative solutions that will benefit students (see also Chapter 9).

As we can see, to take the IDP seriously has major implications for the school culture. In fact, it may be overwhelming, and it may be difficult to see where to start. At this stage the IDP process is well under way; however, is the process of cultural change in progress?

## WHERE DO WE START?

From the brief discussion above, we see that the challenges that schools are faced with today probably assume fairly basic changes in the culture of the school. Since we know that these changes of values and norms will have implications for nearly all aspects of school life, the task is challenging and comprehensive. But how do we do it in practice?

In one 'IDP school' the following situation had developed:

> *It soon became clear to the faculty that something was going wrong with the ambitious change programme. The Steering Committee had successfully launched a process of joint diagnosis; a very interesting analysis had resulted in a fairly clear 'plan of action'. However, as this programme was being implemented, a number of disagreements surfaced, also within the Steering Committee. In fact it became clear that the committee itself was unclear about procedures and norms. Members disagreed about simple things like voting rules and decision-making, and conflicts were not resolved.*

In another school:

> *Following the last Steering Committee meeting teacher Hansen took me aside and told me that he had decided to leave the group. This was extremely sad because Hansen really was an important resource person. I tried to convince him that he should stay on, but he refused even to discuss it. He had made up his mind. I suddenly realized that for Mr Hansen this group was not an open group, where everything could be discussed. And that was exactly one of the cultural changes we had decided to work on in the school development project.*

In another school:

> *The first discussion about project results in the faculty was a disaster. So many complained that they knew nothing about the progress of the school development work. And I felt it was so unfair: we could prove that the Steering Committee had done a lot to communicate, to invite teachers to meetings, to discuss preliminary results, and we had sent around three 'newsletters', and still the teachers complained. I started to wonder: Is there something wrong with this culture, or is something wrong with the way we approach the tasks? Or maybe there is something more fundamental underneath ...*

In another school:

> *I was uncertain about the last decision by the headmaster. He wanted to write a contract with a computer firm, to get computers into the school and to 'show the community that we care' about the wishes of parents and industry. When one of the teachers responded, 'Computers seem to be a wonderful answer, what is the question?', the headmaster really got angry and left the room. How can we, on one hand, respond*

*to the community, and on the other respond to real needs and find innovative answers? Moreover, how can build the headmaster into the process?*

Schools soon discover that project implementation illustrates a number of basic issues related to the culture of the school, issues that relate to individual behaviour (in the classroom and in the project groups), to relationships, structures, strategies and the environment. As the school tries to work with these issues, new dimensions are often discovered that lead the way to values and norms, to the very nature of the culture.

We find that these issues can best and first be dealt with in the basic work unit responsible for the change process — the Steering Committee. In our terms, this 'temporary system' has the responsibility to plan, develop, implement and evaluate those projects that the school decides to devote resources to. In this process, however, the committee will often work with the more basic issues related to the school culture: how values and norms can be internalized, how relationships can be improved, how conflicts can be dealt with, how the leadership can better respond to needs, and how the school can better deal with the demands from parents and interest groups outside the school.

The Steering Committee, in other words, begins to discover that successfully to implement projects aiming at school improvement, and, it is hoped, a practice that improves classrooms and student learning, a whole set of issues related to the school culture must be dealt with *simultaneously*. Sometimes some pressing issues related to norms will have to be dealt with first. However, the Steering Committee is also under pressure to 'produce results'. The strategy is therefore to deal with 'processes' as much as 'content' in an integrated way.

The Steering Committee has no mandate to interfere with the regular management and decision-making process in the school. It is the *motor of development*, a temporary group, that uses its insight into the change process to move the school towards desired objectives. The Steering Committee is always dependent on easy and productive communication with all groups in the school, to clarify, to listen, to help, to redefine and to mobilize energy. The faculty 'holds on to the steering wheel'. The Steering Committee is delegated the responsibility to act; to be the motor. As we have seen, however, the tasks of the Steering Committee are closely connected with the work to develop the culture of the school. The Steering Committee, therefore, as well as having responsibility for project planning and implementation will also be responsible for developing a productive school culture. It is simply strategically impossible to separate the two issues. As the consequences for the school culture begin to appear, both the staff and, of course, the management team will discuss, clarify and agree on what needs to be done.

One condition is that the Steering Committee itself, through its own work, reflects the values and norms of a learning organization. Therefore the first priority is the internal development of the Steering Committee. Is the Steering Committee itself an effective work group? Is it the real motor for the change process? Are different perspectives taken seriously? Is there real co-operation? Are conflicts being dealt with constructively? Are the members and the group

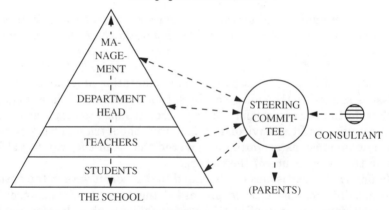

Figure 6.2 *Relations among the school, the Steering Committee and the consultant*

open to learning? Is there openness and trust among the members of the group? Has the group a productive relationship to 'its environment' (the faculty, students, etc.)? Maybe even more important: Is the Steering Committee in the process of 'learning how to learn', the essential message of the IDP?

The Steering Committee can best be *effective* in IDP terms by being a *model* for the school. Therefore it needs to take its own development seriously. This is often the first task in which the consultant can play an important role. Figure 6.2 illustrates the position of the Steering Committee as a 'temporary system' within the school (see also Miles, 1964). Usually it is composed of members from different groups within the school, has a role of communicating actively with the entire school community, and can draw actively on the resources of the consultant.

The actions of the Steering Committee are *visible*. If this group cannot master its own internal processes it may have fundamental negative effects on the entire school development process, as its members are usually 'connected' with most of the school. If, on the other hand, it is able to develop productive norms internally and in its relationship to the rest of the school, the chances are that it may have positive effects on the school organization, not only in terms of the projects it develops but on the internalization of values and norms as well. How, then, can the Steering Committee look after its own development? In our view this can best be done by taking group development processes seriously.

## GROUP DEVELOPMENT

The development of the Steering Committee is no different from the development of other work groups in the school, but it plays a 'modelling role' as a 'pilot' in school development. We will therefore deal with some of the generic processes in group development, and illustrate some consequences for the Steering Committee.

The change process is a learning process. We are dealing with humans testing the unknown, doing things for the first time, working with new people under often difficult and conflicting conditions. Progress is often challenged by the internal dynamics of change. It is essential to deal effectively with inter-human processes, in smaller groups, and in the staff as a whole. The more we work with schools, the more obvious it seems to us that the essential 'production' takes place in small groups. First and foremost: most teaching takes place in groups of from ten to thirty students. Most task forces have from four to six members. The management team is seldom larger than two to five people; a subject department most likely has anywhere from three to twelve members. These groups are the components of the work organization of the school. The quality of their practices and their relationships will to a large extent define the productivity of the school (its ability to reach desired objectives).

One of the important tasks of any school management, but in particular those concerned with managing change, is to ensure optimum working conditions in each operative group. In fact, in a school improvement programme, many task forces, several classrooms, several departments, and indeed the Steering Committee itself constitute the 'operative groups' assigned to contribute to the change objectives. This means that the quality and acceptance of the school development programme, will, to a large extent, depend on the quality of these groups.

In this section we highlight some of the issues of group growth that the Steering Committee, the management and the consultant in our experience need to be particularly sensitive to, and where interventions (and thereby skills) are needed.

## Membership

In formal terms anyone assigned to a group is a 'member'. But it may not feel that way. Here are some common reactions: Maybe my contribution is not recognized? Is it clear what it means to be a member of this group, and will I be accepted? Is there sufficient openness for me to say what I really want to say? Will I be trusted — or punished? How can I find answers to my questions? How much room is there for me to be myself?

These are some of the issues related to 'membership', and they often appear in many forms. Group leadership or consultant interventions are often useful in identifying these issues, by helping members to share feelings, in listening carefully and in helping the group to see what is going on.

## Roles

In temporary groups roles are usually quite unclear. It is also unclear what roles individuals can play and want to play. More important, it is unclear how different members will relate to each other. Here are some common reactions: How clear am I about my own role? What does 'the group' expect me to do? Are there different expectations among different group members? What about the roles of other group members? Are expectations realistic? Do they overlap? Is there competition and overlapping? Are there functions related to the tasks of the group that are not fulfilled by anyone? Is someone overloaded?

Group leadership or consultant interventions may help clarify roles, e.g. by having each member stating his or her expectations for his or her role, and by calling on others' expectations concerning the role of that person. Also, the person in question will have a chance to talk about his or her expectations concerning the others, as they may contribute to his or her role. Also, role expectations, overload and feelings need to be monitored and more realistic expectations developed.

## Communication

The passing of information among people in a group is an essential part of group behaviour. Who talks to whom about what? Are some members more important (receiving and sending more information) than others? What about the non-verbal messages — what form do they take? What personal style of communication is used? Are people trying to clarify messages (really listening and checking out)? What are the accepted norms of communication? Is it effective in relation to the tasks?

Group leadership or consultant interventions may help groups to be more sensitive to messages, to listen carefully and to make perception checks, to paraphrase and to observe non-verbal behaviour. To provide timely and effective feedback to individuals and groups is difficult and an important skill that can be learned. It is essential in day-to-day teacher practice and in the work of leaders. The conflicts in groups that are caused by communication problems can be resolved at a fairly technical level by a trained consultant.

## Influence

The influence structure is a part of any group and any organization. It is a regular part of any group, but is it accepted? What kind of influence is accepted? Are there certain types of behaviour that upset the group? Is certain behaviour accepted in some, and rejected when others use the same behaviour? How does leadership surface in the group? Is formal group leadership associated with influence, or are other members more influential?

Groups differ in terms of their values as they relate to influence. It is a sensitive issue, and seldom talked about. Therefore there is often lack of clarity about it (and sometimes undemocratic use of influence, since it is not openly discussed). Group leadership or consultant interventions may help clarify the norms around influence, test out 'influence models' (e.g. by role plays) and help members to report their feelings about influence patterns in the group.

## Being myself

Most people 'role play' in groups. A reaction from a participant is illustrative: 'It takes time before I can be myself — as I would like myself to be — in a group. In particular I am concerned about how my feelings can be expressed. What are the norms in the group? Who sets them? What feelings can I not express? How direct and spontaneous can I be? We are all unique in some way. Do we accept that in this group? How much self-interest is tolerated?'

Group leaders or the consultant may helpfully intervene by expressing their feelings, by testing out the norms in the group, discussing their own weaknesses and strengths and accepting that others do the same. It is also useful to let everyone share their experiences and background, and to encourage everyone to gradually test new behaviour, and ask for feedback. We see this as a part of group growth and maturity, and it should be done gradually over time.

## Goal-oriented behaviour

Groups have a task to accomplish and also have goals of their own, sometimes instrumental for achieving the task, sometimes important for group maintenance. Do members feel productive? Are goals clear, and are they discussed? Are group procedures goal-related and efficient? Are the meetings well planned and managed? How does the group deal with behaviour not contributing to the goals? How realistic are the goals? Can they be dealt with in a concrete and measurable way?

Group leadership or consultant interventions may reflect what is seen and heard in the group, enquiring about specific activities and behaviours, involving the group in goal definition, assessing progress, helping to develop criteria for assessing the work, helping the group deal with goal confusion and goal conflicts, and contributing to an understanding of both task goals and maintenance goals.

These are a few essential dimensions of group development, dimensions important not only in the Steering Committee but for all work groups in the school. Staff and students need to learn how to work in groups. Much of their own learning is based on group work. The consultant may have a facilitative role in certain groups; however, most likely he or she will work intensively with the Steering Committee, helping some members of that group to assist other groups in their growth.

Taking these and similar issues in group development seriously has a very strong and positive effect on the climate in the group and in the school as a whole. Gradually new norms of group behaviour become internalized. We started this chapter by saying that a strategy to change the culture of the school is to work with the values and norms of the various groups in the school, so that they reflect openness, trust and problem-solving behaviour. By systematic and serious work with groups a gradual development of trust and openness in the school will develop, which to us is the first condition necessary for cultural change.

It may help to use a consultant in the early phases of group development, or in periods of stress and/or conflicts. The role of the consultant will normally be that of an *observer* or *process facilitator*, a person who may help to structure group work, who may listen and intervene to illustrate what is happening in the group. He or she is also responsible for helping the group to 'discover itself' and to enable the group to work with its own development. We often find a 'here and now' discussion useful. This is a chance for members to express what they feel about an issue when a situation occurs. In all process interventions it is essential to *debrief* people concerning what has happened and to try to draw some lessons from it. Many groups develop internal norms that they write up on a large sheet of paper, and revisit once in a while!

There are many ways to develop a group. It goes beyond the purpose of this book to discuss all the different techniques used in IDP and in organizational development interventions; however, the reader is referred to excellent literature, exercises and training programmes in the area (e.g. Pfeiffer and Jones, 1972; Cohen and Smith, 1976; Stensaasen and Sletta, 1983; Egan, 1985; Schmuck and Runkel, 1985; French and Bell, 1990; Schein, 1990). This process, however, goes beyond the discussion of group development. There is a need for effective work groups, effective learning cells (e.g. classrooms) and effective collegial decision-making within any school.

IDP supporters advocate the development of group norms as an *entry strategy* to develop common values and norms throughout the entire school. The process usually starts in the Steering Committee. Through the Steering Committee a capacity for change is developed for the entire school. As new norms are gradually put into practice, they may have a very positive effect on the school as a whole. How can the process be extended to the entire school?

## THE TRANSFER PROCESS

Changes in the culture of a group take time. There must be a gradual process of developing openness and trust, which helps a group to become more sensitive and effective as a group. The Steering Committee, in addition, has another responsibility: to transfer attitudes and behaviour to the school as a whole.

This task cannot be accomplished by means of the knowledge and skills arising from a single project, or even several projects. The objective is rather to help the school to grow towards a problem-solving *culture*, through the development of school improvement projects.

The IDP brings a new element into the school. Even at an early stage the entire faculty is faced with new challenges. They soon realize that only through active co-operation, and by involving themselves in extensive work together, will they get results. A number of meetings, within the Steering Committee and between the Steering Committee and the faculty, will usually give many teachers an interest in getting further involved.

So-called 'study days' or the 'feedback conferences' are such early opportunities. It is important to reach some consensus about *what to do* (i.e. a plan of action); however, it is also important to develop a positive motivation for further development work, at the group level and at the individual teacher level. The climate and norms that evolve during the intensive hours of survey feedback, discussions and problem-solving are essential as a platform for further work. That is why the Steering Committee and the consultant need to plan carefully and develop strategies to implement these plans. What are the additional opportunities for a transfer process to involve the 'whole school' in the development process? We relate a single actual example.

In one of the IDP schools the following occurred after the feedback conference:

*One teacher, Johnson, had been sceptical from the start. Not only was he against the whole idea of involving the school in IDP, he was also withdrawing from the process. The headmaster was worried because Johnson was one of the best teachers in the school, and he had support from many parents. The headmaster learned that influential members of the Steering Committee at this stage wanted to ignore teacher Johnson. The head instead invited Johnson, two members of the Steering Committee and the consultant to his office — 'for a long, relaxed and friendly chat', as he expressed it. It became a hard and difficult meeting, well monitored by the consultant. Towards the end, the headmaster realized what important resources the school was failing to utilize owing to Johnson's withdrawal and he suddenly proposed: 'I would like an ongoing evaluation of IDP. Would you, Johnson, be interested in being the chairman of an evaluation group?' It came as a surprise to the others in the room. It turned out to be the most productive decision in changing the culture of the school.*

The transfer process is clearly about the technical aspects of projects, including the development of needed skills. It is as important, however, to take all members of the school seriously; to listen, to see, to be open to discussion, to assess and to redefine. After all, so far the IDP in the school has only really engaged a few persons within a Steering Committee. The change process of transferring ownership from a small involved group to a large faculty (and moreover to a much larger student and parent group) is highly complex.

Changes in the school culture have to do with values, norms and practical and personal issues (see Chapter 1; Dalin, 1978). The first rule is to *live the norms*. To deal constructively with scepticism and negative reactions is essential. Teachers may have very good reasons for being sceptical! An open and direct dialogue is often the best strategy. Invitations to observe in the classrooms in order to assess the process; to invite alternatives and then to discuss them; to welcome ideas and suggestions — in other words, to build down any barrier between the 'development core group' and the rest — are practical ways of involving the entire faculty.

A number of the staff will be offered an opportunity to participate in project groups. It is essential that someone from the Steering Committee (or the consultant) monitors the group processes and helps these groups to function well.

## CHANGING VALUES AND NORMS AT THE INDIVIDUAL LEVEL

As the school becomes deeply involved in project work, a number of factors will influence the process of change. The extent to which the ordinary practitioner will alter his or her behaviour will often be the essential indicator of change. How would an *individual teacher* change values and norms? In our experience, this happens through a learning process that starts with practice (see also Crandall *et al.*, 1983). Figure 6.3 illustrates the traditional change process as experienced by most teachers. Small-step changes happen in the practice of teaching as a result of *self-evaluation*. The teacher responds to his or her

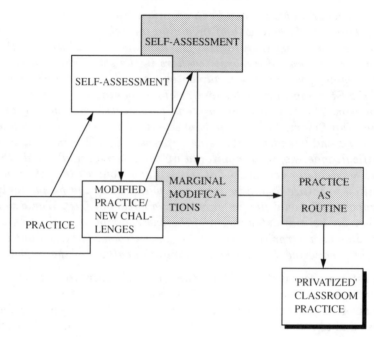

Figure 6.3 *Self-assessment*

subjective judgement, to a feeling of success and failure, to episodes in the classroom and to daily pressures. As this process continues over the years the teacher is less likely to discover new improvement potentials, he or she gradually engages more and more in routine behaviour, the job is seen as less interesting and challenging, and the teacher increasingly works in isolation. Gradually life 'behind the classroom door' becomes 'private territory'.

The IDP is an effort to add alternative perspectives to the teacher self-evaluation process. For most professionals, without challenges from other professionals the self-assessment process will result in stagnation and routine behaviour. Through joint discussions and analysis of real needs, all teachers are invited to 'open up their classroom doors', to work with colleagues and to reassess practice. The first step towards openness is usually, constructive work with colleagues in small subject-based groups. If these groups are effective learning teams, characterized by openness and trust, it is very likely that the teacher will share experiences, and in some cases invite other teachers to discuss their practices, or even observe practices. This is a big step for an individual, who is often an isolated practitioner. This process will not happen if he or she does not feel the need, and feel that the work is useful. The teacher must also have a trusting relationship with his or her colleagues. Even at this first step the importance of values and norms of learning is clear. It also becomes clear that, without openness and trust within the small workgroups, little change will occur.

As the teacher, through the IDP process, begins to work more closely with one or more colleagues, new perspectives are brought into his or her teaching,

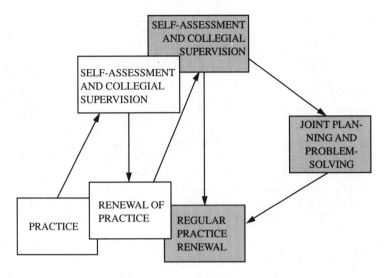

Figure 6.4 *Renewal of practice through collegial co-operation*

needs for change become clearer, and needs for discussions about improvement and needs for co-ordination therefore lead to a process where colleagues plan together. This is the second cycle of learning — the project school cycle (see Chapter 1). Figure 6.4 illustrates how this element of joint planning and problem-solving grows out of interaction and open dialogue. In some countries a 'teacher appraisal' system is now institutionalized, and may lead to the same kinds of results (Evans and Tomlinson, 1989).

As more groups in the school work with their IDP projects, as the Steering Committee assists the groups to ensure productive work, and as many alternative experiences now begin to surface, the need to *reassess goals* becomes clearer. Not only is it important to plan together, it is even more important to have common goals for development. Although these goals were stated in general terms at the beginning of the IDP process, as we learn from practice, realities give new meaning to goals and the need for common goals becomes clearer (Figure 6.5).

The school is now in the third cycle of learning — the learning organization cycle (see Chapter 1). In this cycle the school staff continually question goals, compare goals with actual performance (through an ongoing joint evaluation), and start to formulate the *values and norms* that should guide the operational goals, plans and practice. This is now likely because participants have practised new norms throughout the process and understand from practice, for example, the importance of an open and trustworthy climate. The school has come to a point where it is realizing cultural change (Figure 6.6).

It is important to note that this process does not start with 'stating the objectives', as is so often advocated by the 'management by objectives' movement. In fact, in normal life we do not consciously set new goals. Changes start with growing uneasiness with practice. This often happens because we have a 'built-in' standard, against which we intuitively assess our practice. Dealt with

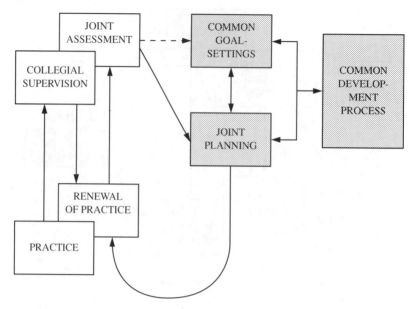

Figure 6.5  *From joint planning to common goals*

in a meaningful way, taking teacher experience and learning seriously, it develops into a process where basic values and norms guide new behaviour. The process that we have described, and developed within several IDP schools, is not unlike the process described by Stallings (1989) in her attempt to implement a systematic collegial learning system and staff development.

However, this does not mean that goal-setting at the outset of the IDP process is a futile activity. It is indeed important, but it serves a limited purpose: to get the school moving in the right direction. Later, as the individuals learn from new practice with colleagues, goals become clearer and more meaningful, and, thereby, 'ownership' of common goals develops.

Also, this process of developing ownership of goals does not mean that real changes only happen from the bottom. Changes in an organization need co-ordinated efforts; they are systemic in nature, and build on forces for change from the environment as well as from the individual practitioner (see Chapter 1).

The core of the IDP deals with changing the school culture. When the IDP started in 1974, it was basically a strategy to develop and implement new educational practice. We assumed that it would imply changes in the attitudes and behaviour of participants; however, we were not fully aware that the consequences had to be comprehensive challenges to the school culture, if new practices were to be institutionalized. Slowly we discovered that schools differ considerably in their readiness for change, from fairly fragmented schools to fairly advanced learning organizations. We understood and learned through practice that the culture of the school was also different in these various types of schools, although some common elements were present. Our next challenge was to discover how cultural change could be influenced in the various schools we were working in. We found that there was no one way; that one could not

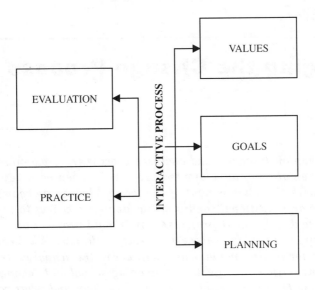

Figure 6.6 *Changing the school culture*

work on one aspect alone, but needed to work simultaneously at all levels: the individual, the group and the organizational level.

## THE ROLE OF THE CONSULTANT

The role of the consultant is often the key to the success of the IDP. Although the consultant needs to master a series of 'technical' dimensions of the IDP, it is his or her *process role* that is instrumental in the helping relationship. Moreover, these skills are often much wanted by school people, since few have had training in these areas, and since individuals may be limited in their ability to function in this role, because they are part of a culture that needs to change.

Changing the school culture is not a 'stage' of the IDP. It is a process dimension within the entire programme, from the very start, until institutionalization. It becomes particularly critical when a large number of participants join in, but it begins as soon as two persons start on the road towards improvement.

# Chapter 7

# Managing the Change Process

*This chapter describes and analyses process from planning to implementation of development projects. It even goes beyond that: it deals with the management of change in a learning organization. What are the organizational conditions needed for a school to implement concrete development projects? How should projects be planned and structured to achieve successful implementation? What are the tools needed for project management? How can the school go from implementation of projects to managing school-wide change? How can we strengthen the change capacity of a school and what role could internal evaluation play?*

In one IDP school the following dynamics were observed:

*At the beginning of the school development programme the Steering Committee had problems of its own. The consultant worked more with the group dynamics of the Steering Committee than with the diagnosis of the school data. Gradually, however, particularly after the two weekend seminars with the Steering Committee, the group started to take control of its own work, informal leaders emerged and the chairman showed both initiative and good problem-solving skills. Following the two-day staff seminar a plan of action had emerged and the Steering Committee had been given full support for its leadership role.*

*The Steering Committee now had to undertake a totally new role, from a pure committee function to a management function. The Steering Committee would be responsible for actually implementing three significant and difficult projects, with the use of the three project groups. What would that mean? Did the committee have the knowledge and skills needed? What about time? And what about the relationship to the school leader and his administrative team? And now, when the real hard work begins, will the school have staff who can carry out the work, and will it have the skills needed?*

In another IDP school the following scenario took place during this period:

*The last three weeks had been very difficult for everyone in the school. It had become quite clear that the school leader insisted on a role in the Steering Committee for the further development of the programme. There were also quite good reasons for it: after all, he was the one who knew the school inspector, a person quite central to the implementation of at least one of the projects the staff wanted to implement. The headmaster also is an effective manager, and management skills are now needed. The relations, however, between the headmaster and the chairman of the Steering Committee have never been warm. How would we be able to deal with the internal conflicts? The school had already achieved a lot in this programme, and a leadership conflict at this stage could well block the whole programme.*

In a third IDP school we experienced the following:

*The staff seminar was a success. It took lots of planning and it was at times quite unnerving. . . . Some very basic conflicts came out; however, they were dealt with in a productive manner. As a result the staff group 'opened up'. It became much easier to develop common goals and to find agreement on an action plan. We left the seminar with a feeling that we were moving the school the right direction. . . . Now, however, it is up to me as headmaster to lead the way from here. Can I meet the high expectations? Reality is after all pretty difficult. Everyone is busy. I have very little extra resources. How can I build on the experiences we already have and mobilize for development?*

These are three quite typical situations in this cycle of development as the school moves from *planning* to *implementation*. At this time issues related to *management* become important to resolve. On the one hand, the school has normally built up a Steering Committee that has worked hard and has become committed to the programme. It also wants to see its work through, and to be responsible for its implementation. On the other hand, it is vital to bring *regular management* into action. To become a natural part of the 'new school', the head and his or her team obviously need to be part of it. These are just two of many factors to consider in this cycle of development.

## FROM PLANNING TO IMPLEMENTATION

A school has many choices as it starts on the road towards improvement of pedagogical practices. It is a complex and long journey; often it takes 4-6 years before a new classroom practice is implemented and benefits all students in a school. Quite often it has to do with changes in the school culture (see Chapter 6). To organize the change process so that *organizational learning* becomes a natural part of daily life is easier said than done, and it needs skilful and supporting leadership. There is no quick fix.

In reading this chapter a misunderstanding may easily arise: to implement improvement projects can be done through fairly straightforward management techniques! We will present several tools that we have found useful at this stage of the process. We should remind the reader, however, that the conditions needed for such techniques to be of use are many. Some of the conditions that the school at this 'stage' has worked at for a considerable amount of time through joint sessions, Steering Committee meetings, problem-solving, workshops, etc. are vital for project management to succeed. If project management techniques are to work and thereby project implementation to succeed, at this stage the following should have been achieved.

## Real needs

Hopefully the school has, by now, arrived at an understanding of its strengths and weaknesses and has settled for some priority goals that reflect *real needs* as understood by the actors (e.g. staff, students, parents, etc.). We realize that what are understood as real needs may well change over time, as new experiences evolve. As a starting point, however, the school has a good understanding of its needs and has designed an action plan to meet them.

This is clearly a major advantage of school-based development in general. Schools have often been asked to adopt new practices determined by school authorities. The results have been major adaptations to fit with the culture of the individual school. Evaluations of educational innovations have therefore seldom found high implementation or high impact at the classroom level. The IDP assumes that the process we have described above places responsibility for innovative practices where it belongs: in the school itself.

## Ownership

The process by which staff and other participants have analysed and planned the programme has improved the climate in the school, has increased the commitment to the school and the change objectives. The staff are ready to mobilize their resources for the benefit of the school and will invest time and energy towards the goals established. In Chapter 3 this is called the 'mobilization process', and it needs nurturing many times during the programme.

Huberman and Miles (1984) found that commitment was not necessary at the outset of the change process, but that it was a condition for implementation. The IDP can document the same. We find that the *process of change* to a large extent determines the degree of ownership that participants will have to new practices. Although the innovative practice itself (its values, norms and characteristics) is clearly important, the process by which it is conceptualized, developed and implemented has a major impact on the motivation of teachers and other participants (see below).

## Planning and development skills

The programme has so far used a number of planning and development techniques, often new to school staff, but quite useful for project development work. There are several skills related to development work that will facilitate implementation, some of them possibly already learned (e.g. by the Steering Committee) at this stage of the process (see below). Most of the learning so far is preliminary, at the *individual* level and not widespread. Usually both individual and group skills are related to the Steering Committee and staff development for all staff lies ahead.

Most school people are not aware of the skills embedded in planning and development activities. Management is often unprepared for these challenges. Our experience in the IDP is that consultants need to work systematically to build up skills in the Steering Committee and in the management team. As the school moves into implementation of innovative projects the needs for staff development are 'discovered' (see Chapter 8).

## Norms and climate

Usually at this stage new norms and an open, development-oriented climate emerge. Although most work has been going on in the Steering Committee, the result is often that innovative work becomes a new or renewed norm in the school (see Chapter 5).

We find that most schools using the IDP have achieved much in this area. If we talk about 'impact' of the programme at this stage it is a positive development of the climate in the *adult group* (teachers and management). It seldom has an impact at the classroom level, although this depends somewhat on the degree of involvement of students in the process. In schools where students (and/or parents) are involved, we find a positive development of the climate among these participants as well. Well processed, the IDP 'opens up', and develops trust and a commitment to work together.

## Management attitudes and behaviour

As a prerequisite for further work we assume a leader who is committed to common goals, believes them to be important, has trust in his or her staff, is open to new ideas and has learned to work closely with other people (interpersonal skills). We assume that the head and his or her associates want to learn more to improve their change management skills (see below).

The extent to which the management team has developed positive attitudes towards the school development programme depends on a number of factors. One factor, clearly, is the extent to which management was involved from the beginning and saw the IDP activities as important and useful. It may also depend on the degree to which management has been actively involved in the Steering Committee, or at least has been communicating with the committee. We see a committed management as critical during the stage of implementation, and IDP consultants have a role to play should there be conflicts at this stage between the management team (or within it) and the Steering Committee.

A school that, at the outset, may be called a 'fragmented school' is at this stage of development moving towards becoming what we in Chapter 2 called a 'project school'. Experiences move from pure individual teacher practice to more collaborative work and experiences. This mobilizes the staff further, new common visions and norms emerge and there is a greater chance to obtain a joint experience base for further work. The vehicle is one or several *projects*, which in fact is a *strategy* towards the 'organic school', or the new learning organization. If some of these projects also involve collegial co-operation and supervision, there is a good chance of gradually changing the school culture.

## PROJECT MANAGEMENT

A project is primarily a strategy to achieve defined goals for the school. A 'project' has clear and limited goals. A major development objective may be broken down into smaller, *achievable* projects (which are then related to each other). The school development plan has stated some more general objectives, often including an analysis of 'problem statements' (see Chapter 3), a discussion of strategies for achieving the objectives, and a timetable (flowchart, see Chapter 4) for reaching the desired outcomes. One or several projects are usually the best way to *operationalize* the objectives.

A project also has a limited life span. It does not go on for ever, it is not part of the regular work, it is special, and it needs particular attention for a limited time period. It is also an activity that takes place only once in the lifetime of a school, and will therefore, most likely, have built-in surprises and challenges. A project usually cuts across organizational boundaries. It is a task that brings participants from different subject areas and different departments together. It also brings people with different roles together (e.g. teachers, parents, students). Some school projects, however, are simply a modification of practices within the existing structure, within a department and/or discipline. A project may not call for extensive co-operation with teachers from other departments and/or students. In many cases it can be dealt with as part of the regular ongoing improvement process and as part of the regular work of the department, and should probably have status other than that of a 'project'.

A project needs a separate budget; participants need to have time off from other duties, rather than have yet another task added to their their existing obligations. It is imperative for teachers and others to be able to work with the development tasks during normal school hours. Most schools have a very limited free budget. The really important resource is *time*. This resource is also tied up quite rigidly to instructional hours and leaves little flexibility. It is another illustration of how status-quo-oriented schools are. A major task for the Steering Committee, school management and the consultant is to design projects in such a way that resources (mostly time) can be given to project implementation.

A project is a *planned intervention*. It is not something that happens by chance. Through systematic project planning and monitoring techniques, a project can be followed, intermediate results can be discussed, preliminary experiences may help to adjust the course of action, and necessary alterations can be made in the implementation plan. This cannot be done without ongoing monitoring, which means some form of ongoing assessment, feedback of preliminary results, discussions of data and decisions to improve the project (formative evaluation). In Chapter 8 we describe how the IDP works with formative evaluation (see below).

A project is also a *learning opportunity* for individuals and groups. It usually brings exciting opportunities for tackling new issues, often with extra resources, and collaboration with people other than those who work together daily. It also gives opportunities for *organizational learning*, providing opportunities to develop new procedures, new norms and new relations. How do we learn from our work? How can we deal with the evergrowing needs for staff development? How can a school, which should be leading us into a world of new information and new knowledge, cope with the rapid pace of change? The IDP has an approach to staff development that is dealt with in Chapter 8.

A project should also lead to concrete results. These may be related to the curriculum, to the work in the classroom, to structural changes (e.g. new organization of the work-day), to changes in processes, methods or procedures and to changes in leadership, the climate or ethos of the school. Here are some real case examples.

*... The new timetable helped both students and teachers. It provided opportunities for joint planning, for more collaborative work, and gave the students more time for optional activities. It increased the scheduling problems, but with the use of the newly developed computer program there is good hope that these difficulties will be ironed out ...*

*... The diagnostic phase clarified that absenteeism was a major problem, in particular among the immigrant children. The project helped the school to communicate more regularly with the parents; in fact, it involved parents regularly in the work of the school and increased their motivation for schooling. The project was a success; however, it also made it clear that the teachers know far too little about the multicultural home environments that influence student motivation. The teachers have decided to start a new project and study the various home environments ...*

*... Those first computers were really quite hopeless. They broke down so often that only computer experts could use them. Now with the new hardware, new software and, above all, comprehensive training and coaching, more than 60 per cent of the teachers are using the technology in their classrooms. The project has also demonstrated how insufficient the software situation is, and the school is presently applying for money for a software development project ...*

These are illustrations of project characteristics and project outcomes. School projects are not necessarily complex from a *technical* point of view; however, they may be highly complex from a *human relations* point of view.

Berger and Borkel (1988) have summarized some of the conditions that are necessary to structure a project well.

1 A clearly formulated project concept should be available, in which the goals, tasks, needed skills, as well as the necessary tools and resources for the project are described.

2 An elected project leader (usually a member of the Steering Committee), who is responsible for the process, can take decisions and co-ordinate if necessary.

3 Clarity is gained, in advance, about whether any experts should participate in the project, and if so in what way, and also if expertise from the outside should be drawn in.

4 At least in larger schools, one person from the management is appointed as a contact person who receives regular information about the project.

5 A time plan exists, e.g. a visual flow chart.

6 A clear view is gained, in advance, of how the information and decision-making routines should be, particularly in relationship to management and the Steering Committee.

7 Agreement is arrived at, in advance, on how the necessary control should be carried out.

8 Documentation is available that gives both participants and others information about the project.

9 Information and feedback exist, so that both participants and non-participants can see the results of the project.

10 Project evaluation is engaged in at the end to document how successful the project has been, and what the practical experiences are that might have an impact on future projects.

This list of points gives a picture of the *structural* conditions. We agree with Berger and Borkel that it is necessary for schools to be clear about how projects are structured. Equally important, as we shall see later in this chapter, are the human relations issues connected to the management of change. It is important that projects are structured clearly. Projects are never part of the routine, and management and participants will always have to live with insecurity, surprises and the unfinished. A clear structure is a strategy to reduce insecurity but it can never eliminate the insecurity that always is connected with working with the unknown. We have seen schools that have used too much time to structure projects, possibly as a defence mechanism since they are anxious about doing something quite different from routine work. Structuring therefore can be a defence *against* change — change in our attitudes and our behaviour. The irony here is that a school may well be able to implement a project as planned, without changing anything (see also Chapter 6)! Project structuring, therefore, must always be used as a *strategy for change*, not only for organizing the limited resources for a short-sighted goal.

## DEVELOPING JOINT UNDERSTANDING AND THE USE OF PROJECT MODELS

While it may be clear what one wants to achieve through a project plan and a flow chart, it is not always clear *how* one is going to achieve it. One assumes that 'somebody' will take the necessary steps, but often the *implementation process* is overlooked. And it is usually more complex than we prefer to believe!

A project model is basically an attempt to clarify more precisely how the project is supposed to *achieve its goals* in the school. It is a technique to understand the underlying assumptions and the hypothesis of the planned intervention; and to 'detect' the critical process variables and the *administrative steps* needed to secure implementation. A very simple project model is illustrated in Figure 7.1.

A project model goes, in other words, beyond a flow chart, in that it represents the 'project theory', and can therefore help us to explain *why* certain

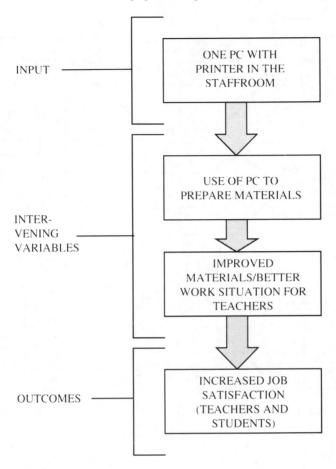

Figure 7.1   *One-dimensional model*

activities and tasks are needed. The 'process variables' describe a project's expected preliminary goals, which aim to lead to the final outcome of the project, or they describe the necessary project activities that lead to the goals. This helps us to better assess whether the necessary skills and resources are at hand and to find out what type of assistance the school needs.

The project model tells us what steps need to be taken when a project gets started. When a project starts there is usually consensus about the final project outcomes. It is, however, not always clear what needs to be done to achieve these goals. It is assumed that certain activities build on a positive effect, and that somebody takes the necessary steps. A project model helps us to explain how a project should run to reach the objectives. A project model goes a step further than a flow chart, which tells us *what* should be done, but not *why* it should be done. We explained in Chapter 5 the close relationship between pedagogical goals and means, and that means quite often represent goals and vice versa. A project model helps us to analyse the relationship between goals and means and see if the necessary relationship is present.

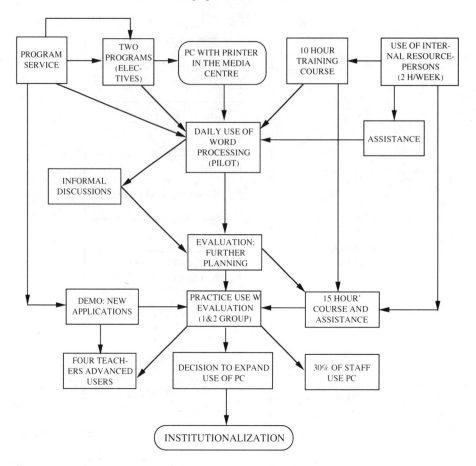

Figure 7.2 *Multi-dimensional model*

# A PROJECT EXAMPLE

We will cite one example of a project with *one input* only. The input is a personal computer (PC) with a printer in the staffroom. The assumption is that this will lead to teacher use of the PC for class preparation; which again will lead to reduced workload and better products (materials); again leading to teacher and student satisfaction. Will this work? Let us look at the hypothesis under-lying this model (the process variables). We obviously assume that the teachers already know *how* to use the PC, that they will have time to use it; indeed that they will use the 'public space' in the staffroom for their class preparation, that the equipment will work, that the use of the PC will reduce teacher work-load and produce better materials, and that it finally will lead to a more satis-fying situation for teachers and students.

Are these assumptions realistic? Probably not. Most school projects are better planned than this one, but they are also often quite optimistic in terms of their value! Figure 7.2 shows a more realistic model using the same example.

While the 'one-input' model is usually the level of sophistication that one

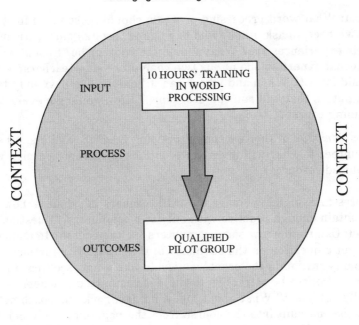

INPUT

10 HOURS' TRAINING
IN WORD-
PROCESSING

CONTEXT

PROCESS

CONTEXT

OUTCOMES

QUALIFIED
PILOT GROUP

Figure 7.3 *Mini-model*

can read from a school development plan, the 'multi-dimensional' model is the result of extensive work by the Steering Committee or the task force appointed by the Steering Committee to undertake the project work. The consultant usually plays an instrumental part in developing the first project models. Through a problem-solving technique he or she helps the school sort out needed inputs, discusses the rationale for inputs, helps the participants to answer the 'why' questions (e.g. 'why do you need an internal resource person?') and to understand the assumptions behind the model (a model reflects a given view of how change comes about in a school), develops a change strategy (our multi-model is based on a 'pilot strategy'), and *relates* the different variables to each other.

If we assume that the 'multi-dimensional' model is a realistic one, and that it reflects the expected processes and outcomes, what does project management do to secure and monitor this process? To answer this question we need to understand the strengths and weaknesses of the school in relation to this process, to analyse the needs for resources (see above) and to take the necessary administrative steps. As an example: we now assume that all teachers need to be offered a 10-hour course in the use of a reasonably good and user-friendly word processing program. Which one? What are the experiences of computer-using staff? Do those using a PC use different programs? Does it make much difference to them? Can/should the school install several programs? These are all questions relevant to the implementation of this project. To clarify the process dimensions of a subpart of this project, we develop a mini-model to see what the questions may be (Figure 7.3).

The mini-model helps us to understand some of the critical dimensions in a subpart of the project. Here are some issues:

**Input:** What word processing program should be selected for training? Do we need to ask others who have gone through similar training what their experiences are? What should the content be? Should we use an external expert or one of our two computer-using teachers? What would it cost? When and where can it be done (we have only two computers that will run the programs)? How would we evaluate the training course?

*Decision:* One of the two computer-using teachers and one other volunteer teacher will investigate options and propose a plan with the required resources.

**Process:** Assuming we have up to 10 teachers in a course, how can they all obtain enough practice with only two computers? (Question to the head: Can we borrow some computers for the course? Immediately we get a question on the adequacy of the *input*.) For further implementation in the school we would like a few 'sceptics' to join. How can the course be attractive to the non-committed teacher? Is a course really sufficient? What about follow-up, feedback and coaching? How can that be built into the course from the beginning? If a 'helping norm' is essential for future use, how can we build a relaxed and supportive atmosphere in the course? How can we avoid a *general* course and make a teacher-relevant course?

*Decisions:* We set up an early demonstration with one of the computer-using teachers producing worksheets for a science class (and drawing on a database with nice figures), thereby making the demonstration a pedagogically attractive opportunity. We plan a course *with* the teachers. We work in pairs in the course. We use our own computer-using teachers as our mentors and coaches.

**Outcomes:** What do we mean by 'practice'? Do we expect all teachers in the course to practise daily? How is that possible with only two computers? Is it even possible that queues may discourage a teacher from using what he or she has learned? If support and coaching is needed, how can we be secure that it is available when it is needed? What would happen if only very few teachers started to practise? What happens if several of those who try give up through frustration? How can the course prepare for the potential problems ahead?

*Decisions:* We need to clarify the size of the pilot group, taking into account that probably only two computers are available. Again, can we borrow or rent some computers for a short period? The head will clarify the budget situation and the availability of computers. We will give priority to the daily support of the first users, and set aside 30 minutes in the mid-break to consult and provide support (in pairs and with the resource teachers).

**Context:** How motivated are the staff to engage in yet another innovation at this time? Do we really have the resources to support the project? What will happen if it is really a success? Can the school follow through? What can we do to avoid division between the 'computer experts' in the faculty and the 'others' (the present conflicts do not help the project)? Parents are very positive to student use of computers; could they help and support this project? Can and should we use some of the talented students to help the teachers? What would the reactions be in the faculty?

*Decisions:* We are more worried about a large volunteer group than a small one. We will *role play* the consequences of a large following with the faculty and the parent committee, and involve them in developing ideas for follow-up. We will also begin to develop a common user's vocabulary with the computer experts and other teachers, to break down the language barriers between the two groups.

As we have seen, a project model illustrates a number of critical issues in the input, process, outcomes and context dimensions of a project. It is an important vehicle to tackle some of the key management decisions in a project.

## PROJECT MODELS AND FLOW CHARTS

The flow chart helps us to clarify the concrete steps that need to be taken in a project, gives us some realistic perceptions about time and resources, and also helps us to decide who should do what in a project. It is a means, at an early planning stage, to understand the goals and the means and their relationship. A flow chart could very easily be the starting point for a project model; however, a project model can also be developed without the use of a flow chart.

While a flow chart has certain decision points and the 'boxes' are basically *activities* that show the relationships among tasks, and the time sequence of events, a project model has *preliminary* goals as 'stations' and *final outcomes* as the 'end station'. While the flow chart is a practical project management tool that helps us to define activities, the project model represents the *project theory*, helps us to explain *why*, and thereby places the activities into a meaningful framework. It will serve as a 'yardstick' as the project develops.

As we start to use 'mini-models', to ask the fairly detailed questions necessary to implement a component of a project, the process may lead to a renewed flow chart, this time much more detailed, to illustrate only a part of what has been illustrated in Figure 5.4. As the project leadership works with the overall project model and mini-models, a new and important clarification of the relationship between goals and means develops. What the assumptions and the processes are becomes clear, and the learning that takes place helps the group to take decisions based on better information. Now we know not only *what* should take place, but also *why* it should happen and in what *context* it should be done.

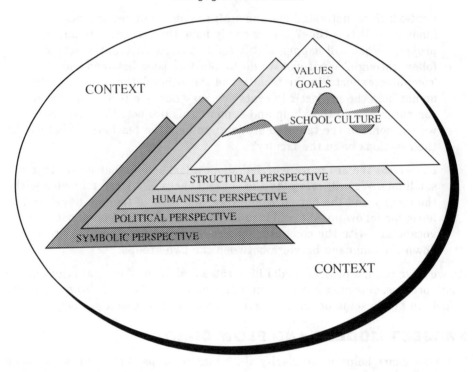

Figure 7.4  *Management perspectives*

## LEADING THE SCHOOL IMPROVEMENT PROCESS AND DEVELOPING LEADERSHIP

To lead development processes is an unusual challenge in schools. In books about 'project management' the technical, the economic and the structural sides are often described. Even if these aspects also are important in change projects in schools, they are usually not the most important. There are two aspects of change management in school improvement that we are concerned with:

1  Change deals with changes in participants' attitudes and behaviour as individuals and as partners in 'joint ventures'. Perspectives other than the more technical ones are then important (see below).

2  'Project management' is important; however, it is only part of the complex task to lead change processes in an organization. In a school the task is primarily to influence *organizational behaviour* at the same time as a project is implemented, which means that management needs to look beyond projects to be able to manage the change process.

The management of change is intended to facilitate appropriate changes in the culture of the school. In Figure 7.4 we have tried to visualize the complex interaction of processes and activities that need to be taken into account in the school improvement process. This figure is related to the perspectives discussed in Chapter 3.

## Structural perspective

In most management literature the term 'project management' is often exchanged for the term 'change management'. The topics dealt with are usually quite technical in nature (often issues related to monitoring complex technical projects in industry), and concentrate on the structural and formal part of the organization. Although this structural perspective is important, it is only one side of the coin. In fact, if we compare schools to, let us say, an industrial organization, we find that structural aspects are possibly less important in schools.

## Human perspective

The human relations perspective is also a part of what we define as an important perspective on 'change management'. The management's ability to mobilize staff towards change objectives, to assist groups in developing their productivity, to assist in problem-solving and conflict resolutions, to be sensitive to the informal 'messages', to be able to 'take the temperature' and to communicate well internally and externally are just a few important change management skills.

## Political perspective

This perspective provides us with another angle from which to look at 'change management'. As schools change, resources are often reallocated and priorities are shifted; some people who were central to the school are less so, and others become quite central. Parts of the curriculum are upgraded, links to new parts of the community may be established and some students may be given special attention. Management needs to be clear about the power shifts connected with changes in organizations, to clarify them, to deal with the frustrations involved, to help minimize problems, and to take decisions when necessary to secure the development of the programme.

## Symbolic perspective

'Symbolic perspective: the more things change the more they stay the same', said the nineteenth-century French writer Alphonse Karr. The *symbolic perspective* on change management can help us to understand some of the basic forces in the school as an organization, to use the 'cultural traits' to support the change effort, and to understand the emotional and symbolic meanings that change activities may have for participants.

Figure 7.4 illustrates a complex interaction of factors that need to be considered in change management.

1 Most people are interested in the *content* of a given innovation. What 'change is about' for most actors is change in the

characteristics of practice. It is to some extent a structural perspective; change is about *replacing* one practice with another.

2  What fewer participants are fully aware of is that new practice often implies a change in values, goals or norms, or the *culture* of the school. It may also alter the way power is distributed. Some may gain and some may lose, as the political perspective would emphasize.

3  We have learned that these perspectives, although very important, are not sufficient to understand how change comes about in schools. The *change process* to a large degree influences the content — or the final outcome. *How* we change may either facilitate or block, make it easier to implement or worse, attract more participants or make people shy away, mobilize energy and resources or isolate new behaviour so the process stagnates. *How* we process change will be instrumental for *what* we achieve, or, as was earlier quoted from a Rand study, 'implementation dominates outcomes' (McLaughlin, 1990).

4  Those who are 'process-oriented' sometimes do not understand the impact the project itself has on the way it is introduced, implemented and institutionalized. A project, for example, that reflects the needs of a great majority in a school is easy for teachers to master. Such a project does not upset normal school life, and may run fairly smoothly with little intervention. On the other hand, a project that is highly complex, central to the mission, values and norms of the school, highly controversial and very difficult to master at the classroom level calls for a different set of activities, or processes.

5  Figure 7.4 also illustrates that schools, like other institutions, are embedded in a *structure*. Some of these are historical and have little meaning today. Some of them are *physical* (e.g. a building with a given layout), some are *organizational* (e.g. the organigram), some are related to the use of resources (e.g. the structure of the budget and regulations for its use), some are related to *time* (e.g. the timetable that regulates who works with what, whom and when), some are related to established procedures, some are quite stable and difficult to change, and some may be altered fairly easily.

All projects will sooner or later, and particularly during implementation and institutionalization, have to deal with several aspects of the school structure. A project may call for a different timetable, a new physical layout, or a new organigram (e.g. with changing roles and functions). Change management needs to understand how institutionalized practice of a change programme will *interact* and influence the structure, and vice versa. Often structures are *perceived* as constraints. The task of the management is to use the structures skilfully for project goals, and/or to alter structures that are needed for implementation to succeed.

6 Beyond the boundaries of the school are *infra-conditions* that may have an impact on the change process. Such conditions include the total resources allocated, the laws and regulations for the school system, the work conditions laid down by national (or local) unions and the ministry (the district), and the more general rules regulating the school environment.

Beyond these conditions, which deal directly with the schools, are also unwritten laws that regulate our *perception* of what schools are about, what we can possibly do (and change), and how we can do it.

Change management will often have to deal with these boundary issues. They often seem difficult to alter; they may well block initiative and hamper creativity. School leaders often interact successfully with groups in the local environment and at the system level to provide more 'space' and thereby more room for manoeuvre.

Management needs to understand the complexities of the process, to avoid a role reduction that may either be inadequate or irrelevant. It is a skilful art. It calls for a whole set of functions and skills, which probably only practice combined with on-the-job training can provide.

(a) *Sensitivity* to what happens in the school, how a project may alter traditional values and norms, how people conceive the project, how people relate, how influence is distributed, how subgroups are formed, how feelings are expressed and/or suppressed, what implementation problems occur, and sensitivity to what is heard and seen.

(b) *Diagnostic skills* that help management to really *understand* what goes on in the school. The ability to put data together, to make sense out of often messy situations and share this 'meaning' among staff, to actively seek joint understanding and mobilize energy for improvement is another skilful act.

(c) *Ability to act*, or to know how to *intervene* in a social system, to be able to communicate well, to problem-solve, to resolve conflicts, to work with others and to structure activities — to mention just a few of the skills that are needed.

## MANAGEMENT ATTITUDES AND SKILLS

The word 'management' is often defined in terms of *skills*. Indeed, management skills are needed and important. Skills in isolation, however, may be reduced to *instrumentalism*. In particular, in the field of organizational development it is vital that management does not become a mere sophisticated manipulation tool. In fact, the structure of the IDP, namely as an ongoing *sharing* of knowledge and skills, should help to avoid such potential negative side-effects.

Fundamental to change management are some basic beliefs and attitudes, that form values and norms, and therefore are guides to the ethics of the

133

profession. Those who have management responsibility for school change should understand and believe:

- that school improvement is vital, and that success is dependent on the school working on its 'real needs';
- that the outcomes are partly dependent on the starting point: does the school respond to its 'real needs'?
- that the school itself has the main resources to accomplish the objectives;
- that co-operation among staff, students and parents is critical to success;
- that openness and trust is essential to the development of the school as an organization;
- that staff development is essential for quality outcomes;
- that all actors are dependent on support and feedback from colleagues;
- that both colleagues and management are responsible for ongoing supervision and assessment;
- that management has a responsibility for structuring the process and thereby clarifying conditions, expectations and the action steps necessary;
- that management has a major role in developing the work climate, in groups and in the school as a whole;
- that management has the responsibility for group growth;
- that management has a particular responsibility for resolving conflicts and to assist in problem-solving;
- that the task is a long-term job of changing the school culture;
- that management has the ultimate responsibility for securing the needed resources, 'sheltering' the process from undue external interventions, and marketing the project to the external environment.

Above all, we need school leaders who have a *vision* for their school, that is shaped and developed in close co-operation with staff, students and parents. A school leader is needed to give birth to the vision, to facilitate the process towards this vision and to be a 'backup' whenever needed. A learning organization having a leader who has a sense of personal commitment and mission is well served.

We mention these understandings and beliefs as examples to remind the reader that tasks and skills cannot, and should not, be seen in isolation. It is also important to note that we do not necessarily mean that the formal leadership should always perform these tasks. In fact, it may be counterproductive. Often these skills are represented among staff, and work can be delegated. We are, therefore, not talking about what the head as a person should do, but what kinds of *management functions* are essential and what kind of skills change management needs.

Our experience with leaders undergoing management courses is that they experience one heavy burden after another loaded on to their backs as they progress through the course, and many feel: 'This I cannot do. I will never be a successful leader.' It is more realistic to ask the question: 'How can I build on all the talents (including informal leadership talents) in my faculty to provide the school with the needed management skills?'

## THE FORMAL AND INFORMAL

The management of change deals with structuring and with facilitating the process. It is often a major change from working with routines in a fairly stable organization towards a rather dynamic situation. The essence is to develop an integrated work structure where one can draw on all talents and resources towards common goals, to develop a culture of pride, commitment and teamwork.

Quite often the most effective improvement-oriented organizations live with a considerable degree of ambiguity, expecting everyone to contribute with new ideas. Often the practical steps may be unclear, but the vision and the outcomes are clear to everyone. Integrated structures encourage people to share, facilitate communication and relationships, and make it easier to co-ordinate activities and to share authority and responsibilities.

Clearly, a school must also have a stable organization that structures work in a routine way. This is needed as we begin to *institutionalize* programmes. It is the degree of stability and structure that distinguishes an effective change-oriented organization from one that deals with only routine programmes.

In many comments so far we have made references to the 'formal' and the 'informal' part of the organization. A manager needs to work with both. Formal management processes are characterized by:

- their regularity (e.g. the teachers' council meets once a month);
- their stability over time (e.g. a change in procedure needs recognized mechanisms to make formal decisions);
- their rationality (e.g. promotion is built on agreed-upon rules and regulations); and
- their emphasis on quantitative data (e.g. assessment described as student achievement scores) (Snyder, 1988).

A school improvement programme lives side by side with the regular life of the school. Management needs to secure an orderly high-quality teaching-learning process for all students, parallel with experimentation and development work that may involve a large part of the school. Although management will also use the formal part of the organization in the school development programme, informal management processes are equally essential, and:

- they are more qualitative in nature (e.g. they work with communication processes);
- they often deal with more unstable situations;

- they are more intuitive and less clear;
- they are more dependent on creativity and contribute to an ongoing learning process;
- they are more 'holistic' in their approach.

The image of a systematic, rational and strong leader is being replaced by that of a leader who can take advantage of the formal as well as the informal organization; who knows how to structure, but also how to deal with processes; who is responsible for quality outcomes; and who is also concerned with the support needed at all levels to achieve them.

We now turn to the more practical issues. What do managers actually *do* to facilitate the change process?

## ANALYSING CHANGE CAPABILITY

How ready is the school to move into implementation? Our theory, as well as our practice, tells us that schools differ widely in terms of their readiness and capabilities (see Chapter 2). Let us look at some of the critical dimensions at this stage and later see what management and consultants can do about it.

### The organizational learning process

In Chapters 1 and 2 we discussed the process of change in schools as we have experienced it. We find that schools generally 'behave' differently depending on their 'maturity' in relation to the change process, and that it takes several years for a school to move from the first individual experiences of change towards a collective experience base. A school needs quite different forms of assistance depending on its 'maturity'. An important task therefore is to determine:

1  The extent of involvement of staff in previous change efforts (and their experiences). What types of projects have been implemented successfully? Have some projects failed? Do we know what the resources of staff are? Are they used?

2  The attitudes and behaviours related to the present projects. (These should be clear from the earlier phases of the IDP.) Are there still participants who are against or lukewarm towards the projects? What do we do about it?

3  The degree of common norms and common goals for the development phase. Is anyone monitoring this in group meetings and elsewhere?

4  The extent to which change efforts so far have led to organizational changes and/or institutionalization. Is there new practice that most teachers now use? Has this led to change in structures and procedures? Should it? What can be learned from these processes?

### Change capabilities

Our view of the capability for change is an essential part of our concept of readiness. We think about 'capabilities' both in terms of *individual skills* to perform a given task (e.g. in the classroom, the community, the staff, etc.) and *group skills*, or participants doing something *together* (e.g. the classroom, the staff, etc.) (see also Chapter 5).

## Resources

Change means the use of *energy*. It has costs. Some costs can simply be money for materials or consultants. Most often we see staff time as the most common and the largest cost item. Quite often it is necessary to free teachers from their daily teaching load and to adjust the work load for most participants. In fact the use of time is as we see it a major issue in 'change management'. Both the total time available, how it is distributed among staff, and at what periods of the process can have a major impact on the outcomes.

## Mapping external resources

In the daily routines of schooling most schools work without external assistance. The most common form of assistance is in-service training in its various forms. However, it is seldom developed systematically and usually reflects individual needs for further development. During active periods of development work, and in the daily life of a 'problem-solving' school, interaction with external resource persons is a normal part of life. Some of these resources may be free of charge, e.g. the inspectorate (in some countries), and some assistance from pedagogical centres and teacher-training institutions. Increasingly, however, resources (people and materials) from these institutions cost money and can increasingly be regarded as part of the *external consultant market*. Whatever institution consultancy comes from, public or private, it is imperative for a school to know *what it is* and *how good it is*. Mapping external consultancy is vital if the the school is to have a chance to identify resources needed. In fact, one of the important roles of the consultant during this period is one of linkage to the external resource network.

## STAFF DEVELOPMENT

Staff development is already taking place in the school at this stage through the project groups and various forms of work groups (e.g. the Steering Committee) that have been established for the school improvement programme. The more we work with schools, the more we realize how much of 'production' takes place in smaller groups. Even classroom instruction is quite often broken down into smaller work groups, the staff work in subject-based teams, the management group is small, and special project groups are fairly small.

One of the most important conditions for change, therefore, is to make each work group a productive group.

The more basic question is: how do we normally learn in a work situation, and how can we best organize work for effective learning? To answer these question we use some theories and analytical methods that, over the year, have received considerable attention in industries and other private organizations, developed by (among others) Åke Dalin (1987).This point of view is represented in Figure 7.5.

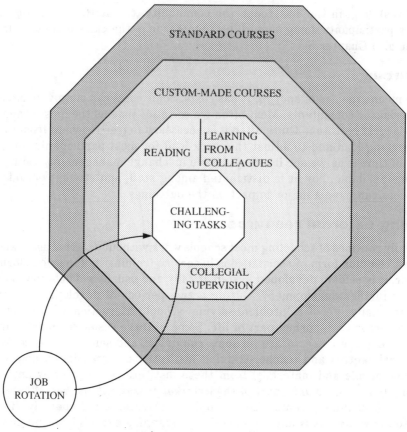

Figure 7.5 *On-the-job learning (Å. Dalin, 1987)*

1 Learning first and foremost starts with a *challenging task*. If the work is routine with no challenge, little job-related learning takes place and the chances of real improvement of output are minimal.

2 The next most effective means of learning comes from *interaction among colleagues*, in an open climate based on trust. This implies that adults work together to learn from each other and to have a common experiences base, as they reflect together upon their work.

3 Following colleague learning, *personal reading* and immediate *supervision* are the most effective forms of learning. The last component may well be peer supervision and critique. The essence is *feedback* and someone who cares for the work he or she is supervising.

4 Tailor-made, work-specific courses (often organized at the school) are the next most effective vehicle for job-related learning. These courses are rare, and often involve *consultancy* more than training.

5 Job rotation becomes equally important in Åke Dalin's analysis. This of course very often provides another challenging opportunity, and the same learning opportunities as discussed above apply.

6  Finally, the least effective training consists of general courses held at some public or private organization, removed from the workplace, often given to an individual (and not a team), and often presenting more general theory and/or 'packaged' solutions.

School development work provides a unique chance for staff development. The faculty is faced with new and challenging tasks. Most work is performed in co-operation with others, sometimes in interdisciplinary teams. The chances for colleague learning and peer supervision are very good. Also, management will have the basis for designing tailor-made workshops which are school-based.

Some opportunities are rare in schools, such as job rotation. We see, however, temporary task forces, development groups, etc. as learning opportunities that have similarities to job rotation. Job rotation provides totally new challenges and provides the support structure as well (if well managed).

Most schools think only of the least productive form of staff development, namely in-service training offered by some training institution, usually as a standard course. These courses may be very good for personal growth and career advancement, but are seldom very effective in relation to a school development programme.

## ORGANIZATION OF WORK AND LEARNING

There are clearly many ways in which in-service training can be improved methodologically, and much work has been done to improve the quality of staff development (e.g. Joyce and Murphy, 1990). These efforts are important and should continue.

We are concerned about a different dimension of staff development. There is clearly a limitation to the time that staff members can spend on courses and seminars, as well as a limitation in resources. Added to this is the fact that much staff development is ineffective.

The effectiveness of staff development is linked directly to the way work is organized in the school. The extent to which staff members are *challenged* is clearly, as Åke Dalin has pointed out, an important motivational factor. This also is related to expectations. In a school where leadership is concerned with high quality, staff members will also be expected to improve their work and achievement. To provide challenging tasks for as many staff members as possible should therefore be a daily concern of school management.

To provide challenging tasks is not the only condition. The individual cannot be left alone with new and difficult tasks. He or she should be supported through interaction with other colleagues, through literature, internal and external support, and, if needed, tailor-made courses. We can expect, however, that if school management is able to design the tasks and to organize the work in such a manner that collegial resources and motivation are used well, most of the resources needed would be available within the school.

Schools lack economic incentives for doing a better job. They have, however, plenty of intrinsic motivational opportunities, e.g. to see results in the development of the students, or to work with challenging and interesting tasks. The only real chance for higher productivity in schools with limited and declining resources is to take another look at the way they organize the way they work.

One important aspect of work organization is *feedback*. Just as students need feedback on their work to be able to improve, so do adults as individuals and in groups. It is necessary to set standards, to agree on how improvement can be measured, to thoroughly discuss preliminary results, and to have freedom and the resources to modify behaviour and to spread good practice. In other words, the work organization needs to include formative evaluation.

## INTERNAL PROJECT EVALUATION

All schools use *evaluation* as an important activity to guide learning and to assess the outcomes, in terms of student learning. Schools have a long history of practice in assessing *individual learning and individual practices* (e.g. teacher performance); however, few schools use evaluation as a strategy for learning at other levels of the organization.

There is little practice of *peer review*; that is, colleagues who trust each other review each other's work and coach each other. Teachers are most often working alone. It is a lonely profession.

There is little practice of *supervision* in schools, i.e. someone in authority observing and commenting upon the work of teachers. This is usually part of the mandate of the head but is seldom practised. Few heads know from their own experience what is going on in the classrooms; most information is rumour. In Germany, it is the role of the inspectors to assess individual teacher performance; however, it is done as seldom as every 4-5 years, and it is not looked upon as an effective strategy for improvement.

Few schools use evaluation to assess *group* performance or *organizational* performance. Therefore, they also have minimal practice in evaluating *innovative projects*. In fact, at all these levels evaluation may be a very effective strategy for improvement. In this context we deal with the evaluation of projects during the implementation period.

The IDP is about learning. We know that feedback is important for individual growth. It is imperative for organizational learning. There are usually a number of expectations as a school moves towards implementation. Some are shared, some never talked about, and some quite unclear. Our perceptions and expectations are essential as we informally assess the value of an activity.

Our expectations change over time. They change with learning, and with new activities. What seemed important six months ago may not be so important today. The development process is dynamic in nature, full of surprises and unexpected events. Why then *evaluate*?

There are many reasons — internal and external. A school improvement programme is based on a number of assumptions. The first issue is whether new practices hold up against expectations. The second is what has actually been implemented. Often evaluation looks at outcomes, but forgets to consider whether the programme has been tried as intended! Also, as our project model indicated, a programme has many intermediate goals. To what extent are they achieved? The programme also has certain stated objectives. How far does the project contribute towards these objectives? Are they still important? Are others becoming more central? What is then learned? Finally, it is likely that a dynamic change process will also have produced some unintended (positive and negative) effects. How did these happen? What value do we put on them? What are the consequences?

An external body, for example a funding body, may well be more interested in the final outcomes and the consequences for the school as a whole. These data may well be gathered and analysed as part of the assessment process (summative evaluation).

We believe that all schools need a *quality control system* designed to analyse all relevant aspects of school life at the organization, the group and individual performance levels. This system needs to be linked to the external quality control system (see Chapter 8); however, the internal system has more functions than that of support of external quality control. Our experience tells us that most schools have very limited experience with evaluation (except for extensive testing of students). To build a *culture* of evaluation, as part of daily and regular life, is a remote goal. We discuss a more elaborate system in Chapter 8 (institutionalization). At this stage, we are approaching a more modest undertaking: to obtain a picture of how school improvement programmes fare throughout the organization. We often see a systematic evaluation of the school improvement programme as the first attempt to try systematic evaluation at the organizational level, and therefore a unique learning opportunity.

## A PRACTICAL EVALUATION PROCESS

We assume that the school has built a *project model* or possibly even a total *school improvement model* (linking the various project models into one programme model). A project model has several advantages as a starting point for evaluation:

1  It visualizes the hypothesis behind the work, and it makes it public (for participants and non-participants).

2  It builds on a *common understanding* among participants, and therefore represents the best joint picture.

3  It operationalizes both process variables and outcomes. It is possible to identify what it is in practice.

The IDP uses project and programme models as the basis for internal assessment. The basic steps in the evaluation process in the IDP are:

1  *Joint programme understanding*: The basis is the project model which all participants have been working with (which is very important).

2  *Setting priorities*: Not all aspects of a programme can and should be evaluated. The first 'evaluation exercise' is to set priorities for evaluation, short term and long term. There are several ways of arriving at priorities; here are some examples:

(a) Clarify what worries actors most (e.g. 'What aspects of the implementation of the programme cause you most concern, knowing that you will be responsible?').

(b) Place participants in a situation where they have to *slim the programme* (e.g. 'We are faced with a 20 per cent cut in project resources. How can we cut and still achieve what we really want?').

(c) Turning from quantity to quality aspects (e.g. 'We may get this seminar for teachers, but what is needed to make the *transfer* to the classrooms?').

3 *Defining terms*: In constructing an evaluation design we need to be clear about what we are talking about. If we are going to assess an outcome such as 'improved climate in the classrooms', we need to be more specific. We need to find *indicators* and somehow reduce the areas of investigation, without losing the meaning. Also, we need to define the *standards*. How much of a given indicator do we want to see before we define the results as 'good', 'satisfactory' or 'excellent'? Standards give us a *measure* to evaluate an activity. Again, these are activities where all participants need to be involved (or at least all should be invited to participate).

4 *Identifying the evaluation questions*: First there are some main questions that should guide the evaluation process. There may be two or three main questions to which other questions are tied. Here are some examples from IDP schools:

(a) 'What constitutes an effective supervision system in our school?'

(b) 'What is the impact of computer use on the workload and quality of teacher preparation?'

(c) 'What consequences for student achievement does our new "interdisciplinary project work" have?'

Within each of these main questions a series of more detailed questions would be raised. We use Stufflebeam's (1974) CIPP model to develop questions relevant to *context*, *input*, *process* and *products*. It is simply one way of organizing questions. All questions need to be considered by those involved before a final list of main, and more detailed, questions emerges.

It should be noted that the IDP does not use the CIPP model as intended for summative evaluation. We see it rather as a tool for an intensive dialogue between key actors. It is simply a framework for organizing evaluation questions that enables a group to sort out ideas and opinions.

5 *Developing an evaluation design*: 'Who should be asked what kind of questions and when?' These are the basic issues involved in design. For internal formative purposes we find it more than adequate to design the evaluation as a continuous data-gathering process

alongside each project (with no control group or other sophisticated techniques, often advocated in 'summative' evaluation). In the IDP, evaluation is *a learning activity* to help the school to modify and improve the process. To us, reliability is a question of creating an open atmosphere where all relevant information can be gathered, shared and analysed.

6 *Selecting evaluation methods and developing instrumentation*: This does not have to be a lengthy process. There is standard instrumentation that the school might like to use. The GIL instrument, for example, since it is often used as a starting point, could be used as 'baseline data' (e.g. on 'leadership' if that is a concern in the evaluation process), and administered once or twice during implementation. The IDP also has several smaller instruments developed to measure dimensions like 'climate', 'training', the 'decision-making process', 'group growth', etc. Usually, however, for formative evaluation purposes, home-made instrumentation (sometimes with external assistance) suffices.

7 *Implementation*: To us the implementation of the evaluation process includes data-gathering, feedback of data to participants and problem-solving. We have discussed this process in Chapter 3, and shall not repeat it here.

The data from the internal assessment process belong to the school. If external authorities are also interested in the results, the school will have to decide to what extent the internal evaluation should provide such data (it often changes the climate for evaluation, but it does not need to). We discuss the relationship between internal and external quality control in Chapter 8.

# Chapter 8

# Institutionalization

*It is not obvious that new practice that is mastered by a few teachers will be used by all teachers in the school. It is not automatic, either, that rules, procedures and norms change so that new practice becomes a natural part of everyday life. Within the IDP the term 'institutionalization' means more than implementing a project; it means that the school has 'learned how to learn', and has developed the necessary competence to manage change processes.*

*How does a school with such a capacity work? What happens in the classroom, in the staffroom and in the management team? How is it possible to build up a culture of change also to include school-based evaluation processes? What role ought external evaluation to play?*

The projects that were planned within the IDP in the early phase take perhaps from six to twelve months to implement. The projects are usually tested by a few teachers, assessed and revised and then, perhaps, tested by more teachers. Through several rounds of projects, both motivation and competence are developed and the projects improve in quality. We often calculate that projects at the classroom level that really change the role and behaviour of teachers and students could take from four to five years to be implemented throughout the entire school. By 'implemented' we mean changes in attitudes and behaviour by teachers and students in all relevant groups.

Many school projects do not demand major behavioural changes by teachers and students. To implement a new timetable is possibly difficult from a technical point of view, but it could probably be done for the entire school within a couple of months (or from the next school year), with little skill needed, except possibly by the person making the schedule!

## FROM IMPLEMENTATION TO INSTITUTIONALIZATION

The projects that are most difficult to implement in a school are those that challenge the existing school culture, the methods used in the classroom, the demands on the students, the quality of the human relations, ways that roles and functions are divided, and the way decisions are taken and the school managed. Such changes often demand new structures (e.g. a new decision-making mechanism), which can be met with considerable resistance from individuals and groups who benefit from the existing structure.

Such changes also often demand *new procedures*, or changes in the way work is implemented. If a school decides to introduce collegial supervision, its success depends on agreement on how it should be done, the procedures one should use and the competence of the colleagues involved.

Most changes at the classroom level demand staff development. Probably one of the most important criteria for a teacher when deciding whether he or she wants to take part in school improvement programmes is the extent to which the quality of his or her instruction will be improved. The hope is that both students and teachers will benefit from the reform. Teachers have good reason to look at school improvement with scepticism. Bringing about changes in the culture of the school, in the way teaching is conducted, in the attitudes or behaviour of teachers and students is complicated and demands support and assistance over a long period. Many teachers feel that quality is *reduced* as they move into new practice. This could certainly be true and is known as the concept of 'the implementation dip'. This is one of the reasons why teachers may be hesitant and why, therefore, the *quality* of the implementation process is vital (Fullan, 1982).

Other changes need reallocation of resources. Normally a school will have to shift resources from one activity to another. In some cases it may be necessary to negotiate with the local education authority (LEA), with groups of teachers or teachers' unions, whereupon changes in the school budget are decided.

We have given these examples to illustrate that a school undergoing several changes will begin to realize that it is the way the school functions as an organization that needs to undergo change. Figure 8.1 illustrates the relationships in this process.

Figure 8.1 illustrates the ad hoc nature of development strategies as they are used to implement given projects. Let us look at the figure to illustrate our point: we assume that the school development programme has resulted in the decision to implement three priority projects in the school. The first project, e.g. one that deals with 'student active learning', may result in the decision to provide training for the involved teachers in thinking skills and individualized instruction. The second project, e.g. one that attempts to increase 'school-based curriculum development', is facilitated through a course in didactics and materials development. Likewise, the third project is supported by a training programme in group dynamics and process consultation.

All these activities are in themselves very important to secure the implementation of projects. We know, however, that they all demand a lot of energy, and moreover, after project evaluation and an overall assessment, the school may well in a year's time decide to start another series of projects. This time the inputs may be the same or different. Each time the school has to construct a new support programme, as it is not a regular part of the school organization.

To *institutionalize* the change process in a school is to make it a regular part of daily life. A more general definition of 'institutionalization' is expressed by Matthew B. Miles: 'a stabilized modification, aiming at improvement of an institution or parts of it — its processes, products or capacities' (Miles *et al.*, 1987). Institutionalization within the IDP has as its major goal that, beyond normal and daily use of a new practice, the school has improved its ability

145

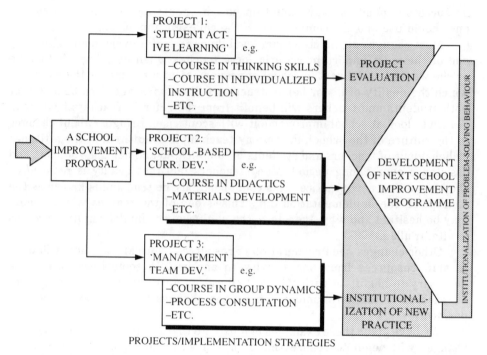

Figure 8.1  *From implementation to institutionalization*

to learn. This is vital, because every time a project is to be planned, implemented and institutionalized, new development strategies are needed, and new resources and a new division of tasks are demanded. The need for a more general approach to the support of innovation processes within a school becomes important. The question is how to 'institutionalize the institutionalization'! Schools have to live with change, and learn how to learn and to generalize improvement processes.

## THE LEARNING ORGANIZATION

A school that to a large extent is able to organize its own improvement processes and mobilize internal knowledge and skills for such work was called in Chapter 1 an 'organic school', or a new learning organization. This type of school is the ultimate objective for the IDP.

Also at this point we need to modify our statements. We know few 'organic schools', but we have seen many schools that are well under way! The learning organization is a development ideal, and development ideals are like stars: one may never reach them, but they may well give us good direction. Without knowing the direction, it is difficult to know if improvement takes place, or if it is only a series of hectic activities that may not even be heading in a desired direction!

The ideal of an organic school has structures and change capabilities that make it possible to initiate changes when needed (see Figure 1.7). The school is regularly working with its own values and norms. An organic school is an institution that takes the needs of students, parents and teachers seriously. It is a school that has a conscious and consequent relationship to the environment; it has an organizational culture and management that is open to innovation and change. It is a school where joint commitments make it possible to develop new visions, and where these are realized against the background of a realistic assessment of its strengths and weaknesses. It is a school that has the capacity to mobilize the staff as well as the students and the needed material resources for a programme. And moreover, these activities are clearly improving the quality of instruction.

We know that this picture of a learning organization may sound unrealistic to most school people. Schools are as a rule stable, and sometimes also rigid, organizations. Reforms are usually decided and implemented externally, and the role of the school is to adapt to such demands for change. The organic school represents a totally different school culture, a culture where initiative, creativity and development are the dominant norms. The remaining part of this chapter deals in some detail with critical aspects of the school as a learning organization.

## SCHOOL-BASED CURRICULUM DEVELOPMENT AND THE INSTRUCTIONAL PRACTICE

Wherever the curriculum is decided, at the national level, as in some countries, regionally, locally, or at the school level, the most important curriculum decisions in a school are made in the classroom (see Chapter 4 for further discussion). Curriculum research has for years shown that there are large differences in the implementation of the curriculum from school to school and from group to group within the same school. We find it useful in this connection to distinguish between three curriculum concepts.

1 *The intended curriculum:* This is the curriculum written down in a text and adopted by the appropriate authority (from Parliament all the way down to the individual school in some countries). A few years ago the intended curriculum was rather specific, outlining not only general and subject-specific objectives, but also types of content, depth of study, length of time for each component and even methodological advice. Increasingly, the written curriculum is seen as a *guide* to practice. It seldom goes beyond general and subject objectives, advice on content and advice on the length of study. Most modern curriculum texts are open to school and teacher interpretations.

2 *The implemented curriculum:* This is actually what happens in the classroom. Research into classroom practice shows us clearly that 'the curriculum' as implemented is widely different from classroom to classroom, mainly influenced by the interpretation, knowledge and skills of the teacher, the characteristics of the student population, the resources (time and materials) available for the instructional processes, and the evaluation process.

At this level, the school and classroom level, the need for

school-based curriculum development becomes clearer as the school begins to analyse its strengths and weaknesses. If the school, for example, analyses 'time on task' (i.e. the time used in each classroom for instructional tasks) and finds that it varies between 40 per cent and 80 per cent within the same subject and grade level in the same school, it becomes obvious that something needs to improve. Such variance is not uncommon. If, on the other hand, it becomes clear that some part of the student population is not benefiting from the instruction in a given subject area, clearly there is a need for improvement of the curriculum to meet the needs of special student populations.

The needs for changes in the curriculum may also be directly related to *teacher needs*. It may be that a given part of a subject curriculum is both needed and relevant, but that it is very difficult to get across to the students. Both content and methodological adaptations may improve the situation.

3 *The achieved curriculum:* Achievement outcomes give us at least one picture of how the curriculum is mastered by the students. A detailed analysis of results may show not only problems at the individual student level, but issues that are of more general concern to the school.

It may be that parts of the curriculum need more time, that some aspects need less attention, that some parts may be strengthened by better co-ordination with other subjects, that the *timing* of the content is problematic, that *sequence* is less than appropriate for some students and that some teachers need assistance in certain aspects of the subject taught.

Most schools are fully aware that the existing examination system only measures certain aspects of the curriculum. School objectives are more than the sum of achievement scores! As the school analyses the impact of instruction on students, the informed teacher, sensitive to student developments, will have much information and reflection to offer as a total analysis of outcomes is discussed. An analysis of the data may also lead the staff to look more carefully into the evaluation system. Is the evaluation too narrow? Does it give information about all relevant and important aspects of the objectives? Is it valid to take decisions about improvements?

What importance does an analysis of the curriculum have in relation to the school and the individual teacher? Possibly the most important insight to be gained is that it could lead to a school-based adaptation of the curriculum and of the evaluation procedures in relationship to the student group and the teachers who work with them. We have seen the importance of drawing the student actively into a dialogue with teachers about the curriculum and about instruction. We see the analysis of the curriculum as an important subject for discussion among teachers and students.

## STUDENT READINESS

Both the motivation and the abilities of students to learn are influenced by a number of factors in and external to the school. Research over many years has shown that the socio-economic factors (e.g. the home, the peer group, etc.) have a major influence on student learning. The self-concept of the student, also partly influenced by socio-economic factors, is important for his or her readiness to learn. Many students have a background of school failures. Through such failures they have indirectly learned that they have little value, and a vicious circle starts. One of the most important tasks for any teacher is to change this vicious circle. This is dependent on a real dialogue between students and teachers in an atmosphere of openness and security.

We are convinced that such a climate can best be nurtured in a school where the adult climate also is open and secure. In relation to students we are particularly interested in the *full use* of students as resource persons in the classroom. The research on co-operative learning, for example, shows that this form of learning not only has major advantages in the emotional and social area, but it also seems to have very positive effects on cognitive achievement (Levin *et al.*, 1984; Johnson and Johnson, 1986).

Many teachers need to change their role in the classroom. This is hard for one single teacher, but is easier when teachers work together with students to achieve role changes and improved relationships. One effect of the efforts of the IDP is clearly to change the norms and the skills needed to influence the teaching-learning climate of the classroom. One strategy is increased teacher co-operation, collegial supervision, staff development and joint projects. These and other activities help the teachers to work with students as partners. As these experiences are promoted and discussed over time, there is a great chance that student readiness will improve.

It is not the task of this book to describe and analyse various models of teaching and learning. When we stress the importance of teacher co-operation on the one hand, and co-operative work with students on the other, it is because we see these as important objectives for the future of the school. These and other models of teaching clearly need to be analysed in relation to specific pedagogical and subject goals (see Joyce (1990) for further reading).

## PROFESSIONALIZATION

One of the cornerstones of the 'real needs' model of change is the development of *competencies* to master the change process (change capacity), and this is an integral part of the 'learning organization' (see Figure 1.7). Throughout this book we have on numerous occasions made clear how important this factor is in school development. The schools' main mission is to foster *learning*. It goes without saying that a high-quality learning institution must have high-level *competence* in the area of work.

Further professionalization of the staff, therefore, becomes a key strategy for success, and must be built into the school as routinized practice. It needs to be secured through institutionalized procedures.

For a school to facilitate the professionalization of its staff is basically a

149

question of how work is organized (see Chapter 7). It is not a question of how many in-service training courses are offered! We advise a school to institutionalize the following activities and procedures to facilitate staff development (and achieve school improvement at the same time).

1 *A school assessment process* that leads into a yearly school development plan. This activity should involve all staff (and often also students and parents). A 'Steering Committee' may be responsible for the process (with rotating membership to give most staff an opportunity for learning and contribution). We recommend that a tailor-made school survey is administered every year (e.g. the GIL), which will provide the school with data comparable over time.

2 *Project groups* that provide staff with a development and learning opportunity, often with staff and resource persons they do not normally work with, and with tasks that are challenging. If possible *every* staff member should have one such appointment per year.

3 *Co-operative planning work* at the department level to deal with school-based curriculum development and the planning of instruction (as illustrated above). Such co-operative mechanisms give each teacher a true collegial setting in which to test professional issues and an opportunity for further professionalization. Collegial groups also provide an opportunity for personal growth and training in group dynamics. This depends on good group leadership with process skills.

4 *Peer supervision* that helps each teacher to be critically assessed by a trusted colleague. This is the core of the professionalization strategy (see below).

5 *Planning and development of tailor-made courses* to import needed knowledge and skills appropriate to the development tasks that the school is involved in. In Europe, for some years the discussion of *school-based* courses has been predominant, although *practice* of in-service training has not changed that much. There are good reasons to work closely with each school to provide more *relevance* in staff development. Hopefully, this will not lead to the opposite rigidity: that staff development is good just *because* it is school-based, and any external course by definition is bad! Quality probably has more to do with the choice of persons (and institutions) than with where they work.

Professionalization is dependent on a *system of learning* within a working organization that gives each teacher challenging tasks, and provides ongoing collegial support, supervision and coaching in a real dialogue, also with external experts. We now discuss one aspect, 'peer supervision', in more detail.

## PEER SUPERVISION

Both research and practice show us that the effects of organizational learning will slowly disappear if there is not a continuous and systematic evaluation or supervision in the organization (Boss, 1983). The term 'supervision' is in many European countries primarily known within social work and has been relatively little used within the school sector (Weigand, 1987). It is much more common in North America, at least in the literature. However, we find it necessary to discuss the term before we give it a meaning within the IDP. For further discussions see, for example, Caplan (1970), Cogan (1973), Lauterburg (1985) and Lauvås and Handal (1990).

Lauterburg discusses two concepts, namely 'supervision' and 'intervision'. These are concepts that at least in non-English-speaking countries are little known and difficult to distinguish, By supervision Lauterburg means critical control of an activity. A 'supervisor' has the task of controlling the work of others, or of leading a group in order to control the work of the group members. When two or more colleagues give each other mutual advice, Lauterburg uses the term 'intervision'. Other terms quite often used in English are 'peer supervision' or 'peer review', and sometimes also 'clinical supervision'. For our use in the IDP we choose to use the term *peer supervision*.

This distinction between supervision and peer supervision reflects the distinction between hierarchical positions in power and horizontal positions within an organization, discussed among others by Caplan (1970) and also by Lauvås and Handal (1990). The problems of combining collegial help and control, which are at the heart of much of the debate about school evaluation, are much in the forefront of the discussion.

Within the IDP we talk mainly about peer supervision, or a partnership between two colleagues or within small groups of colleagues, i.e. we speak either of a two-teacher concept of peer supervision, or about small 'supervision groups' that have the following tasks:

- to systematically control one's own work;

- to get ideas from others for one's own work;

- to learn from observation and discussion of others' work;

- to learn by giving other people advice.

These are ambitious goals. Such goals are only possible when the institutional conditions are present, the foremost being that anxiety and insecurity are reduced to a minimum. Learning best takes place when there is regular and critical feedback in secure environments. One of the reasons why peer supervision fails in many schools, or is started and then slowly disappears, is simply that the ground work has not been done. Within the IDP supervision is placed in a context of school improvement. We do not recommend peer supervision in isolation. However, at this stage of IDP development work, the school has worked so much with itself that management and teachers have created a climate of mutual trust and understanding. At this stage we find that many schools go into peer supervision with little planning, because it is a natural need. It can be done by organizing a 'project group' and drawing on staff members who have particular experience in the area, or who can help to train colleagues from each 'supervision group' in process consultation.

Participation in peer supervision groups is based on the assumption that participants bring in their own work for discussion. It is not necessary to have a large and comprehensive project for discussion. What is important is that the teacher has a challenging task that he or she wants to bring into the discussion with a few trusted colleagues. An important aspect of supervision is that it takes place *over time*, not with a series of one-shot cases, but with an ongoing discussion of a major aspect of teaching and learning.

We have found certain ground rules to be important for peer supervision groups to function.

1   *Regular meetings:* each member needs to be committed to regular meetings. Our experience is that an interval of between six and eight weeks is fairly ideal and possible from a scheduling point of view.

2   *Continuity:* We find that continuity is important, that each member has a major project or challenging task that he or she wants to discuss thoroughly with colleagues, that he or she brings materials or new data to the next meeting, and thereby help other members to get inside the case. As the case discussion continues over time, it is useful to make a short summarized one-page log of the discussion.

3   *Group size:* The ideal size may be four to six members. It is important that there are enough members to provide new and sometimes surprising ideas, but that the group is not too large; this would make it impossible to discuss every participant's case. A critical dimension of group supervision is how big the group is and how often the group meets. If the group is too large, and the time between meetings is too long, then it is impossible to do the job thoroughly.

4   *Peer supervision in the classroom:* Our experience with supervision groups is that many colleagues begin to 'see each other' in their classrooms. One might use a structured approach (e.g. 'clinical supervision'), or fairly straightforward agreements between two teachers about the goal of the visit, the procedures and the feedback. We find that the discussion in the supervision groups, if it is backed by peer supervision in the classroom, is richer, more open and more fun! A discussion of techniques for classroom observation and peer supervision in the classroom is given in other publications (see among others Goldhammer *et al.*, 1980; Evans and Tomlinson, 1989; Lauvås and Handal, 1990).

5   *Students as partners:* Part of professionalization, and a very important part of supervision, is the use of students as partners in a real dialogue about the improvement of classroom instruction and learning. Student perspectives give the analysis a broader and richer basis, and are often the starting point for regular assessment of instruction and learning, in close co-operation among teachers and students in a single class. We know many schools and teachers who

practise a systematic and regular dialogue with students about instruction; however, we are surprised at how few teachers have tried such an obvious effort. In the IDP we have developed materials for two approaches to student participation:

(a) Simple questionnaires (1-2 pages) that are used regularly. These questionnaires give the student the chance to reflect over his or her own preparation for the lesson, the difficulties he or she had during the instructional hour, what the teacher did that was useful, what one would like to have more of, and what the students would propose as follow-up work by the teacher and the student. The teacher gathers the information at the end of the class period and feeds results back to the students (and to teachers in the supervision group), if possible during the next lesson or at least within a week's time. The feedback session gives one opportunity to give meaning to the data, to help students to articulate their points of view, and gives the teacher a chance to clarify and to get closer to some of the sensitive issues in the classroom.

(b) The investigations of classroom climate and instructional and learning practices. This is a form of 'mini-GIL survey' that is performed in co-operation with the teacher and students in a given class. The questions deal directly with the classroom climate, classroom leadership (both the formal and informal), dynamic issues, methods of instruction, styles and practices of learning and preparation by the students, roles and relations within the group, ways decisions are made, and, foremost, with the values and norms of the class. Since the factors that contribute to learning are many and complex, and certainly because learning is influenced by the students' motivation and attitudes to the school and to their class, the work of students and teachers together to improve the classroom climate is an important contribution to the quantitative development of instruction.

Peer supervision may take many forms; the information may come from colleagues as well as students. Where the data come from and how they are discussed are factors dependent on the trust and openness that exists in the group. Our advice to teachers is to build trust gradually, taking one step at a time, so that it is possible to implement valid data-gathering and analysis with the broadest possible participation. Only a step-by-step process leads to trust and openness, and a reflection based on valid data that helps teachers and students.

Peer supervision is a necessary and institutionalized part of a learning organization. It may be that the implementation has consequences for the way work is organized, according to the choice of group members, as well as for the timetable. Peer supervision must be planned; commitment to the work and the process is necessary at the management level, the teacher level and the student level (students are participants in parts of the process). It is not an easy process to implement. Many schools therefore opt for training, and many teachers work over a period of time to get the fullest advantage from peer supervision.

Many researchers and staff developers argue that 'structured supervision', with the use of external expertise on 'effective instruction', has many advantages. Some argue that peer supervision could lead to a rigid stagnation and ineffective practice (Little, 1989). Also, Joyce (1990) argues for assessing instruction against our knowledge of effective models of teaching and learning. We agree with this point of view. The start, however, should be collegial co-operation based on the level of trust in each of the peer supervision groups. We find that sometimes it is necessary to 'hold up a mirror', to reflect from a different perspective what goes on in the peer supervision groups, and to provide some alternative information. IDP consultants do this mainly by providing lists of suggested reading, and encouraging the group to look at an issue from an alternative perspective. This is the role of the IDP consultant: to provide *alternative information*, not to teach alternative methods. Quite often the IDP consultant is not an expert on alternative instructional and learning models anyway, and would have to refer to expertise in the area. Sometimes colleagues ask for further information and even courses that will help them to provide and develop alternatives. This is of course an ideal situation where more research-based information can be brought in.

We have found that an alternative method may be used before external expertise is brought in. We have positive experience with 'intergroup visitations'. In this case one teacher in a supervision group volunteers to present his or her case to colleagues from another supervision group. The case is presented and the colleagues from both groups look at strengths and weaknesses and put forward some alternatives. Simply having other colleagues in the discussion often facilitates a very creative process that provides a number of new ideas which may be tested against validated practice or research before ideas are tested in reality.

## INTERNAL SCHOOL EVALUATION

At this stage of the IDP the school has gone through several cycles of development, several projects have been tested, assessed and evaluated, and the school has experience with the development of project models and has evaluated several innovative projects (see Chapter 7). Gradually a new norm is developing, that ongoing assessment, feedback and discussions are vital for the quality of the school. We are at a stage when an internal school review process should be institutionalized (see also Figure 1.7).

We have seen how a school can establish procedures of assessing its practices at five different levels of activities:

1 *School-wide assessment:* This is the basis for the IDP process, for example via an organizational survey (e.g. the GIL), or use of other methods (see Chapter 4). Staff (and often students and parents) obtain data to assess the strengths and weaknesses of the school. The information is available to all; everyone has the same right and

opportunity to provide data and to participate in the diagnostic phase.

We advocate that the school needs to establish a regular practice of school-wide assessment. It may be that certain aspects are looked upon as so important that an assessment should be made once every year (e.g. 'climate'). Knowing how quickly the student population is changing (in a six-year primary school half of the organizational members are new in the school in three years), we advocate that a school should *institutionalize* a practice of school-wide assessment at least once every third year.

If this is done, data become available on a *longitudinal basis*. It is possible to 'compare notes', to see how different aspects of the school become important, and to see how the school is coping with its priority issues over time.

The mechanisms needed for the school review are basically: Steering Committee (newly elected, hopefully with some overlap), instrumentation and other materials to brief new participants, access to an external consultant, file of earlier data and new relevant data, training, resources and time. It *does* take time. However, it is well worth it, if *organizational* learning is a priority.

2 *Assessment of group productivity:* We have seen how important groups are in schools. Most learning, as we have noted, takes place in relatively small groups. Teachers are either participants in work groups (e.g. in a department) or 'production leaders' in learning groups (e.g. the classroom). We have also seen how important the composition of the group is, and how important are the dynamics of the group and the leadership of group processes.

The IDP provides consultants with skills in assessing groups. In some schools it also becomes important to transfer these skills to the Steering Committee or other participants as part of the school improvement programme. In the development of group practices there are several ways in which group performance can be assessed.

(a) *Through observation* by a trained observer, who will also provide feedback to the group. This again provides an opportunity to improve group performance.

(b) *Through joint reflection* by using an agreed-upon process and instrumentation. This also implies the sharing of information, discussion of strengths and weaknesses, and opportunities for improvement of group performance.

(c) *Through process interventions* by analysing behaviour as it occurs, and thereby providing opportunities for the group to assess its own behaviour as it happens. Process interventions of this kind should be initiated by a qualified group trainer; however, the skill of intervention can be learned and is something that most teachers (and students) should be able to master.

Group processes are fundamental to the development of school-wide norms and behaviour. The climate and the practices of groups are so essential to the health of the school that they need ongoing monitoring. The institutionalization of group assessment practices is dependent on the following: a willingness of all teachers to qualify themselves as group trainers (which in any case is critical for their classroom performance); an opportunity for group training for all teachers (and of course for school leaders); instrumentation and materials in group development that can be applied at the classroom level; and a system of regular monitoring of group performance conducted by the teachers and shared in regular staff meetings.

3 *Project evaluation:* This is achieved through an ongoing dialogue by using project models and a systematic evaluation process (see Chapter 6). This model of internal evaluation provides participants with a joint picture of the project and with the data needed for ongoing revisions and improvements of a project.

In a problem-solving school a number of development projects are started as a regular activity. The danger is that little is known about what is actually done and what is achieved through the projects. The mechanisms for institutionalization are the following: project participants are trained in using project models and an evaluation process (see Chapter 7). As a regular part of project work these activities are performed by the participants in a project. Data are provided, at least twice a year, for the Steering Committee (or school management if the school does not have a Steering Committee at this stage). On the basis of such 'progress reports' decisions are made on how the project can be improved.

4 *Peer supervision:* This helps groups of teachers to obtain data about their teaching practices to enable them to improve their own practice (see above). Peer supervision can be further developed by using classroom data from students. The process of peer supervision is an essential part of a system of internal school assessment; however, it will only be effective if openness, trust and skills are present.

The institutionalization of peer supervision is dependent on the success of the pilot experiences that some teachers have had through the implementation of projects. It is a fairly threatening concept for many teachers and it is through modelling behaviour of trusted colleagues that new teachers engage in peer supervision. Attempts to institutionalize these practices are less useful if they are not done on a voluntary basis. Also, training in supervision practices is important for the quality of the process (see above).

5 *Assessment of student performance:* This is done through regular school assessment procedures. These evaluation practices are clearly well known and used. Practice from country to country varies considerably, and so does practice among schools in a given country, as well as internal practices in schools.

It is important to see student evaluation data as part of the total information picture that evolves in a school. By structuring and analysing data at all these levels the school can begin to use the assessment process as an active tool for the improvement of the school at all levels of the organization.

## EXTERNAL EVALUATION

The individual school is part of a system, and has responsibility to its governing board, the LEA or maybe even directly to the minister of education. It also has a responsibility towards the parents who send their children to school, towards local institutions that support the school, and towards those institutions which receive students either through further training or work. A school assessment process that neglects the wishes and demands of the environment will soon be in trouble (see discussion in Chapter 2).

How the internal school assessment process can and should be related to the *control functions* that are the responsibility of the governing board or the LEA or the ministry is the critical issue. The question is: *Who* has the right to *what* data? If we talk about a purely internal process, where only those who are assessed and those who assess have access to the data, there is a chance that the process could lead to an open and honest evaluation process (but this is not guaranteed). The moment *other actors* have access to the same data, inside or outside the school, critical aspects of clarification are needed. Usually it is possible over time to share information openly within an organization. Our experience is that it takes a long time and that many teachers will always hesitate to share honestly the strengths and weaknesses of their own instruction.

How would a school react to a proposal of bringing the school inspector into the assessment process? How would an eventual formal coercive role influence the process of change? Would the inspector have the right to all types of data? How would he or she acquire the data? If he or she obtains some data, can teacher be sure that other data would be kept confidential in the school? Would teachers dare to be *open with each other* if they knew that data would leak to someone who has authority over jobs?

These are some of the many questions that teachers and school leaders ask us as the IDP is dealing with the boundary functions. If we go back to our theory of the school as an organization (Chapter 1), we assume that the school has an interest in a continuous dialogue with the 'environment'. We have also said, however, that the head has a job during the change process to *shelter* the school from attacks and undue criticism. Any innovation needs protection before it is tested.

The 'environment' consists of many dimensions. The school inspector represents the formal part of the environment and has both a right and an interest in the change process that goes on within the school. The question is not whether the school is going to share information with the inspector, but what information, under what circumstances, at what time and for what purpose the information is going to be shared. The IDP advocates the following structure and practice:

1 *Internal review*: The school itself, as we have described it in this book, periodically has internal reviews (most often with the assistance of an external consultant) as a basis for school development. We have indicated that this should take place at least once every three years. In this process the inspector is informed, he or she may have an input to the planning process (e.g. certain issues that he or she wants analysed), but is not involved in the process and does not see any of the data at this stage.

2 *External review*: At regular intervals (e.g. the same intervals as the school review process) the inspector will review the school. (In some countries this function is performed by an external 'review committee' with broad representation, e.g. the school authorities, colleagues from other schools, parents, etc.) He or she will obviously have visited the school several times during the past three years, and usually he or she will know the head and several teachers and will be acquainted with some of the issues that the school is working with.

In good time prior to the visit, usually *before* the internal review is conducted, the inspector will ask the school to provide data about certain aspects of the school (e.g. achievement scores in mathematics, drop-out rate for bilingual children, staff development needs, needs for materials, issues that would need external assistance, etc.).

The job of the school inspector is *not* to gather raw data, but to ensure that the school has an effective internal review process that provides the best possible data about priority issues.

The external review will involve the inspector in a dialogue with the school management, individual teachers and groups of teachers (e.g. the mathematics department), and will be offered to students, parents and the school as a whole. It lasts for a minimum of two days, often three or four days. In some countries the inspector wants to review the school with colleagues from other schools and/or parents at the school (see, for example, Liket, 1992).

## Assuring quality data

The inspector is responsible for the process of external review, in order to provide the school authorities with a balanced picture of the school, to assist the school in getting needed resources, to help the school to live with existing regulations, to try to modify the existing structure and regulations, and to enable school development processes to succeed.

For these tasks to be accomplished successfully, the inspector needs to trust the data he or she is working with. The following dilemmas need to be solved:

1 *Detailed and aggregated data*: The more detailed the data are, the better the inspector will understand the issues. However, the more detailed the data, the less likely that participants will be open about their problems. Only when individual data are aggregated and made into more general issues will the data be reliable. It is essential

to define the level of generality of data. The closer and more trustworthy the relationship the inspector has with the school, the easier it is to resolve this dilemma.

2 *Ensuring an internal quality review process*: This is vital to ensure quality data. As we have seen throughout this book, to obtain quality data is not simple. The inspector will have to be an expert on the school as an organization and the strategies and techniques of evaluation. He or she will have to review the process with the head, help to strengthen the process (e.g. provide training in evaluation) and provide needed resources, while still remaining *outside* the internal assessment.

3 *The use of data*: This is equally important to ensure quality data. People will not provide data if they are used against them. They will lose interest in the entire process if it does not lead to something better. The inspector has a major responsibility in helping the school to design a better future, by being the bridge to the school administration, modifying rules and regulations when needed, fighting for extra resources when he or she feels that this is vital, and being supportive of the school development process.

These are some of the functions that the inspector can and will play in the process of school-based development. It will change the inspectorate. The inspector is no longer the expert who gives advice; he or she is not primarily working with individual teachers or individual subjects. The inspector is working at the level of the organization, with all staff, looking at broad developmental issues, discussing the strengths and weaknesses of the school and providing help and assistance on the basis of the real needs of the school, as understood by the school and the inspectorate together.

## SUPPORTING MANAGEMENT DEVELOPMENT

The IDP is a comprehensive strategy to modify the school culture in order to achieve improved and desired school outcomes. To institutionalize a process of renewal, the school also needs capabilities in the following areas.

1 *Management development*: Changing an organization puts considerable pressure on the management from within the school as well as from the environment. We have described the roles and functions of change management (Chapter 6). These are functions that are shared by the staff; however, the head and his or her team need to master key processes.

It is unlikely that one person, or even a small team of leaders, will be capable of handling all sides of a school development process. It is to be expected, however, that resources and opportunities exist to develop those skills that are needed.

We see this as being similar to the development of *teacher capabilities*, as outlined above. Management development will take place through co-operation with teachers on development tasks, through peer supervision (e.g. with heads from other schools working together with the head), and through supervision (e.g. through the inspectorate). Through such processes needs for tailor-made courses emerge, and they may range from courses in specific planning techniques to courses in personal growth.

2 *Group development*: We have noted that most 'production' in a school takes place in small groups. The skills of working with groups and learning from groups are highly important for all students, teachers and for school management.

We advise a school to *institutionalize* a capacity to deal with group issues, to train teachers for effective group management, to assist management in group diagnosis and group leadership and to select and develop relevant materials for group development. We encourage the investigation of the productivity and climate of groups as a starting point to improve effectiveness, and advise offering a tailor-made in-service training programme for all staff. The best solution is to have at least one staff member with expertise in this area, and/or to secure resources to hire trainers.

3 *Organizational development*: A significant part of the IDP is organizational development (OD), although this goes beyond the traditional definition of OD. Nevertheless, OD is fundamental as a strategy for institutional renewal. In fact the whole process of school development, if effective, provides training to staff in OD strategies and techniques.

The institutionalization of OD practices is basically achieved through a structure that secures regular reviews of the school as an organization, capabilities that ensure the skills needed for the process, and resources needed for internal and external work input.

We have described a number of institutionalized procedures and processes that characterize the 'organic school', or the new learning organization. Unless such procedures become a part of daily life in the school, school improvement becomes 'adhocracy': special occasional 'happenings' for the few.

# Chapter 9

# Towards a Learning Organization

*The ultimate goal of the IDP is to develop a 'learning organization'.*
*What have we learned about this process, and what can we as IDP*
*developers do to improve our work? We need to work more with*
*management development. We need to be clear about why, when and*
*how a school should use external consultancy. We must work more at*
*the system level responsible for the support to the individual school.*
*We also need a better understanding of the role of the 'school owner'.*
*And this is where the IDP is currently going.*

We have come to the end of our survey. We have attempted to describe, explain and discuss the Institutional Development Program (IDP) as we have experienced it over the past fifteen years. The purpose of this chapter is not to summarize, but to reflect. We reflect on some of the basic assumptions and practices of the IDP, in some areas going beyond our empirical data and reflecting on the value and consequences of the IDP for schools, and in particular we discuss the implications of the IDP at the *policy level*, and what needs to be done at the system level.

## THE LEARNING ORGANIZATION

In our adult life we are faced with more challenges and changes than any generation before us. Private firms, as well as public agencies, are facing demands for renewal at a speed and on a scale unimaginable only a few years ago. Pressures for increased productivity, challenges from competing economies, changes in trade and the use of new technologies are only part of the picture.

At the same time the industrialized countries are experiencing social and cultural changes that set new standards and expectations for our institutional lives. We see changes in the way work is being organized, how enterprises are dealing with human resource development, how women are becoming more active in leadership positions, and how we conceive leadership and participation in organizations.

How can we best prepare our students for a future that most likely will become even more demanding, and where individual and institutional changes will become the norm? We must prepare for a future that will be both 'hierarchical' (but in a different way) and 'horizontal', where power is more evenly distributed, where influence rather than authority becomes important, and where negotiation skills and problem-solving skills become necessities. To us the answer is obvious: beyond a more relevant curriculum and real participation in everyday school life, students have to live and participate in a learning institution. Institutional development, with full participation of teachers and students, is the very best preparation for future roles, be it in the home, the leisure group, or at work.

The often-mentioned 'hidden curriculum' — what students *really* learn from school life, beyond the official curriculum — must become an official part of learning. It is by living through the processes of learning about real needs, by gathering data, analysing data, identifying individual and institutional strengths and weaknesses, formulating goals, plans and activities, participating in pilot schemes, working to develop group norms and discovering assumptions and values, and behaving in creative and responsible ways that students learn to *live* future roles.

The IDP has in several cases, in particular in Norway, involved students actively. It has been a very rich learning experience for the young as well as for adults. We encourage schools to involve students at the classroom level, as well as at the institutional level. We know that some school faculties are not ready for this; it will be a long time before the climate gives sufficient security for students to participate. There should be no doubt, however, that a learning organization has active students involved in the change process.

All schools have objectives that give high priority, in principle, to personal growth and social development. These objectives, in terms of curriculum inten- tions, are stressed in all national curricula. Seldom, however, have they been given a real place in the daily life of schools. Here, subject matter dominates. We question whether personal growth and social development can be 'learned' as part of a 'curriculum'. These goals, in our view, can best be met in practice, through active involvement and interaction with peers and adults in institu- tional life, and beyond the boundaries of the school, in the community. The IDP provides a framework, activities, methods and materials that allow this to happen. In fact, we believe that in addition to a curriculum that stresses 'learn- ing by participation' (Dalin and Skrindo, 1983), the IDP approach gives the school a real opportunity to take these priority objectives seriously.

In the next few years IMTEC will give priority to schools that want to pilot approaches and materials that involve students as well as parents. We have already argued for the importance of involving parents actively in the change process. IMTEC has experiences with parent participation in the IDP, at the primary and lower secondary level (the first nine years of schooling). For schools to take the *users* of their services seriously, not to mention the benefits of close co-operation in achieving better learning for students, is a characteristic of a healthy learning organization.

## THE IDP AND INSTITUTIONAL LEADERSHIP

This book has illustrated in practice and theory how important leadership is to institutional development. We have seen that leadership at times is performed by those in roles other than the formal school leadership. In early phases of the IDP, responsibility for the change process is usually delegated to a tempo- rary system, the Steering Committee. Gradually the formal school leadership takes over responsibility. In other cases the head and his or her team take the leadership role from the start, work within the Steering Committee and take on the responsibility for project planning implementation, and institutionalization.

It is not so important *who* performs the leadership task at a given point in time, but that the needs for leadership are met. We have seen that several leadership functions may be shared, that the school can draw on the informal leadership of the organization, and that to develop a sense of ownership often means to delegate and to share responsibility.

We see the IDP as a 'leadership training institute'! It provides a unique opportunity for the school leadership to learn. Here are some unique aspects of this 'management training institute'.

1  Training is not performed away from reality, in comfortable external management training institutions, but amid real-life situations.

2  At several stages the participants analyse their real need for leadership by assessing the 'here and now', and presenting the notion of an 'ideal' situation (e.g. through the GIL). The meaning of effective leadership is not defined by research or theory, but by those who need leadership in a given context.

3  The formal leaders have to step back, not get fully involved in early phases; they have the luxury to reflect, and to work with a trained development consultant, the only focus being on 'my' institution and 'my' leadership, drawing on the best of leadership theory.

4  The IDP is a school-based competency development programme, where essential skills in planning, design, development, group leadership, norms and value clarifications, project implementation — to mention a few needed change management skills — are introduced, practised and assessed.

5  The school leadership can practise skills such as openness and trust as the school improves. The 'training ground' is more secure, it is not like jumping into deep water; it provides a condition of readiness for problem-solving, and there is a trained support system standing by.

6  Finally, and probably most important, as school leaders learn new skills, and help the school to discover new values and norms, they will receive regular feedback and thereby the needed stimulation for further growth.

We are often asked if the school leadership should not be treated separately within the IDP. In certain phases of development, the consultant may well work directly with the leadership team. As far as training is concerned, we do not see any difference between the need of leaders and that of any other participant. It is through co-operation in an open climate that new skills are tested and learned. The goal, of course, is to qualify the management team for *change leadership*, to be able to work with the school day to day without the support of external consultancy.

School management is also accountable to the governing board or the 'school owner'. Although change management can be learned in the process, the policy and monitoring functions may well set boundaries that need to be handled. In fact, such 'boundary conditions' are needed elements in the process as the school works within the 'mutual adaptation and development' model of change (see Chapter 1).

## THE CONSULTANT

An essential part of the IDP is the use of trained consultants. We do not advocate that all schools use an external consultant, but our experience is that most will benefit from it, at least in certain critical phases of the process (which may differ from school to school).

Our first observation is that we propose a school use a *well-qualified consultant*. As Miles once said: A 'little organizational development may be worse than nothing' (see also Fullan *et al.*, 1980). IMTEC's two-year training programme, followed by a combination of training seminars, supervised practice, interviews and coaching lasting at least a year once the training programme is over, seems to us to be a minimum training programme. To facilitate the IDP is a highly complex undertaking.

Our second observation is that IDP consultancy is built on a set of tested assumptions. Those assumptions are based on our hypotheses and theories of how changes take place in schools, what characterizes schools as organizations, how institutional learning takes place and how interventions may help schools to develop. They have implications for the consultant role and behaviour.

As discussed in this book we advocate a careful definition of consultant-school relationships and division of labour, and emphasize the need to review the 'contract' several times during the programme. We advocate the use of a trained consultant because it may *facilitate* the processes:

- when the school has a desire to start a process, but is unable to get the process going;
- when there is a lack of know-how;
- when a 'third party' is needed, because participants feel generally that they are 'part of the problem';
- when potential internal consultants feel that they will have to play double roles (e.g. lead a process, and at the same time participate with their own interests);
- when the very basis for the organization is questioned, and there is a danger that the school has a too limited perspective, and that the internal analysis may be inadequate;
- when the climate, the understanding of the process and the problem-solving capability is inadequate.

It is likely that a trained consultant has competencies that are needed, has experience from several organizations, has no particular self-interest in the future of the school and has access to the methods and tools needed to facilitate the process.

Although the IDP consultant is a *process consultant* (Schein, 1970), he or she also represents needed expertise. He or she may at times act as a teacher, as a data-gatherer, as an analyst, and/or as a personal adviser, but always with the perspective of helping the individuals and the organization to master the process themselves.

As we have illustrated in this book, the art of intervention is highly complex. In fact, it illustrates the limitations and possibilities of any external actor. A person from a formal hierarchical external position has clear limitations in his or her ability to assist schools in development, as do external consultants. School systems, however, need both types of expertise.

## THE SCHOOL

As the representatives of a school seek assistance from a consultant we have described the school as the 'client'. Several times in this book we have raised questions about the very word *client*. An institution that needs help is not necessarily sick, handicapped, or in need of advice. Staff members may only need someone to talk to, to receive help in finding the first steps along the road, to discuss some experiences, to be reassured, or to become more confident about what they are doing.

There are all types of 'clients'. We like to call a school the 'client' as we start the relationship, and then our 'partner' as we grow into the process. This should indicate what we mean by a healthy relationship.

The 'school', however, is never the client in real terms. Somebody in the school is. He or she may be the head to start with, and we have called him or her the 'contact client'. The Steering Committee in the school is usually our 'primary client'. As long as this group broadly represents the interests in the school, we can say that we work with 'the school'. The 'ultimate client', however, is the student. We are often concerned that the road is long, and the process difficult, to achieve something that really benefits students. This is why we advocate bringing students actively into the process.

We want to work with 'real needs'. The basic assumption holds true: schools are often asked to do something new that has not been tested against the needs of students and teachers. We have seen, however, from the discussion in this book that what seem to be real priority needs as the process starts may be looked upon as *preliminary* needs just a year later. We discover our needs as we learn about ourselves and the school. And we discover that needs differ, that priorities are hard to agree upon, and that it takes a lot of energy to readdress the process to meet new needs.

We also discover the road as we walk it. Each school is unique, and each consultancy is unique. The most important skill, on the consultant side and on the side of the partner, is to *live with the unfinished* — to have the guts to be open about the fact that we do not know; to live with the anxiety of not having the right answer all the time, as we try to define the right question; to learn together with our partners, as we all try to discover and rediscover needs and values. It is a unique learning process.

# NECESSARY PERSPECTIVES

Our starting point in school development is that real innovations happen in a meeting between internal and external needs (Chapter 1). Even though the school is the unit for change, it does not mean that the school lives in isolation. It is imperative for the individual school to understand and to react productively *vis-à-vis* the environment, otherwise the danger of becoming blind is too great. Any healthy organization works actively in its relation to the environment. Should an analysis of needs and possible development goals lead to basic innovations, the school has to take into account a number of perspectives:

1  *The perspectives and needs of the individual teacher*: Our starting point is participants' picture of reality. Participants need to work on clarifying their own perspective.

2  *The opinions and needs of colleagues*: Through a gradual development of openness and trust we have a chance to better understand other points of view. We have shown in this book how peer supervision and collegial co-operation can lead to new points of view.

3  *Students' and parents' needs and perspectives*: If schools have clients they are the parents (primary school), and those who receive our students (e.g. universities and industry). The IDP stresses the importance of participation of students, parents and representatives of the 'environment'. This can happen through direct participation in the process, which is often the case for students, or by these groups giving their opinions in interviews or surveys.

4  *Experiences and research results*: Teachers normally do not use research data; however, there is relevant research that tells us something about 'effective schools', and about relevant and high-quality instruction and learning. It is not necessary to discover everything from scratch! Our experience is that mature Steering Committees quite often discuss their ideas with researchers or consult with the literature about 'good practices'. These can give new and important perspectives to a school.

5  *The perspectives and needs of politicians and decision-makers*: These perspectives are often written down as general objectives, in curriculum plans and in rules and regulations, but they are also represented by political parties and the school administration. We have shown that central decisions are seldom fully implemented in school practice. Implementation is unlikely to be secured by increased control. The best strategy is *improved communication*, to enable both decision-makers and school people to understand each other better.

The IDP builds on the assumption that all the above five perspectives are necessary, if school improvement is going to contribute to real innovation and quality improvement. This is one of the reasons why we feel that external consultancy is important to 'open up the window' and make us comfortable using alternative perspectives.

# THE IDP AND DECENTRALIZATION

The starting point for reform is the school as the unit of change. It is a new vision for most school systems and often strikes a chord with ministries of education, although seeing the school as the unit of change appears to be getting easier as school systems are delegating decision-making down the system. 'Decentralization', however, may have several meanings. It can simply mean to maintain the existing hierarchical decision-making system, but make it somewhat shorter; that is, it may mean giving the district powers that the ministry possessed before. This kind of decentralization may not help schools at all. In fact it may *increase* the detailed and often unproductive control of schools.

Decentralization may also mean to delegate authority to the 'building manager': the principal. School-based management has become very popular in the last few years, in particular in North America. It is indeed important to give the school full authority over its own resources. It is, however, not sufficient.

To us, the really important issue is what kind of leadership a learning institution needs. Leadership starts in the classroom. This is where the important leadership function is carried out. The teacher is the 'production leader', a person who knows how to motivate and involve students and other teachers, who understands the dynamics of groups, and who can lead, structure, encourage, use creative ideas and lead a process that produces results. The school leadership team is a support team for the classroom teacher, who is also able to lead, to motivate, to involve and to interact. We advocate leadership that begins at the classroom level.

This, however, is not enough. A leader of an *institution* has at least two additional responsibilities: to ensure that the *institution* has a policy and that it lives by it, and to ensure accountability in relation to its governing body.

Although effective educational leadership starts in the classroom, it does not end there. The school leadership team clearly has the responsibility to ensure that the institution as a whole has a *vision*, sets targets for itself, mobilizes energy towards common ends and maintains a positive climate within the organization. School leadership, therefore, although based on classroom leadership, has a clear dimension beyond the classroom.

Furthermore, the institutional leader is responsible to the 'environment', and in this case the governing body of the school, for what goes on in the school. A school lives with a 'contract' with its owners and, increasingly, must serve its clients: parents and the local community. Institutional leadership has an increasingly difficult job to argue for the role of the school in a competitive environment. This is a more interesting job.

A school development process, like the IDP, that so basically works to improve the values, norms and practices of the school needs to *communicate* with school authorities, parents and other interest groups. The head of the institution has a major responsibility that can only be carried out effectively if he or she has full ownership of the process and its outcomes. This calls for an active and involved school leadership in the IDP.

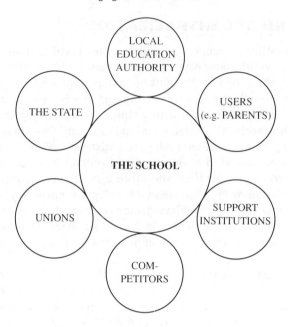

Figure 9.1 *The school 'environment'*

## THE IDP AND THE SYSTEM LEVEL

The school is the unit of change, but it does not live a life in isolation, nor do we assume that school development happens in isolation. In fact, the mutual adaptation and development perspective (Chapter 1) makes it clear that real innovative solutions are found in a creative response to internal and external forces and needs.

Schools are accountable, first of all, to students and parents, and to their governing boards (or similar institutions), which represent broader societal interests. In fact, schools need to take several external institutions into account in their efforts to relate to the 'environment' (Figure 9.1).

In some countries the state has minimal direct influence over schools; however, in most countries the curriculum reflects the interests of groups at the national level. National educational laws and regulations play an important part in defining the 'boundary conditions'. The 'school owner' (e.g. the local education authority (LEA)) in most member countries of the Organisation for Economic Co-operation and Development (OECD) has a significant influence on implementation of school policies, and most schools are accountable to their local authority. There is, in several countries, a clear tendency to delegate authority from the local district to the school (e.g. in the form of a governing board for each school).

The school, however, has to reflect other groups and institutions as well, including unions, which have an increasingly important role in school development, support institutions that deliver services and materials to the educational process (e.g. in-service training institutions), and, as a new phenomenon in some countries (e.g. the Netherlands), compete in a declining market for schooling where parents and students can choose schools at their own will.

In fact, both students and parents will play a more significant role as *customers* in the future. As choices increase, as schools increasingly come to depend on direct 'payments' from parents (possibly through some form of voucher system), what students and parents *believe* to be true will form the basis for decisions. Whatever the structural solution may be, the need to improve communication with parents and students becomes a priority.

Increasingly, schools need to take many actors into account. As we have seen earlier in this book, because of social, technological, economic and ecological changes in our societies those who represent these institutions are themselves undergoing change, and this reflects uncertainties and a dynamic which is new for most schools.

It goes beyond the purpose of this book to discuss the structure and organization of the system level of education. Our concern is more limited: how can the individual school relate to the 'school owner' (usually at the district level) in such a way that it supports the change process and secures a quality control process?

We have several times in this book described the school as a 'learning organization'; a school that supports an innovative organizational culture, management and teacher qualifications through three processes:

1  School-based curriculum and staff development support (e.g. through peer supervision).

2  Management and organizational development support to enable each learning cell and the school to function as a productive learning organization.

3  An internal assessment process that helps the school to obtain data about its own work from the work of the individual learner and teacher, the classroom and the organization.

Figure 9.2 illustrates the relationship between the 'organic' school (the new learning organization) and the 'school owner'. The lower box in the figure corresponds to the 'school as a learning organization' in Figure 1.7. The upper box illustrates the main functions performed by the school owner (e.g. the LEA).

The 'school owner' has a political, an administrative and a professional role and needs to reflect four major forces:

1  The needs of parents who have their children in the school system must be considered. Parent interests are seldom organized effectively; however, they usually express themselves through a political process.

2  The needs of society in broader terms must be considered, usually through the tax payer, and generally reflected through the political process.

3  The needs of the unions must be taken into account, in particular those of the teacher unions.

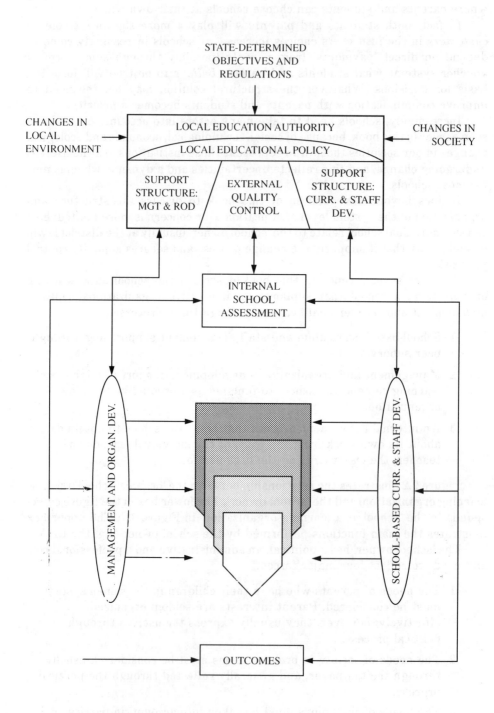

STATE-DETERMINED
OBJECTIVES AND
REGULATIONS

CHANGES IN
LOCAL
ENVIRONMENT

LOCAL EDUCATION AUTHORITY

LOCAL EDUCATIONAL POLICY

CHANGES IN
SOCIETY

SUPPORT
STRUCTURE:
MGT & ROD

EXTERNAL
QUALITY
CONTROL

SUPPORT
STRUCTURE:
CURR. & STAFF
DEV.

INTERNAL
SCHOOL
ASSESSMENT

MANAGEMENT AND ORGAN. DEV.

SCHOOL-BASED CURR. & STAFF DEV.

OUTCOMES

Figure 9.2  *The school and the LEA*

4 The needs of the state must be considered, usually reflected in the curriculum, school laws and regulations. Included are *high standards*, often reflected by research data on 'good practices'.

The 'school owner', in other words, reflects most of the institutions and interest groups we have discussed and illustrated above (Figure 9.1). How can these forces best be 'translated' into a productive relationship between the individual school and the school owner?

1 *Policy*: Increasingly, school owners need to work with alternative *scenarios* about the future. Since changes in schools take considerable time, to build policies on historical data has only limited value. Educational policies need to take possible developments in society at large, and in the local community, into account, including demographic data, the mix of ethnic groups, local economic developments, the family situation, the growing up of children and youth in the community, and the services of other public and private agencies. Clearly, some of the educational policies are laid down through a curriculum (often mandated by the state); however, the 'school owner' in most industrialized countries has more flexibility to develop a policy that will best serve the students in its community.

2 *Curriculum and staff support*: We have seen how essential *staff capabilities* are to educational development. A locally adapted curriculum is increasingly seen as essential to meet the needs of individual students. Most schools need external support, both in terms of resources and professional support, to be able to cope with the challenges of the change process. Although the 'school owner' in many cases will draw on resources from other schools, colleges, universities, teacher centres and the like, it needs a comprehensive professional support structure to cope with the needs of individual schools.

3 *Management support*: To support the development of an innovative organizational culture, to give the school management team, as well as the Steering Committee, help to design, diagnose, develop and implement needed changes, management and OD consultancy expertise are needed. This book represents an example of the resources needed in this area.

4 *Quality control*: The role of quality control is to ensure that the school has data about itself that are reliable and have consequences for quality improvement. The important issue is not necessarily to gather new data about the school. External control measures that are based on the assumption that external agencies or persons will get valid raw data from the school are largely ineffective if the purpose is to improve the teaching-learning process. The 'school owner', as an alternative, may regularly inspect the school, not to gather data, but to have access to agreed-upon data, to ensure that the school has an effective internal assessment process, to conduct a

dialogue about strengths and weaknesses and, if needed, to provide training and advice.

The role of the 'school owner' in 'quality control' is to be a quality assurance agency that sets the criteria, provides assistance in building internal systems of assessment, and ensures that the data the school are using have validity and reliability (see Chapter 8).

Based on internal data sometimes coupled with occasional external reviews (e.g. the American system of accreditation or the British system of course validation), a form of *meta-evaluation* can be brought to bear upon educational policies, at least at the 'school owner' level.

Taking seriously the idea that the school is the unit of change will, in other words, also have implications at the system level. From a tradition of influencing the system through laws, regulations and direct inspection, the system level will increasingly have a future-oriented policy function, a support function and a 'quality assurance' role.

## CULTURAL FACTORS

We have worked with school improvement in many cultures. IMTEC, based in Oslo, Norway, has in fact worked with projects in more than thirty countries in Europe, North America, Africa and Asia. The IDP has been used on somewhat more limited basis. However, we do have considerable experience in using the programme in different cultures. We have also used the IDP at different school levels within the same culture, as well as in public and private organizations and industries. Our experience corresponds with that of certain other international undertakings. Hofstede (1980), for example, has studied the characteristics of 'national cultures'. His starting point was original: he investigated national culture by studying IBM personnel in 40 countries. The assumptions were that 'IBM people' have a fairly common enterprise culture; any differences would probably therefore be related to 'national cultures'. He found that four factors could distinguish cultures in relation to change processes in organizations:

1 The acceptance of power differences, or the degree to which a culture accepts that power, is unequally distributed in an organization and in a society.

2 Degree of individuality — whether it is expected that the individual has to take care of him- or herself, or that the group, the factory or the society (the collective) has the responsibility to care for the individual.

3 Degree of 'masculinity', or the degree to which the dominant traits of the culture are concerned with money, prestige, careers and material things ('masculinity'), in contrast to those traits representing an interest in people, quality of life, expressing emotions, etc. ('femininity').

4 The tendency to avoid insecurity, or the tendency to plan for a

secure career, to develop secure networks, to control behaviour and to ensure that rules are followed.

Many have criticized the work of Hofstede. Triandis, for example, says that Hofstede's categories are too limited (Triandis, 1982), and that it is easy to obtain a biased sample with the choice of a company like IBM (Hunt, 1981). We are interested in Hofstede's analysis if it can help us to explain what happens to the IDP in different cultures. We have, therefore, found the work of Jaeger of great interest. Jaeger tried to characterize OD in relationship to Hofstede's analysis (Jaeger, 1986), and found that OD has the following characteristics.

1 Implicitly, OD does not accept large power differences in an organization.

2 OD is neither 'individualistic' nor 'collectivistic', but tries to find a balance between the two points of view in a given situation.

3 OD is to a large extent interested in the human side of an organization, for example the ability of members to express feelings, and therefore to tend to be 'feminine' in Hofstede's terms (although OD in many projects works with the 'harder side' of the organization as well).

4 OD is concerned with openness, the ability to confront different opinions, to take a calculated risk, to try something new, and is thus concerned with avoiding insecurity.

Jaeger then uses Hofstede's culture analysis to show that OD has greater dissemination power in some cultures than in others. In Scandinavia and the Netherlands, for example, OD is useful to a large extent, at least in private firms and organizations. He feels OD is in harmony with the values of these cultures.

To us these general analyses of national cultures are of little interest. It is too easy to get into stereotypes that create barriers rather than possibilities for improvement. What is interesting to us is to study *different organizational cultures* within the same country.

We are convinced that certain cultural traits within the school as an organization are of great importance for its ability to renew itself (see Chapter 6). What we call the 'autonomous teacher' is a cultural trait that may correspond with 'individuality' in Hofstede's analysis. The teacher may drift into an isolated job over time, which we have seen as a major hindrance for school improvement.

Teachers are, in our opinion, sceptical of large power differences, and therefore work in harmony with an important OD value. Teachers also place value on the human side of the organization, and all their work is therefore in harmony with an important OD value. However, teachers, in our view, have a tendency to avoid insecurity. We do not have systematic data from the IDP to support these observations. It is, however, our experience from working with school management and teachers that teachers often try to avoid conflicts, and to look for long-term security (e.g. fixed, regular appointments, a pension, etc.). This basic tendency to avoid insecurity may be a major hindrance for schools trying to involve themselves in major development work in general.

If it is true that the school, compared to other organizations, tries to 'insure itself', the question is why. The explanation lies partly in the mandate of the school — to transmit the culture of a country, its values and traditions — but it could also have something to do with the way teachers are recruited, the way the school organization is structured, and the norms that have developed over time. To us it is unclear how the many long-term forces influence the school's ability to live with insecurity and the unfinished, an important challenge for all organizations in modern life.

The more we have worked with the IDP, and the further we have come in describing and analysing the programme, the more we understand how comprehensive the IDP is. We have also found that our experiences differ from one country to another. There are *cultural determinants* that, at least to some degree, will influence the success of programmes such as the IDP. We hope to be able to do more systematic comparative research to enable us to understand these factors better (for a discussion of OD and culture, see Jaeger, 1986).

## A FINAL COMMENT

The IDP is a *change strategy* for schools. As with all methods of intervention it has weaknesses, many of which we have described and analysed in this book. The IDP is not a recipe; it cannot be adopted or copied, it has to be *adapted* in a creative way, with insight, to the particular context where it is used.

The IDP also has strengths as a change strategy. It is grounded in both theory and practice. It has been tested over fifteen years in several cultures, in the OECD countries as well as in a few developing nations. We who work with the IDP know that the IDP will be useful for many schools in the years to come. We know that programmes such as the IDP work. And we are beginning to understand *why*.

# Bibliography

Abbott, J. (1991) The creation of effective modern learning communities: constructivism in practice. Hertfordshire, UK: Paper from 'Education 2000'.

Arfwedson, G. and Lundman, L. (1983) *Varför er skolar olika? En bok om skolkodor.* Stockholm: Liber Utbildningsförlaget.

Argyris, C. and Schön, D. A. (1974) *Theory in Practice: Increasing Professional Effectiveness.* San Francisco: Jossey-Bass.

Argyris, C. and Schön, D. A. (1978) *Organizational Learning: A Theory of Action Perspective.* Reading, MA: Addison-Wesley.

Aurin, K. (1990) *Gute Schulen — worauf beruht ihre Wirksamkeit?* Bad Heibrunn: Klinkhardt.

Beckhard, R. (1972) *Organisationsentwicklung: Strategien und Modelle.* Bad Homburg.

Beckhard, R. and Harris, R. T. (1987) *Organizational Transitions.* Reading, MA: Addison-Wesley.

Bennis, W. and Nanus, B. (1985) *Leaders.* New York: Harper & Row.

Bennis, G., Benne, D. and Chin, R. (1969) *The Planning of Change.* London: Holt, Rinehart & Winston.

Berger, R. and Borkel, W. (1988) *Grundwissen Betriebsorganisation.* Munich: Heyne.

Berman, P. and McLaughlin, M. W. (1975) *Federal Programs Supporting Educational Change.* Vol. III: *The Process of Change.* Santa Monica, CA: Rand Corporation.

Block, P. (1981) *Flawless Consulting.* Pfeiffer & Co.

Bloom, B. S. (1976) *Human Characteristics and School Learning.* New York: McGraw-Hill.

Bohnsack, F. (1989) Pädagogische Strukturen einer guten Schule heute, in Tillmann, K. J. (ed.) *Was ist eine gute Schule?* Hamburg.

Bolman, G. and Deal, E. (1984) *Modern Approaches to Understanding and Managing Organizations.* San Francisco: Jossey-Bass.

Boss, C. W. (1983) Team building and the problem of regression. *Journal of the Applied Behavioral Sciences,* 19, 1.

Brookover, W., Beady, C., Flood, P., Schweitzer, J. and Wisenbaker, J. (1979) *School Social System and Student Achievement: Schools Can Make a Difference.* New York: Bergin Publishers.

Buchen, H. (1986) Organisationsentwicklung als Gegenstand von Schulleiterfortbildung. *Schulmanagement,* 18, 3.

Bulla, H. G. (1982) *Probleme einer Organisationsentwicklung in der Schule: Zur Strategie des Survey Feedbacks*. Frankfurt: Suhrkamp.

Caplan, G. (1970) *The Theory and Practice of Mental Health Consultation*. New York: Basic Books.

Christensen, D. (1982) Peer-validation in Indonesia: striving toward quality development in teacher education. *IMTEC Occasional Paper No. 340*, Oslo.

Cogan, M. (1973) *Clinical Supervision*. Boston: Houghton Mifflin.

Cohen, A. M. and Smith, R. D. (1976) *The Critical Incident in Growth Groups*. La Jolla, CA: University Associates.

Coleman, J. (1987) Family and schools. *Educational Researcher*, August/ September 1987.

Corbett, D. and Rossmann, G. (1989) Three path to implementing change: a research note. *Curriculum Inquiry*, 19 (2), 163-90.

Crandall, D. *et al.* (1983) *People, Policies and Practices: Examining the Chain of School Improvement* (10 vols). Andover, MA: The Network.

Dalin, Å. (1987) *Kompetanseutvikling i arbeidslivet*. Oslo: Cappelen.

Dalin, P. (1978) *Limits to Educational Change*. London: Macmillan.

Dalin, P. (1986) *Skoleutvikling*. Oslo: Universitetsforlaget.

Dalin, P. (1987) *Handlingsprogrammet: En systemstudie*. Oslo: IMTEC.

Dalin, P. (1990) Zukunft der Schule, *Zukunftwissen und Bildungsperspektiven*. FORUM ZUKUNFT, Nomos Verlagsgesellschaft. Baden-Baden, 1988.

Dalin, P. and Rust, V. (1983) *Can Schools Learn?* London: NFER-Nelson.

Dalin, P. and Skrindo, M. (1983) *Laering ved deltaking*. Oslo: Universitets-forlaget.

Deal, T. E. and Kennedy, A. A. (1982) *Corporate Cultures: The Rites and Rituals of Corporate Life*. London: Addison-Wesley.

Döring, P. A. (1978) *Planungaufgaben der Schulleitung*. (Vol. 7 of *Schulleiter-handbuch*.) Braunschweig: Westermann.

Dyer, W. (1987) *Teambuilding: Issues and Alternatives*. Reading, MA: Addison-Wesley.

Edmonds, R. R. (1982) Programs of school improvement: an overview. *Educational Leadership*, 40 (3), 4-11.

Egan, G. (1985) *Exercises in Helping Skills*. Monterey, CA: Brooks/Cole.

Ekholm, M. and Fransson, A. (1987) *Skolans socialpsykologi*. Kristianstad: Raben & Sjögren.

Evans, A. and Tomlinson, J. (1989) *Teacher Appraisal: A Nationwide Approach*. London: Jessica Kingsley.

Flinders, D. (1988) Teacher isolation and the new reform. *Journal of Curriculum and Supervision*, 5 (4), 17-29.

Foltz, J. A., Harvey, J. B. and McLaughlin, J. (1974) Organization development, in Adams, J. D. (ed.) *Theory and Method in OD*. Arlington, VA: NTL Institute for Applied Behavioral Sciences.

French, W. L. and Bell, C. H., Jr. (1990) *Organization Development: Behavioral*

*Science Interventions for Organizational Improvement.* 4th edn. Englewood Cliffs, NJ: Prentice-Hall.

Fullan, M. (1982) *The Meaning of Educational Change.* Toronto: OISE Press.

Fullan, M. (1991) *The New Meaning of Educational Change.* London: Cassell;
New York: Teachers College Press.

Fullan, M. (1992) *What's Worth Fighting For?* Toronto: Ontario Public Schools
Teachers' Federation.

Fullan, M., Miles, M.B. and Taylor, G. (1980) Organizational development in
schools: the state of the art. *Review of Educational Research*, 50 (1),
121-83.


Geissler, K. H. (1989) *Anfangssituationen.* Weinheim: Beltz.

Gjessing, H. J., Nygaard, H.D. and Solheim, R. (1988) *Studier av barn med
dysleksi og andre laerevansker.* Oslo: Universitetsforlaget.

Glaser, S. R. and Eblen, A. (1988) *Toward Communication Competency.* New
York: Holt, Rinehart & Winston.

Glasl, F. (1975) Selbstdiagnose einer Schule, in Glasl, F. and de la Hussaye, L.
(eds) *Organisationsentwicklung.* Bern and Stuttgart: Haupt.

Goldhammer, R., Anderson, R. H. and Krajewski, R. J. (1980) *Clinical Supervision: Special Methods.* New York: Holt, Rinehart & Winston.

Good, T. and Brophy, J. (1986) School effects, in Wittrock, M. C. (ed.) *Handbook
of Research on Teaching*, 3rd edition. New York: Macmillan.

Goodlad, J. (1975) *The Dynamics of Educational Change.* New York:
McGraw-Hill.

Goodlad, J. (1979) *Curriculum Inquiry.* New York: McGraw-Hill.

Goodlad, J. (1983) *A Place Called School: Projects for the Future.* New York:
McGraw-Hill.

Goodlad, J. and Klein, F. (1970) *Behind the Classroom Door.* Worthington, OH:
Charles A. Jones.


Haenisch, H. (1989) Gute und schlechte Schulen im Spiegel der empirischen
Forschung, in Tillmann, K. J. (ed.) *Was ist eine gute Schule?* Hamburg.

Hargreaves, D. H. (1975) *Interpersonal Relations and Education.* London:
Routledge & Kegan Paul.

Hedley, B., Caldwell, B. J. and Millikan, R. H. (1989) *Creating an Excellent
School: Some New Management Techniques.* London: Routledge
Education.

Heller, F. A. (1972) Gruppen-Feedback-Analyse als Methode der Veränderung.
*Gruppendynamikk*, 1972-3.

Hodgkinson, C. (1978) *Towards a Philosophy of Administration.* Oxford:
Blackwell.

Hodgkinson, C. (1983) *The Philosophy of Leadership.* Oxford: Blackwell.

Hofstede, G. (1980) *Culture's Consequences.* Beverly Hills, CA: Sage.

Horkheimer, M. (1967) Mittel und Zwecke, in Horkheimer, M. (ed.) *Zur Kritik
der instrumentellen Vernunft.* Frankfurt: Suhrkamp.

House, E. (1981) Three perspectives on innovation, in Lehming, R. and Kane, M.
(eds) *Improving Schools.* London and Beverly Hills, CA: Sage.

Huberman, M. and Miles, M. B. (1984) *Innovations Up Close*. New York: Plenum Press.

Hunt, J. W. (1981) Applying American behavioral science: some cross-cultural implications. *Organizational Dynamics*, 10 (1), 55-62.

Hutchins, C. L. (1989) *Achieving Excellence*. Kansas City: McREL.

Hutchins, C. L. (1990) Redesigning schools for school year 2020. *Noteworthy*. Kansas City: McREL.


Jaeger, A. M. (1986) Organization development and national culture: where's the fit? *Academy of Management Review*, 11 (1), 178-90.

Johnson, D. W. and Johnson, R. (1986) *Learning Together and Alone: Cooperation, Competition and Individualization*. Englewood Cliffs, NJ: Prentice-Hall.

Joyce, B. (1990) *Changing School Culture through Staff Development*. Alexandria, VA: Yearbook of ASCD.

Joyce, B. and Murphy, C. (1990) Epilogue: the curious complexities of cultural change, in *Changing School Culture through Staff Development*. Alexandria, VA: Yearbook of ASCD.

Joyce, B. and Showers, B. (1980 ) Improving inservice training: the message from research. *Educational Leadership*, 37, 379-85.

Joyce, B. and Showers, B. (1984 ) Transfer of training: the contribution of coaching, in Hopkins, D. and Wideen, M. (eds) *Alternative Perspectives on School Improvement*. London: Falmer Press.

Joyce, B., Bennett, B. and Rolheisen-Bennett, C. (1990) The self-educating teacher: empowering teachers through research, in *Changing School Culture through Staff Development*. Alexandria, VA: Yearbook of ASCD.


Kant, I. (1923) Was ist Aufklärung? In *Kants gesammelte Schriften*, vol. VIII, Berlin and Leipzig, p. 35.

Klafki, W. (1989) Kann Erziehungswissenschaft zur Begründung pädagogischer Zielsetzungen beitragen?, in Röhrs, H. and Scheuerl, H. (eds) *Richtungsstreit in der Erziehungswissenschaft und pädagogische Verständigung*. Frankfurt: Lang-Verlag.

Kolb, D. A., Rubin, I.M. and Osland, J. (1991) *Organizational Behavior*. Englewood Cliffs, NJ: Prentice-Hall.

Kubr, M. (ed.) (1986) *Management Consulting*. Geneva: International Labour Organisation.

Küpper, W. and Ortmann, G. (1988) *Mikropolitik: Rationalität, Macht und Spiele in Organisationen*. Opladen: Westdeutscher Verlag.


Landesinstitut für Schule und Weiterbildung (LSW) (1988) *Gemeinsam Schule machen: Arbeitshilfen zur Entwicklung des Schulprogramms von Grundschulen*. Soest.

Langmaack, B. and Braune-Krickau, M. (1987) Bevor ich zusage: Vorklärungen und Kontrakt, in Langmaack, B. and Braune-Krickau, M. (eds) *Wie die Gruppe laufen lernt*. Munich: Beltz.

Lauterburg, C. (1985) Arbeitssupervision im Kollegenkreiss. *Organisationsentwicklung 1985/1*, 53-70.

Lauvås, P. and Handal, G. (1990) *Veiledning og praktisk yrkesteori*. Oslo: Cappelen.

Levin, H. M. *et al.* (1984) Cost-effectiveness of four educational interventions. *CERAS*, Stanford, May 1984.

Lie, S. and Sjoberg, S. (1984) *'Myke' jenter i 'harde' fag*. Oslo: Universitetsforlaget.

Liket, Th. M. E. (1992) *Vrijheid en rekenschap: zelfevaluatie en externe evaluatie in het voortgezet onderwijs*. Amsterdam: Meulenhoff Educatief.

Lippitt, G. and Lippitt, R. (1986) *The Consulting Process in Action*, 2nd edn. San Diego, CA: University Associates.

Litt, T. (n.d.) *Das Bildungsideal der deutschen Klassik und die moderne Arbeidswelt*. Bochum: Kamp O.J.

Little, J. (1989) *The Persistence of Privacy: Autonomy and Initiative in Teachers' Professional Relations*. San Francisco: AERA.

Lorsch, J. W. and Lawrence, P. (1975) Die Diagnose von Organisationsproblemen, in Bennis, W. G. *et al.* (eds) *Änderung des Sozialverhaltens*. Stuttgart.

Lortie, D. (1975) *Schoolteacher*. Chicago: University of Chicago Press.

Marx, E. (1990) *Werken met Modellen in Organisaties*. Amsterdam: Samsom.

McLaughlin, N. W. (1990) The RAND change agent study revisited: macro perspectives and micro realities. *Education Research*, 19 (9), December 1990.

Mead, G. H. (1934) *Mind, Self and Society*. Chicago: University of Chicago Press.

Meyer, H. L. (1972) *Einführung in die Curriculum-Methodologie*. Munich: Piper.

Miles, M. B. (1964) *Innovation in Education*. Columbia University, New York: Teachers College Press.

Miles, M. B. (1981) *Learning to Work in Groups*. Columbia University, New York: Teachers College Press.

Miles, M. B., Ekholm, M. and Vandenberghe, R. (1987) *Lasting School Improvement: Exploring the Process of Institutionalization*. Lauven/Amersfort: ISIP, OECD, ACCO.

Morgan, G. (1986) *Images of Organizations*. Beverly Hills, CA: Sage.

Morris, L. L. and Fitz-Gibbon, C. T. (1978) *Evaluator's Handbook*. Beverly Hills, CA: Sage.

Mortimore, P., Sammons, P., Stoll, L., Lewis, D. and Elob, R. (1988) *School Matters: The Junior Years*. Wells: Open Books.

Myrdal, G. (1965) Das Zweck-Mittel-Denken in der Nationalökonomie, in Myrdal, G. (ed.) *Das Werkproblem in der Sozialwissenschaft*. Hanover.

Nadler, D. A., Hackman, J. R. and Lawler, E. E., III (1979) *Managing Organizational Behaviour*. Boston: Little, Brown.

Nellessen, L. (1987) Professionalität von Supervisoren/Supervisorinnen. *Supervision* (11).

Neuijen, B. (1993) *Diagnosing Organizational Cultures: Patterns of Continuance and Change.* Groningen: Wolters-Noordhoff.

NHO. *Kunnskapens pris,* September 1990.

OECD (1989) *Schools and Quality: An International Report.* Paris.

Pfeiffer, I. W. and Jones, J. E. (1972) *The Annual Handbook for Group Facilitators.* San Diego: University Associates.

Philipp, E. (1986) Verbesserung de Kooperation von Sekundärschulen. *Schulmanagement,* 18, 3.

Philipp, E. and Rolff, H.-G. (1990) *Schulgestaltung durch Organisationsentwicklung.* Braunschweig: Schulleiter-Verlag.

Pink, W. T. (1989) *Effective Development of Urban School Improvement.* San Francisco: AERA.

Postman, N. (1987) Will the new technologies of communication weaken or destroy what is most worth preserving in education and culture? *IMTEC Occasional Paper,* No. 360, 1987.

Probst, G. J. B. and Gomez, P. (1989) *Vernetztes Denken.* Wiesbaden: Gabler.

Purkey, S. C. and Smith,M. S. (1983) Effective schools: a review. *The Elementary School Journal,* 83, 1983/4, 427-52.

Reynolds, D. and Cuttance, P. (1992) *School Effectiveness: Research, Policy and Practice.* London: Cassell.

Rolff, H.-G. (1983) Realität und Entwicklung von Lehrerkooperation, in Rolff, H.-G. (ed.) *Soziologie der Schulreform.* Weinheim: Beltz.

Rolff, H.-G. (1991) Schulentwicklung als Entwicklung von Einzelnschulen? Theorien und Indikatoren von Entwicklungsprozessen. *Zeitschrift für Pädagogik,* 40, 1991/4.

Rolff, H.-G. and Zimmermann, P. (1990) *Kindheit und Wandel.* Weinheim and Basel: Beltz.

Rosenholtz, S. J. (1989) *Teacher's Workplace: The Social Organization of Schools.* White Plains, NY: Longman.

Rutter, M., Maugham, B., Mortimore, P. and Ouston, J. (1979) *Fifteen Thousand Hours: Secondary Schools and Their Effects on Children.* Wells: Open Books.

Sarason, S. S. (1971) *The Culture of the School and the Problem of Change.* Boston: Allyn & Bacon.

Schein, E. (1990) *Process Consultation.* 2 vols. Reading, MA: Addison-Wesley.

Schelsky, H. (1965) Der Mensch in der wissenschaftliche Zivilisation, in Schelsky, H. (ed.) *Auf der Suche nach Wirklichkeit,* p. 456. Düsseldorf: Bertelsmann.

Schmuck, R. A. and Runkel, P. J. (1985) *The Handbook of Organization Development in Schools,* 3rd edition. Palo Alto, CA: Mayfield.

Schwendter, R. (1987) Zum Für und Wider die Professionalisierung von Supervision. *Supervision* (11).

Senge, P. M. (1990) *The Fifth Discipline: The Art and Practice of the Learning Organisation.* New York: Doubleday.

Siegers, F. and Haan, D. (1983) *Handboek Supervisie*. Alphen aan den Rijn: Samsom.

Snyder, K. J. (1988) *Competency Training for Managing Productive Schools*. Orlando, FL: Harcourt Brace Jovanovich.

Snyder, K. J. and Anderson, R. H. (1988) *Managing Productive Schools*. Orlando, FL: Harcourt Brace Jovanovich.

Staehle, W. (1989) *Management*. Munich: Vahlen.

Stallings, J. A. (1989) School achievement effects and staff development: what are some critical factors? Paper presented at American Research Association annual meeting.

Stensaasen, S. and Sletta, O. (1983) *Gruppeprosesser*. Oslo: Universitetsforlaget.

Steuer, E. (1983) *Organisationsentwicklung für die Schule*. Frankfurt: Lang.

Stufflebeam, D. L. *et al.* (1971) *Educational Evaluation and Decision Making*. Itasca, IL: Peacock.

Stufflebeam, D. L. (1974) *Administrative Checklist for Reviewing Evaluation Plans*. Kalamazoo: Evaluation Center, Western Michigan University.

Svedberg, L. and Zear, M. (eds) (1989) *Skolans själ*. Stockholm: Utbildnings-förlaget.

Tillmann, K. J. (1989) *Was ist eine gute Schule?* Hamburg.

Trebesch, K. (1982) Fünfzig Definitionen der OE — und kein Ende. *Zeitschrift für OE*, 1, 1982/1.

Triandis, G. (1982) Reviews of culture's consequences: international differences in work-related values. *European Business*, 39, 71-9.

Türk, K. (1989) *Neuere Entwicklungen der Organisationsforschung*. Stuttgart: Enke.

Ulrich, H. and Probst, G. J. B. (1988) *Anleitung zum ganzheitlichen Denken und Handeln*. Bern and Stuttgart: Haupt.

Volanen, R. (1987) *Domestic and Global Trends in the Communication Area: Realizing the Descartion Program*. Oslo: IMTEC.

Watzlawick, P., Beavin, J. H. and Jackson, D. D. (1967) *Pragmatics of Human Communications*. New York: W. W. Norton.

Weber, M. (1956) Die 'Objektivität' sozialwissenschaftlicher Erkenntnis, in Weber, M. (ed.) *Soziologie, Weltgeschichtliche Analysen, Politik*. Stuttgart: Kröner.

Weick, K. E. (1976) Educational organizations as loosely coupled systems. *Administrative Science Quarterly*, 21, 1-19.

Weigand, W. (1987) Zur beruflichen Identität des Supervisors. *Supervision*, Fall.

Weisbord, M. R. (1982) The organization development contract, in Plovnick *et al.* (eds) *Organization Development: Exercises, Cases and Readings*. Boston: Little, Brown.

Ziehe, T. (1990) *Kulturanalyser*. Stockholm: Symposium Bokförlag.

# INDEXES

# Name Index

# Subject Index